Melitopol' (Khar'kov; Moskva)
ZAPOROZHSKAIA OBL.
Sheliugi
Chkalovo
Aleksandrovka
Stepanovka
Okhrimovka
Atmanai
Azovskoie
Utliukskii liman
kosa Biriuchii Ostrov
Kherson
M 25
Zhilino
Ordenonosnoie
E 97
DZHANKOI
Dneprovka
Mar'ino
Dmitrievka
Severo-Krymskii kanal
Bolotnoie
Pobednoie
Mirnovka
Yarkoie
Michurinovka
Konstantinovka
Timofeievka
M 26
Azovskii kanal
Tarasovka
Novaia Zhizn'
Rysakova
Novostepnoie
Ozernoie
Blizhnegorodskoie
Dorozhnoie
Kondratovo
Feodosiia
Arbuzovka
Slavianka
Yarkoie Pole
Nakhodka
E 105
Pobednaia
Roschino
Simferopol'
© SSPE "Kartographia," 2003
kosa Arabatskaia Strelka
Izobil'noie
Yemel'ianovka
Dmitrovka
Sovetskii
Urozhainoie
Arabatskii zaliv
m.Kazantip
Mysovoie
SCHELKINO
Kazantipskii zal.
Aktashskoie
Pesochnoie
m.Ziuk
Kurortnoie
oz. Chokrakskoie
Bagerovo
Voikovo
m.Kamennyi
Kuchugury
Zaporozhskaia
Chistopol'ie
KERCH'
Chushka
Kalinovka
Ostanino
Kamenskoie
LENINO
Semisotka
M 17
Leninskoie
Priozernoie
Kerchenskii proliv
kosa Tuzla
Tamanskii zal.
Kirovskoie
Vasil'kovo
Krasnogorka
M 25
Pushkino
Yarkoie Pole
Severo-Krymskii kanal
Batal'noie
Marfovka
oz. Tobechykskoie
m.Tuzla
Taman'
ROSSIIA
Zhuravki
Vladislavovka
Yarkoie
Marievka
Zavetnoie
Primorskii
Yakovenkovo
m.Takyl
m.Zheleznyi Rog
Zolotoie Pole
Privetnoie
Beregovoie
oz. Uzunlarskoie
oz. Kachik
oz. Koiashskoie
Pervomaiskoie
Blizhneie
Feodosiiskii zaliv
STARYI KRYM
FEODOSIIA
Yuzhnoie
m.Chauda
Schebetovka
Ordzhonikidze
Koktebel'
Kurortnoie
m.Kiikatlama
Lesnoie
Dachnoie
SUDAK
Pribrezhnoie
Novyi Svet
m.Meganom
E M O R E

THE GUIDE-BOOK

ISBN 966-96041-9-2

Publisher **"Baltija dryk"**
General Director **Ruta Malikenaite**
Editor-in-chief **Virginiyus Strolya**

Authoress-compiler **Yuliya Ferentseva**
Managing editor **Alisa Grigoruk**
Model and decorative design by **Yelena Zheleznyak**
Make-up and pre-printing preparation
by **Stanislav Stefanovich, Vladimir Suljenko**
Proof-reader **Natalia Ivanchenko**
Head of the advertising department **Dmitry Belokon**
Photography by **Nikolai Ferentsev**, **Sergei Tarasov**, **'van Pilipenko**
Three-dimensional landscape plans by **Sergei Poznyak**
Axonomeries by **Aleksandr Sedak**
Reviewer **Andrei Malgin** (cultural-historical part)

Translation into English and German languages - the Centre of Translation "TRIS"

Maps by the State Scientific-Production Enterprise "Kartografiya" ("Cartography")

The authoress expresses her great thanks to Lidiya Demidova, Aleksei Shorkin, Vladimir Syrkin, and the employees of the enterprise "Dori", to the workers of the I. Franko Crimean Republican Scientific Universal Library for the inestimable assistance in preparation of the publication "Touring the Crimea" rendered by them.

The certificate on including the subject of publishing business in the state list of publishers, producers, and spreaders of the publishing production: series ДК, No. 643 of October 23, 2001 was issued by the State Committee of information policy, television, and broadcasting of Ukraine.

51/2, A. Barbyusa St., Kiev, 03150, Ukraine
tel./fax (044) 252-8832, e-mail: baltija@ukr.net

The editorial staff has made every effort in order to give data, the most correct as of December, 2002, in the guide-book, but the telephone numbers, prices, working hours, etc. could change with the lapse of time.

Touring the Crimea

«BALTIJA DRYK»
Kiev 2003

Dear readers!

You are holding in your hands the second book of the series of guide-books produced by the publishing house "Baltija dryk". The previous guide-book "Touring Kiev" was published in 2002. Why has the Crimea found itself in the zone of our attention? Probably, because it is difficult to find in Ukraine a tourist region including so much recreation factors: an excellent climate, an amazing diversity of natural landscapes, the caressing sea, beaches to any taste, abundance of excellent fruit and wonderful wines, good transport communication, a large quantity of historical, architectural, and archaeological monuments, and many another things.

We hope you will enjoy your promenade!

The book is notable for its simplicity and convenience. It consists of several parts: a brief historical essay tells about the Tavrida's past. The next part narrates about the Crimea's pearls - beautiful towns of the peninsula, a separate chapter is devoted to every of them. The authoress has chosen ten towns: eight of them (Yevpatoriya, Saki, Sevastopol, Yalta, Alushta, Sudak, Feodosiya, Kerch) are situated at the sea-coast, two (Bakhchisarai and Simferopol) are at a distance from the sea.

Every chapter contains information not only about the town itself, but about the whole region. For instance, Greater Yalta includes, in addition to Yalta proper, small towns and settlements from Gurzuf to Foros, the tale about the most interesting of them is given in the form of an out-of-town excursion.

A chapter is constructed as follows: first a brief acquainting essay goes, it contains a map of the town where all the important objects (hotels, architectural monuments, etc.) tourists care about are marked. The information given on pages "Communications", "Residence", "Nourishment", "Entertainment" will help the holiday-makers to determine their choice of transport, lodging, to receive the idea of the most popular cafes and restaurants, night clubs, theatres, concert halls, etc.

A review of the most striking town sights: palaces, museums, monuments, temples, and other places of tourists' mass pilgrimage is given in the next sub-division. In addition to town routes, the guide-book offers to carry out out-of-town

Heading

Three-dimensional landscape plans

Entertaining information (chronicles, legends, etc.)

The map of the town

The name of the chapter

excursions along the picturesque environs of every town.

About 100 colourful illustrations, both present-day ones and given by archives of museums and by private collectors, make the tale visual and more cognitive. Architectural sectional views of famous constructions allow to imagine their interior. Maps-schemes and three-dimensional landscape plans will help to find their bearings on the ground even to those who have come to the Crimea for the first time.

The part "Camp and extreme tourism" is intended for lovers of "wild" rest. Information about permitted parking and spontaneous encampments, and also on rules of behaviour in the peninsula protected zones are collected here. Admirers of the extreme will learn of the regions where the funboarding and glider sports are popular, where they are engaged in rock-climbing or speleotourism, etc.

The reference part "Information from A to Z" contains practical information about transport, communications, sanatoria-health-resort institutions. You will learn where to buy souvenirs, which grades of wines every region of the Crimea is renowned for, familiarize yourselves with the recipe of making dishes of Tatar and Karaite national cuisine.

When compiling the book the authoress tried to cover the widest possible range of questions and themes being of interest to tourists. We hope that the guide-book "Touring the Crimea" will become a reliable assistant during your whole stay in the hospitable Crimean land.

Practical information (addresses, telephones, working hours of museums, hotels, restaurants, etc.)

MAXIMIANVS

Гербъ
Таврической губерніи

History
in figures and facts

History begins when it is already impossible to check up anything...

V. Verkhovsky

■ **Judging by the investigations of the archeologists the Crimean peninsula has always been the Promised Land. Parent history has still been keeping its illustrations. Approximately about 150,000 years ago, long before the birth of Herodotus, universally recognized farther of history, representatives of the human race settled in the local caves and grottoes. Neanderthal sites of Old and Middle Paleolithic epoch were found in many places of the Crimea (Ak-Kaya near Belogorsk, Chokurcha near Simferopol, Staroselye in Bakhchisarai, and others).**

The 1st Millenium B.C. - the epoch of the Cimmerians begins. The Assyrians called in such a way their north neighbors of the State of Urartu. These Iranian language tribes invaded into the peninsula in ancient times. Among the ancient authors, in addition to Herodotus, one can find a record of these people at Homer. In "Odyssey" the poet described a rather dull picture of the Crimea. The country of the Cimmerians, as he described it, was eternally covered with a shroud of mists and a haze of clouds, which a sunbeam could never struggle its way through. Here the great Greek located the threshold of the Aid Kingdom of the Dead. Fortunately, the climate has changed since then...

Harpoon - a powerful weapon of an ancient hunter

This petrified fish was floating in the warm sea-ocean that covered almost all the territory of the Crimean peninsula in prehistorian times (FMRS)

In the 8th - 7th cent. B.C. the Cimmerian nomadic tribes united for the raids to Asia Minor and Middle Asia. Traces of the people partially expelled by the Scythians or assimilated by the aboriginal population preserved in the toponymy of the Crimea: Cimmerian Bosporus (now the city of Kerch), Cimmerian (an ancient settlement on the western slopes of the Opuk mountain, southern coast of the Kerch peninsula), and others. Some scientists are inclined to think that the Cimmerians are

White rock in the suburbs of Belogorsk, in the grottoes of which the traces of Neanderthal sites were found

Discoveries in passing by

A student of Petersburg University Konstantin Merezhkovsky (brother of the writer Dmitry Merezhkovsky) being fond of archeology came to the Crimea in the summer of 1879 to investigate the Crimean caves. Youthful passion for the life of the ancient inhabitants of the peninsula lasted exactly for two seasons, and then enthusiasm vanished. During this time a meticulous student investigated 34 caves, in 9 of them a cultural layer was found. K. Merezhkovsky discovered the first cave site of the Old Stone Age in the territory of the country - Wolf's grotto near the village of Mazanki (now Simferopol district), grotto Suren I in the valley of Belbeka and several more interesting objects. He also discovered a kind of a "factory" of stone tools near the cave complex Kiik-Koba. During a short period of time he did so much that some other archeologists were unable to do for the whole life. Having made such brilliant discoveries, the investigator left excavations and had never ever returned to archeology again, though he has lived in the Crimea for 36 years!

The Tauri and the Cimmerian people lived in the Red cave (Kisil-Koba)

Anthropomorphous stele - a mengir which the ancient people erected over the tomb (CRMRS)

founders of so-called Kyzyl-Kobin culture (7th - 6th cent. B.C.). Other scientists connect it with the Tauri tribes that populated the southern part of the peninsula approximately at the same time (10th - 9th cent. B.C.). By their name (a Tauri means a mountain-mass) the ancient Greeks called the southern part of the mountain and forest area - Tauris. In the Middle Ages, up to the 15th cent. A.D., the name spread over the whole peninsula.

Greek culture firmly came into the history of the Crimea. Aboriginal population did not only adopt the technique of agriculture from the Greeks but a military art as well. Fighting with the Greek settlements, the Scythians appreciated at its true value the advantages of the regular army

Written sources brought the information to us about cruelty and wildness of the Tauri who alleged to practice human sacrifice. Sailors shipwrecked at the rocky coasts of Tauris were brought to the temple of the local goddess Deva, located on the top of the tall rock, and thrown into the sea. People got together to look at that "solemn performance of ceremony". The Greeks used to describe it in such a way but how it happened (if happened at all) in reality - only God knows. On the base of those bloody legends the ancient writers created their works (for example, "Iphigenia in Tauris" by Euripides).

Let us move to the ancient period and to the Middle Ages. Cultures and peoples change each other on that plot of land as in the kaleidoscope.

The first Greek colonies emerged on the coast two and half thousand years ago. The Hellenes brought their civilization to the peninsula. Those who came from Milletus founded Feodosiya, Pantikapeum, Mirmekius, Nimpheus and other colonies on the Kerch peninsula. The colonists from Geracleus explored the west and southwest of Tauris - here they founded Kerkinitidus (modern Yevpatoriya), Chersonese and Kalamitus (modern Sevastopol), Kalos-Limenus (modern Chernomorskoye). In addition to a convenient harbor, those towns were peculiar with the fact that there were lands near by applicable for agriculture. The colonists cultivated grapes, cereals, brought a lot of cultivated species of trees.

8th - 3rd cent. B.C. - the Scythians, that came from the steppe of the northern localities near the Black Sea, emerged on the historical arena. They were nomads and worriers. Having united the Scythians into a big army, czar Atey made some daring raids onto the lands of

Researchers think that the Scythians looked like this (YMRS)

Wars of Diophantus

Diophantus, a military leader of the Pontus czar Mitridat VI of Yevpator, was sent twice with the troops to the Crimea to help the inhabitants of Chersonese in their war with the Scythians. Both campaigns were a success, and in honor of Diophantus his statue was erected in the square in Chersonese. After the third campaigns along with the victory Diophantus brought the State of Bosporus to his czar. Historians intentionally attributed him some other brilliant raids which he probably did not committed. Prestige of an outstanding military leader was so immense that a number of successful military campaigns of that century were given a general name "wars of Diophantus".

Skilur is the most famous czar of the Scythians. On the bas-relief he is shown with his son Palak. In the summer of 1827 an archeological expedition from Odessa was working on the site of an ancient settlement near Simferopol. A bas-relief is one of its numerous windfalls

Chersonese - antiquity and the Middle Ages

the neighbors. But after the defeat, inflicted by Philip of Macedon when Atey was killed, and under the pressure of the Sarmats, the Scythians had to leave the steppe between the mouths of the Danube and the Don. They founded their state in the Crimea. Neapolis Scythian (modern Simferopol) became the capital of the state in the 3rd cent. B.C. The state achieved prosperity under czar Skilur and his son Palak (2nd cent. B.C.). The Scythians were eager to fight their way to the sea and to press the Greeks on the coast. Wars broke out. To repel the pressure of the Scythians in the west, the inhabitants of Chersonese asked for help from the Pontus czar Mitridate VI Yeupatore. His troops were led by a talented commander Diophantus. The Scythians suffered defeat in the battle, and Chersonese got into vassalage from the kingdom of Pontus.

The first roads in the mountains of Tauris were built by the Roman warriors

107 B.C. - the insurrection of the Scythians under the leadership of Savmak started in the kingdom of Pontus. And again Mitridate sent Diophantus to oppress the participants of the insurrection. Annexation of Bosporus by Mitridate, who soon started war against the Rome, was a compensation for the military support. Alas, his own son Farnak, who joined the enemy's side, betrayed an outstanding ruler of ancient times.

63 A.D. - Roman legionaries, invited by the inhabitants of the town to protect them from the attacks of the Barbarians, came to Chersonese. Ruins of the fortress of Pharaks in the cape of Ai-Todor, the road built through Shaitan-Merdven is an evidence of the Romans presence in the Crimea. To strengthen Bosporus the Romans built the fortress of Iluratus in the western shore.

The invasion of the Goths and the Alans put an end to the rule of the Scythians on the vast steppe spaces of the peninsula. Then in 375 the Huns conquered the Crimea. Not only the Scythian state but also the

Greek amphorae lifted from the bottom of the sea where the bigger part of Chersonese is located now

towns of the kingdom of Bosporus were lost in the struggle between the strangers and the local population. The rest of the Scythians escaped into the mountains where they mixed with the Tauri.

In the 5th cent. Byzantine as a successor of the Rome emerged on the political scene of the world. Its influence in the Crimea strengthened at the same time. On the initiative of the Emperor Yustinian (482 - 585) several fortresses were built here: Aluston (modern Alushta), Gorzuvity (modern Gurzuf), fortifications in Chersonese. So-called Long Walls were erected - fortifications blocking the passages through the mountain passes to protect the allies-Goths from the Barbarians.

In the 8th cent. a significant part of the Crimea taken away from Byzantine is under the rule of the Khazars khanate. Later the Khazars had to ally with Byzantine, united themselves against the Arabs. Close ties with the Byzantine Empire promoted widespread of the Christianity in the Crimea that, in fact, existed in Chersonese and Bosporus from the moment of their foundation. There is a legend about Andriy Pervozvanny being here. Finally the Christianity became firmly established in these areas a little later, in time of iconoclasm when the persecuted iconoclasts rushed into the Crimea. They founded many monasteries and temples (Uspensky Skit, Surb-Khach, etc.). The Khazars did not make any obstacles to it. At the same time the breeding grounds of Islam, brought by the Arabs, and Judaism spread among the Khazars emerged in the Crimea. A significant part of the population under it remained pagan. As one can see, there were no significant religious discords on the peninsula.

In the 9th cent. a great Slavonic enlightener, a creator of the Slavonic written language Konstantin (Kirill) the Philosopher visited this area. On the way to the Khazars State he was preaching Christianity. According to the formal version, Prince Vladimir transferred Christianity from here to Kievan Rus. To marry a Byzantine Princess Anna (in terms of politics it was a very important marriage!) in 988 Vladimir had to rush Chersonese (the town called Korsun of Kherson at that time). Thus, the Kievan Prince made the Byzantine Emperor Basil II keep his promise and recognize the political rights of Kiev in Tauris.

Slavonic enlighteners Kirill and Mefody

Middle Ages in the Crimea were marked with numerous historic shocks. The Genoese and the Venetians that started to struggle for the supremacy in the Black Sea changed the Greeks. In addition to the fact that Tauris itself attracted attention of the colonists, there was a famous Silk Road here - a trade artery between the West and the East. Finally Genoa expelled the Venetians and founded coastal commercial settlements in Tauris: Caffa (modern Feodosiya), Soldaya

Yustinian I erected fortifications in the Crimea. In addition to the coastal fortresses the mountain passes were blocked on his order by long fortifications that hampered an access of the nomads to the Gothic towns. The remnants of the powerful fortifications can be viewed even now in the mountains of the Crimea

Chersonese christening site. They traditionally believe that it is here, in Chersonese, Vladimir Svyatoslavovich committed christening and acquired Christianity. It was a crucial moment in the life of the Kievan Rus and in the life of the prince himself. In order to marry Anna who was a Christian he had to leave his previous wife Rogneda who soon went to the nunnery

How the Genoese bought Caffa from the Tatars

The Genoese merchants were smart and keen-witted. Having selected the southwest coast of Tauris, they decided to buy the land of the Old Greek Feodosiya that has already been demolished at that time from its actual owner Timur, nephew of the khan Oran of the Golden Horde. A sly Tatar agreed to make a deal but asked for the following price: the merchants had to cover a bull's skin spread out on the ground with several layers of coins. Then they were to cut the skin into strips, tie together the ends of the strips, and to embrace with such an original rope their future property. But the merchants from Genoa were not frightened by such a proposal. They paid the money and then ordered the best furriers to cut the skin into thin threads. With those threads the merchants embraced so much land that they managed to build a huge city for 70,000 inhabitants!

Genoese fortress in Feodosiya

(modern Sudak), and Chembalo (modern Balaklava). Fortifying their towns from the sea and the land, the Genoese built fortresses, the remaines of which can be viewed today by the tourists. After the Crimea has been conquered by the Mongols-Tatars, Genoa managed to preserve its coastal commercial settlements.

In the 12th cent. a feudal state Feodoro with the capital Mangup was founded in the southwest of the Crimea. The city was located on the mesa and enclosed with the fortifications. The Christian State was a part of the Gothic eparchy.

Nomad tribes showed interest in the rich Tauris steppe. The hordes of the Khazars, Polovtsians, and Pechenegs rushed through the peninsula like waves, changing each other. But in the 13th - 14th cent. the Mongols, brought to the Crimea by Baty-khan, a grandson of Chingiz-khan, firmly settled here. Tauris became a part of the Golden Horde founded by the great khan. Conquer of the peninsula was marked with a black event in the history of the whole Europe. When khan Djanibek of the Golden Horde besieged the Genoese fortress of Caffa, a plague broke out among his worriers. To break down the resistance of the Italians, locked themselves up in the fortress, the Mongols began to throw by means of a catapult the dead bodies of the worriers died from the plague over the walls of the beleaguered city. Soon the epidemic broke out in Caffa as well. Trying to escape from the disease, the Genoese left for Italy by sea. Alas, they brought an awful disease with them there. The plague spread very quickly throughout Europe. Terrible epidemic called "black death" took away 75 million lives...

In 1434 khan Khadzhi-Gerey I began to struggle for the independence of the Crimean khanate. With the help of the Lithuanian prince he managed to capture the Crimean throne nine years later. The most influential families of the Crimean yurta struggled for that throne. (It is known that after the dissolution of the Golden Horde in 1380 and the defeat of khan Mamai in the Kulikovskaya battle, the Mongolian State split into the Crimean, Astrakhan and Kazan yurtas). The Crimean khanate has not stayed independent for a long time. It became a Turkish vassal just under the second ruler - khan Mengli-Gerey. But the dynasty of the Gereys had been ruling the Crimea for more than 300 years.

Having invaded into the Crimea in 1475, the Turks captured the shore with the Genoese fortifications and founded their fortresses there: Enikale in the suburbs of Kerch, Inkerman (belonged to Feodoro Kalamita prince-

Chingiz-khan - a founder of a mysterious Mongol State that managed to conquer big states of Europe and Asia. His grandson Baty brought the Mongols into the Crimea

dom near modern Sevastopol), Gezlev (modern Yevpatoriya), etc.

The Crimean khanate in times of the Turkish supremacy was a scourge of the Russian Empire. Regular raids of the Tatars into the Russian lands weakened the borders and devastated near border villages. But it became much more difficult to make raids beginning from the 16th cent. because Zaporozhskaya Sech, emerged by that time, counteracted them. The cossacks themselves often attacked Caffa, Trapezund, Anatoliya and liberated prisoners from Ukraine, Poland and Muscovite.

To fight its way to the Black Sea and to stop the predatory raids of the "aboriginal inhabitants of the Crimea", Russia repeatedly entered into the wars against Turkey.

Russian-Turkish war of 1768 - 1774 ended with the defeat of the Turkish army and fleet and with signing the Kuchuk-Kainardzhiyskiy peace treaty. In compliance with the treaty conditions the Crimea got its independence.

Meanwhile the struggle for the influence on the policy of the Crimean khanate was going on. The Turkish sultan remained a spiritual father of the Crimean Moslems preserving in such a way his influence on consciousness of a big part of the population of the peninsula. The Russian government in its turn decided to take out all the Christians from the Crimea, allegedly apprehending their oppression and by that reduced by 30 thousand the population of the Crimea. So new settlements emerged on the Russian shore of Azov with the Crimean names of Yalta, Mariampol (Marioupol), etc.

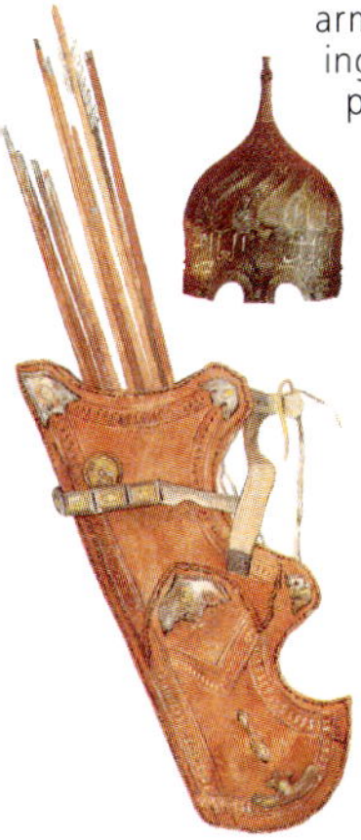

A quiver and a helmet of a Turkish worrier

On February 6, 1783 willing to solve the problem of the Crimea with one shot, Empress Catherine II declared a manifest on the "adoption the Crimea, Taman island, and all the Kuban territory into the Russian State". That was the end of the Crimean khanate. The last ruler Shakhin-Gerey received from the Russian empress a pension and a small house in the city of Kaluga. Soon he decided to go to Turkey where he was executes on the order of sultan. Tens of thousand of the Tatars and the Nogais immigrated to Turkey without such a sad aftermath. The Crimea has been depopulated. The lands began to be filled with the serfs from the Russian provinces, fugitive peasants, and also retired soldiers. So, for example, a village of Izyumovka near the town of Stary Krym (Old Crimea)

Suleiman the Magnificent

Roksolana - a mistress of the Ottoman Empire

The biggest slave market of the Crimea was located in the medieval Caffa (closer to the sea on the place of today's Sea Garden). Its name - Kan (in the Turkic language - "blood") tells for itself. About 150,000 - 200,000 people were taken away from the Russian lands in the course of the Tatar raids for only the first half of the 17th cent. Slave trade was considered to be an extremely profitable business - one could receive from 50 to 120 rubles in the currency of that time for a young man. Meanwhile a price of a cow in the Moscow market was about 60 kopecks...

Men became oars, slaves, janizaries; women replenished the harems of the western sovereigns. So during one of the raids in the 16th cent. the Tatars kidnapped a young girl-Slav that was destined to become a great sultan's wife. Roksolana was sold as a slave at the sadly famous Kan market.

Eyewitnesses affirmed that a beloved wife of the sultan Suleiman the Magnificent was not a beauty but was notable for amazing grace and prettiness. She completely won the heart of a terrible ruler with her charm - for the first time in the history of the harem the sultan married a concubine. Suleiman loved Roksolana until the very time he passed away. He was writing poems in her honor:

"I was a ruler of the Universe
and a beggar at your door.
The most severe storm
will break out in the world
but I will not set my sails;
I dropped my anchor
at the ship of your love".

Sultan's wife became not only a mistress of his heart but also a wise adviser in the state affairs.

A trip of Catherine II to the Crimea

In January 1787 Catherine II with a splendid suit left the Czar's village and went to see her new estates. In addition, the trip pursued a secret object: to show the power and wealth of the Russian Empire to the representatives of the European States. Catherine was accompanied by the envoys of England, Austria, France and also an Emperor of Austria Joseph II - incognito under the name of a count Fankelshtein. The trip was a success; the allies of the Ottoman Empire were impressed by the power of Russia. Fifteen million rubles were allotted for the trip from the state treasury. The money was spent to build the travel palaces throughout the entire journey of the royal persons, to arrange dinners, to fit out carriages...

Russian Empress Catherine II

called in such a way not because they were making exclusively perfect raisins from the local grape, but because the place here was determined to be a permanent residence for the retired soldiers of the Izyumovsky regiment. Later the Greeks, Germans, Bulgarians, French, Checks settled here...

Prince Potyomkin, who was appointed a Governor of the acquired lands, did his best to decorate country estates, peasants' houses and even built new villages. (They say that his Majesty acquired for himself "a little" amount of the public money for his efforts). Since that time there appeared beautiful names of the villages - Priyatnoye Svidaniye (a pleasant meeting), Chistenkoye (a clean tiny place)...

Joining the more developed country in terms of economy, made a favorable impact on the development of the Crimea. By the way, the peninsula was called Tavrida after annexation. New towns emerged on the peninsula and the old ones developed. In 1783 the town of Sevastopol was founded - a Navy port and a fortress. It became the main theatre of operations during the Eastern (Crimean) War, 1853 - 1865. Russia suffered a defeat from the united forces of France, England, Turkey, and Sardinia, but heroic defense of Sevastopol is an example of unprecedented courage of the defenders of the town. After the destruction caused by the war the economy of the Crimea was slowly restored. Towns were rebuilt, peasant households were restored...

The real prosperity of the Tavricheskaya Guberniya (Tavrida Province) began after the emperor's family started to build summer palaces and dachas in the coast. Following the Romanovs, highborn noblemen, rich industrialists and factory owners were going to the Crimea. Dacha settlements with luxurious villas, beautiful parks and spacious bathing-huts emerged along the southern coast on the place of small Tatar villages. Vineyards and tobacco plantations stretched on the slopes of the hills, fruit trees were planted in the valleys. Rich landlords invested money into the development of the region. Winemaking that has been practiced in the Crimea since ancient times but was almost lost in times of the Turkish supremacy began to boom. Many people were engaged in the revival of winemaking, among them: count M. Vorontsov, prince L. Golitsin, industrialist P. Gubonin.

October Coup in 1917 became another shock, and not only for the Crimea. Struggle of the Soviets for establishing their power on the territory of the peninsula was long and bloody. The Bolsheviks allied troops, detachments of the Volunteer Army, partisans, Tatar detachments - the power changes as in the kaleidoscope accompanied with shootings, terror, and robberies. Final establishment of the Soviet power in the Crimea took place in 1920. The remnants of the Volunteer Army as well as noble families, members of the emperor's family caught by the revolution in their Crimean

Palace of Nikolai II in Livadiya

estates, allies and also the citizens that did not accept the Bolsheviks had to leave the Motherland, having departed by the steamers from the Crimean ports. The Civil War ended, and just a month later Lenin signed a Decree "On using the Crimea for the treatment of the working people". In accordance with the Decree the palaces, mansions, and dachas of the rich were to be used as health centers and holiday homes.

On October 18, 1921 the Crimean Autonomous Soviet Socialist Republic (the Crimean ASSR) was created as an integral part of the Russian Federation. The Crimea passed through all the stages of the socialist construction: surplus-appropriation system, collectivization, industrialization, five-year plans... An attempt to transform the autonomy into an industrial region brought a lot of harm to the nature of the unique health resort. But it was impossible to stop the mill of the Soviet policy, the decision of the government were not to be claimed...

Last Russian Emperor Nikolai II

Severe years of the Great Patriotic war did not pass the peninsula aside. Malaya (Little) land - the name of the Crimea in the wartime - means heroic defense of Sevastopol in 1941 - 1942, Kerch and Feodosiya airborn operation, Fire land of Eltigen, an exploit of Adzhimushkai, heroism of partisans and members of clandestine organizations... Cities of Sevastopol and Kerch were awarded with "Hero-city", almost half thousand persons fought on the Crimean land were awarded with the highest award - Hero of the Soviet Union. The Crimea was liberated in May 1944. The population of the peninsula reduced twice, cities and towns were in the ruins, national economy was demolished. In addition, in compliance with Stalin's decrees a great deal of the Crimean population was deported (the Crimean Germans were taken away yet in 1941, and in 1944 the same fate occurred to the Tatars, Bulgarians, Armenians, Greeks of the Crimea). In 1945 the depopulated Crimean ASSR was transformed into the Crimean Region.

In February 1945 the leaders of the three States - U. Churchill (Great Britain), F. Roosevelt (USA), I. Stalin (USSR) got together in Yalta, in Livadiya Palace, to determine the future of not only Germany but that of the whole world

1954 - in compliance with N. Khrushchev's order the Crimea was transferred to the Ukrainian Soviet Socialist Republic (the Ukrainian SSR). National economy of the region was steadily restored. Since 1968 the deported peoples started to return to their native lands. The people of the Crimea managed to stop the construction of the Nuclear Power Plant in the Kerch peninsula. Winemaking of the Crimea was done a lot of harm in the course of Gorbachev's anti-alcoholic campaign. Fortunately, they managed to partially save elite vineyards.

In January 1991 in the framework of the referendum the citizens of the Crimea said in favor of the restoration of the autonomy. Now the former Crimean Region is an Autonomous Republic of Crimea within Ukraine.

State flag of Ukraine and a flag of the Autonomous Republic of Crimea

МУСКАТ

pearls of the Crimea

I am travelling along the south coast
of the Crimea, -
It is not the Crimea but a copy of an
ancient paradise...

V. Mayakovsky

Entablature - the upper part of a building bearing against pillars.

Arse - a semicircular (sometimes multangular) projection in the wall of Christian church buildings.

Arcade - a row of arches, identical by their form and size, bearing against posts or pillars.

Basilica - a special ancient and medieval type of a building, rectangular in plan and divided inside by two longitudinal rows of pillars.

Bas-relief - sculptural (with a low relief) picture on a flat surface.

Baroque - an architectural style of the XVI-XVIII centuries notable for decorative splendour and complexity of forms.

"Byzantine" style - a Russian architecture style of the middle of the XIX century - the beginning of the XX century with usage of ancient Russian and ancient Byzantine architecture motives, is notable for monumental and massive constructions.

Gallery - 1) a long, narrow sheltered passage connecting two separate parts of a building;
2) a long, narrow sheltered corridor or balcony along the facade of a building.

Gothic - an architectural style of the XII-XVI centuries notable for a stressed rush high into the air, for usage of lancet arches and vaults, for abundance of sculptural decor.

High relief - a sculptural picture on a flat surface when the figures project more than by a half of their volume.

Decor - artistic decoration of a building.

Capital - the upper part of a pillar or a pilaster acting as an immediate transition to the roof.

Classicism, classical style - an architectural style of the XVII - the early XIX centuries which developed the traditions of antiquity and was notable for austerity and reserve of forms.

Console - a projection in a wall for supporting some parts of a building (cornice, balcony, etc.) or for mounting on it any decorations.

Constructivism - an architectural style of 1920-1930-ties notable for striving for creation of simple forms functionally justified.

Attic - a garret under a steep broken roof, can act as a dwelling.

Minaret - a tower of a mosque from which muezzins call Moslems for a prayer.

Modern - an architectural trend of the close of the XVIII century - the beginning of the XX century for which an original decor, a free layout, usage of new building materials were characteristic.

Order - a type of a composition based on an artistic processing of carrying pillars and carrying constructions (entablature).

Ramp - an inclined plane by the entrance into the building acting as stairs and also acting for entry of carriages, cars, carriages for invalids, etc.

Pergola - a garden pavilion twined round by greenery or a passage of light lattice lined with climbers.

Pylon - a support in the form of a massive post.

Pilaster - a tetrahedral semi-pillar with a capital fit by its one side into a wall.

Portal - an opening architecturally put into shape and usually being the entrance to a building.

Portico - a shed supported by a colonnade.

Propylon - a colonnade in front of the entrance to a building or to any territory located symmetrically in the direction of the movement.

The Renaissance - an architectural style of the XIX century - the beginning of the XX century notable for monumentality, abundance of relief decorations.

Rotunda - a round construction (building, pavilion, hall) usually surrounded by pillars and crowned by a dome.

Pediment - the completion (as a rule, triangular) of the facade of a building, portico, colonnade limited on each side by two slopes of the roof and by a cornice near the base.

Sherfe - a small balcony encircling the minaret of a mosque.

Simferopol - the gate of the Crimea

There are very many governmental institutions in Simferopol. At the same time it is the main spiritual center of the land.

G. Moskvich

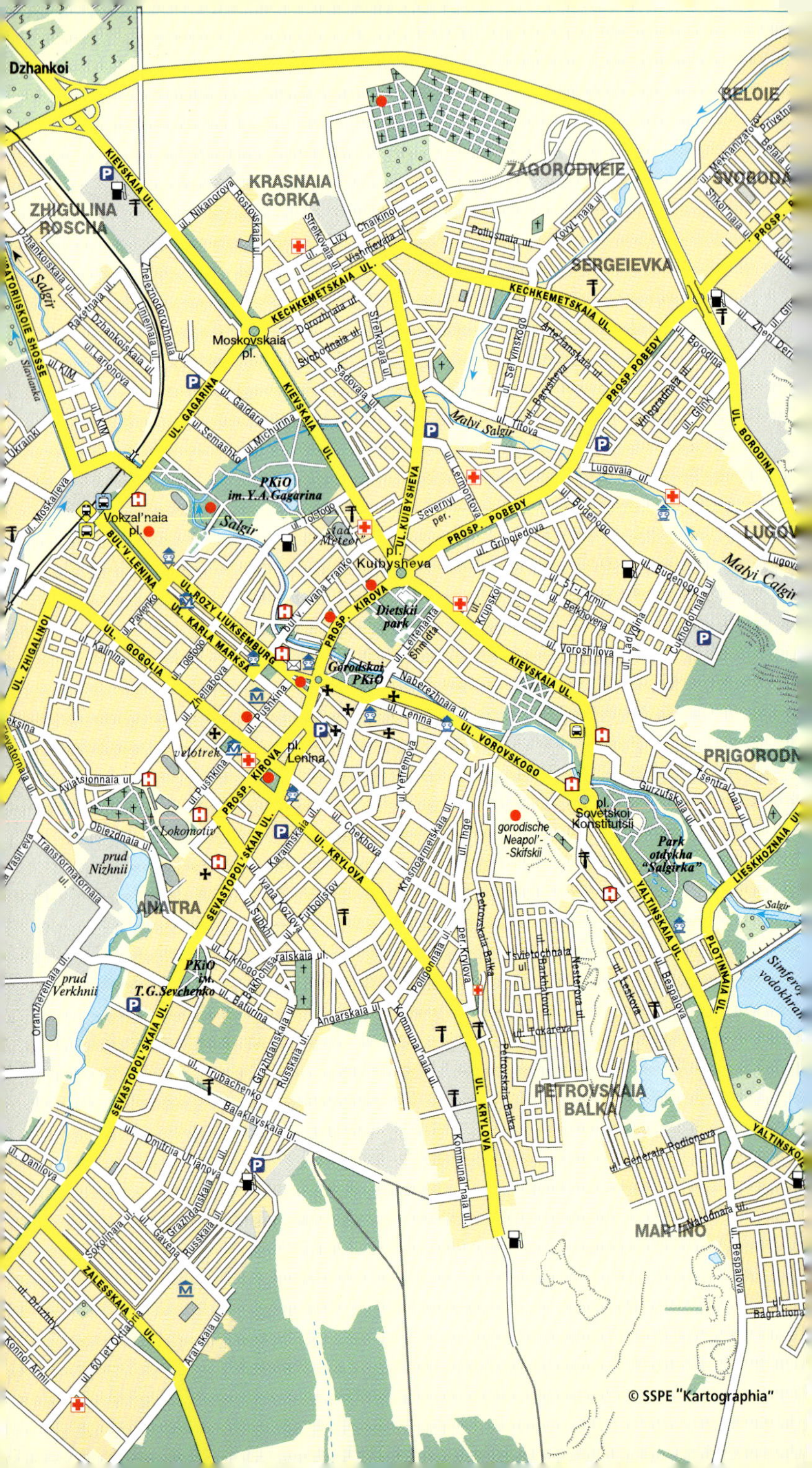
Dzhankoi
BELOIE
ZAGORODNEIE
SVOBODA
KRASNAIA GORKA
ZHIGULINA ROSCHA
SERGEIEVKA
KIEVSKAIA UL.
KECHKEMETSKAIA UL.
KECHKEMETSKAIA UL.
PROSP. POBEDY
UL. BORODINA
Moskovskaia pl.
UL. GAGARINA
KIEVSKAIA UL.
UL. KUIBYSHEVA
PKiO im. Y.A. Gagarina
Salgir
Malyi Salgir
Vokzal'naia pl.
stad. "Meteor"
pl. Kuibysheva
PROSP. POBEDY
BUL'V. LENINA
UL. ROZY LIUKSEMBURG
UL. KARLA MARKSA
PROSP. KIROVA
Dietskii park
Gorodskoi PKiO
KIEVSKAIA UL.
LUGOV
UL. ZHIGALINOI
UL. GOGOLIA
pl. Lenina
velotrek
UL. VOROVSKOGO
PRIGORODN
pl. Sovetskoi Konstitutsii
gorodische Neapol'-Skifskii
Park otdykha "Salgirka"
LIESKHOZNAIA UL.
"Lokomotiv"
prud Nizhnii
ANATRA
SEVASTOPOL'SKAIA UL.
UL. KRYLOVA
YALTINSKAIA UL.
PLOTINNAIA UL.
Simferopol'skoe vodokhran
prud Verkhnii
PKiO im. T.G. Sevchenko
SEVASTOPOL'SKAIA UL.
UL. KRYLOVA
PETROVSKAIA BALKA
YALTINSKOI
MAR'INO
ZALESSKAIA UL.
AVTODOROZHNOIE SHOSSE
© SSPE "Kartographia"

History in a few lines

40 - 50 thousand years ago *ancient people settled in the cave of Chokurcha on the territory of modern Simferopol.*
The 3rd cent. B.C. - *the Scythians founded here the capital of their state - Neapolis of the Scythians, as the Greeks called it. A Scythian name of the town that disappeared six centuries later was lost for the history.*
The 16th cent. - *a Tatar settlement of Ak-Mechet was located here since the beginning of the century. For some time it served as a residence of kalgi-sultan, a governor-general of the Crimean khan.*
February, 1784 - *Catherine II signed a decree on the foundation of Simferopol.*
October, 1874 - *construction of the railway line Kharkov-Simferopol is completed. An economic boom began in the provincial town.*
October, 1921 - *Simferopol became the capital of the Crimean Autonomous Soviet Socialist Republic.*
September 25, 1992 - the city became the capital of the Republic of Crimea and in 1995 - the capital of the Autonomous Republic of Crimea.

A bas-relief on Dolgoruky's obelisk, erected by a grandson of General V. Dolgoruky, commander of the Second Russian Army, in commemoration of a victory in the war against Turkey in 1768 - 1774. It is the first monument in Simferopol, built in 1842.

A view on Simferopol from the top of Peter rocks

It is difficult to determine the age of the city that became the capital of the Autonomy. In fact the age of Simferopol is a little more than two centuries - it is not that much. The age of Neapolis Scythian, a capital of an Old Scythian State located on this site, is two milleniums more. But the Scythians themselves did not settle on a desert place as well...

A favorable geographical location of the city "makes" it play a role of the capital. After the annexation of the Crimean peninsula by the Russian crown, it was necessary to determine an administrative center of the annexed lands. Prince Grigory Potyomkin proposed to build the main city of the Crimea near a small Tatar village of Ak-Mechet. A priest and a historian E. Bulgaris invented the name of the city - Simferopol, in translation from Greek it means "a city-collector". During the whole period of its existence the city did not change its status of the regional center.

Nowadays the population of Simferopol is about 400,000 people - it is the biggest city of the Crimea, a center of economic, cultural and scientific life of the republic.

In fact, the tourists do not stay here as far as there is neither a caressing sea, nor majestic mountains or pompous magnificence. Instead, the central offices of big tourist firms are located here, numerous tourist routes start from here. This is the main gate where all the roads, leading to all the corners of the beautiful Crimean land, cross. However, one should not think that there are no interesting things in Simferopol. Temples and parks, well-groomed streets in the central part of the city, a unique Russian Drama Theater and splendid museums, stylish buildings dated back to the beginning of the last century are expected to be seen by those who will decide to stay in Simferopol for several days.

River Salgir

A warning for the automobilists: the streets of the city are overloaded with vehicles in summer, it is stressful to drive.

Addresses, telephones

City Police Department *Tel.:* 27-2040

Duty-officer of the Traffic Police *Tel.:* 27-6568

Ambulance *Tel.:* 22-1366

Drugstore *Tel.:* 0-67

Mine-rescue service *Tel.:* 25-3158

City Inquiry Service *Tel.:* 27-6206

Central Post Service
1 Rosy Lyuksemburg St. Tel.: 27-2255

Creditbank
21 Dekabristov St. *Tel.:* 25-4470

Privatbank
15 Pushkina St. *Tel.:* 27-4340

In the square near the railway terminal

Inquiry Service of the Railway Terminal *Tel.:* 24-3418
Tickets Reservation *Tel.:* 0-55

"Tsentralny" ("Central") Autoterminal
4 Kievskaya St. *Tel.:* 29-5545
Tickets Reservation *Tel.:* 27-2302

Coach stations: "Kurortnaya" ("Resort") *Tel.:* 25-2560
Vokzalnaya Square
"Zapadnaya" *("Western")*
Sevastopolskaya St. *Tel.:* 44-78345

Order of taxi-cabs *Tel.:* 27-5209

As it was already mentioned, practically all the roads in the Crimea lead to Simferopol. Tourists are coming here prior to go to the seashore, and it is from here that they are going home, being sad that the vacation ended so quickly...

"SIMFEROPOL" AIRPORT

One of the biggest international airports in Ukraine is located outside the city. The air flights to Ukraine, Russia, Belarus, the Caucasus as well as to Europe, Asia and America are made from here. Airliners of many air companies of the world are serviced here. Air tickets are sold in the air booking offices of Simferopol or in the air booking offices of the Crimean regional agency of air transportation that are available in all the cities of the peninsula.

One can leave from the airport by coaches or trolleybusses to the resort cities of the seashore. If you want to go to Simferopol, you can go to down town by trolleybus # 9, its stop is located just opposite the building of the air terminal (fee - 40 kopecks). It will take you about half an hour. A stop of the route taxies is located there as well. Their services are twice as expensive but it will take you less time to get to down town.

RAILWAY

A beautiful building of the railway terminal located in Vokzalnaya (Railway Terminal) Square is a pleasant surprise for the guests of the Crimea tired of a long trip. While getting off the railway cars the guests are met by the taxi drivers willing to bring the travelers to any spot of the peninsula. Don't be in a hurry to agree - with each step towards the near railway terminal square the prices of a taxi trip will be lower!

"Tsentralny" ("Central") Airport in Simferopol

One can go from here to Yevpatoriya, Saki and Sevastopol by train. Local traffic ticket-offices are located in the square near the exit from the tunnel.

BUS SERVICE

There are several autoterminals and coach stations in the city. From the "Tsentralny" ("Central") autoterminal the coaches leave for Sevastopol, Kerch, Stary Krym. "Kurortnaya" ("Resort") coach station is located near the railway terminal. You can go from here to Yalta, Yevpatoriya, Saki and Sudak. "Zapadnaya" ("Western") coach station provides services to the passengers going to the western coast of the Crimea: Nikolayevka, Mezhvodnoye, Chernomorskoye.

TROLLEYBUS SERVICE

In the Crimea you have a unique opportunity to have a ride along the mountain roads by a trolleybus for only UAH 5. It is the longest trolleybus route in Europe. It connects Simferopol with Alushta (trip time - one hour and a half) and Yalta (two hours and a half).

LODGING

"Ukraina"

7 Rosy Lyuksemburg St.
Tel.: 51-0165

Business life is boiling up just behind the windows of the hotel. An interior design of the rooms is out of date, but they are rather decent. Air-conditioning is not available. The price of a double room with hot running water, a refrigerator, a TV set and a telephone is UAH 122 per night. The price of a single room without any conveniences is UAH 39 per night. There is a bar and a cafe in the lobby. There is a parking place near the hotel (additional UAH 5 per night to a doorkeeper for looking after your car).

"Tavriya"

21 Bespalova St.
Tel.: 23-2024, 23-3919

The hotel is located near the Yalta highway where there is a trolleybus route leading to the southern shore. Organized tourist groups are basically staying here.

"Paradise"

near the "Tsentralniy" ("Central") Airport
Tel.: 29-5337

The hotel is located near the air terminal building. It is convenient for the tourists who arrived with a night flight.

"Moskva"

2 Kievskaya St.,
Tel.: 32-7520, 23-9795

It is located near the autoterminal, just opposite the "Salgirka" park. The price of a two-room semi-suite with a telephone, a refrigerator, a TV set and hot running water is UAH 200 per night. The price of a suite (three rooms) is UAH 300 per night for the Ukrainians and about UAH 500 per night for foreigners. The price of the cheapest room is UAH 48 per night. Reservation fee is 50% from the cost of the room per night. There is a restaurant in the hotel.

The first street of the city - now Karla Marksa Street - has been restored lately. It is partially closed for the vehicle traffic.

MEALS

There are many cafes and restaurants in the city. Ordinary snack bars, snack bars serving patties, etc. are located in the railway terminal area and are notable for cheap prices.

They serve the dishes of the Ukrainian cuisine in the restaurant **"Knyazha vtikha"** ("Prince's enjoyment") (35 Turgeneva St., Tel.: 29-1489).

For those who like Armenian cuisine we can recommend the restaurant **"Chistiye Prudy"** ("Pure ponds"), which is located to the right from the central entrance of Yuriy Gagarin's park. One can see a show in the evening here.

"Camelot" (1 Gorkogo St., Tel.: 25-4456) attracts the customers by the combination of moderate prices, pleasant interior, and good cuisine.

Fast-food funs are expected to visit **McDonald's** located in Vokzalnaya Square.

ENTERTAINMENT

One can find a shelter from the summer heat in the parks and gardens located along the banks of the Salgir River. If you came here with the children, bring them to the Children's park (trolleybus # 2 can bring you there from the railway terminal).

In the old park "Salgirka" one can be interested in a travel house of M. Vorontsov, former governor of the area, and an estate of Academician P. Pallas who, in fact, laid out this marvelous park.

Theatre-goers will hardly miss an opportunity to visit the Crimean Tatars Music and Drama Theatre (5 Mendeleyeva St., Tel.: 25-6198) where talented actors perform. There are seven stages in the beautiful building of M. Gorky Theatere (15 Pushkina St., Tel.: 27-6702) built by architect A. Beketov's design.

In addition, there are cinemas, a circus, casinos, nightclubs, etc. It is impossible to tell about everyhting - we suggest you to get orientated yourself in the city.

The Academic Russian Drama Theatre

The inhabitants of the Crimean capital are proud of numerous historic and architectural sights of their young city.

A site of an ancient settlement "Neapolis - Scythian"

Somewhere in the past there was a beautiful city here with stone houses and magnificent palaces decorated with splendid wall paintings and statues. After the Goths and then the Huns fought their way through Tauris, destroying everything around them, nothing but mere ruins remained from a Scythian capital. Most of the survived Scythians escaped to the

All that remained from Neapolis - Scythian

mountains, and only a handful of the inhabitants did not leave the ruins... Life was going on. A settlement of Kermenchik ("a small fortress") was set up. The Tatars that came here a thousand years later called it in such a way. The Tatars settled themselves near the stone plateau where a poor site of an ancient settlement was located. The remains of a fortification like an ancient Cyclop protected it.

The Tatars founded a settlement of Ak-Mechet near by. They picked up trimmed stones from the plateau, exterminating little by little a memory about the Scythian capital. The last inhabitants, descendants of an ancient state, left these lands in 1779.

In the beginning of the 19th cent. nothing showed that a big city used to be located above the Petrovskaya gorge. One day a district police officer who was very fond of antiquities saw a bas-relief with a Scythian picture on a bullock cart with stones. He let the scientists know about the finding, and an archeological expedition started its work.

Kebir-Jami mosque

4 Kurchatova St.

The oldest building of the city, that gave its name to a Tatar settlement of Ak-Mechet (White mosque), was built in 1502. The Crimean khan Mengli-Gerey presented these lands to kalgi-sultan - his deputy on military affairs. A settlement was set up on the banks of the Salgir River. A Turkish traveler Evliya Chelebi, who visited the Crimea in 1666, wrote that at that time there were about 1,800 houses, and also 5 mosques and 4 caravanserais (hotels) in Ak-Mechet. The main mosque Kebir-Jami was located in the center of the city. Its modern view differs a little from a canonical one as far as the roof is concerned: a habitual big cupola is not available. Most likely it fell down as early as in the 17th cent. The reconstruction took place at that time as well. Nowadays the mosque is acting.

Kebir-Jami - White mosque of Simferopol

Vorontsov's house

"Salgirka" park

A travel house of General M. Vorontsov, a Governor of Novorosiysk, was located in the ancient landscape park. M. Vorontsov frequently attended Simferopol on his service affairs. Here he also stayed on the way to his southern coast estate (now Vorontsov's Palace in the town of Alupka). It is for those purposes that a country estate of Prince D. Naryshkin, built in 1826 - 1827 by an architect F. Elson, was bought. After the October Coup the faculties of the Tauris National University were located in the estate. Academician V. Vernadsky was the first rector of the university. Now Vorontsov's house belongs to the Crimean Academy of Sciences. In the main building there were preserved fragments of wall paintings in the Ampere style, some details of the interior, for example, a splendid bentwood staircase leading up to the second floor. Wide stone steps lead to the main entrance. Two huge lions guard a pedestal of the steps.

Milgauzen's house

24 Kievskaya St.

A house of Fyodor Karlovich Milgauzen, a famous medical doctor, meteorologist, and botanist was built in 1828. For all that it is not the house itself but an outstanding personality of the house owner which is of historic interest

Svyatotroitskaya Church

for us. F.Milgauzen entered Saint-Petersburg Medical Institute in the age of 14 and being 22 years old he had already started his medical practice. In 1820 he moved into the Crimea because his health had become worth. The Crimean climate did him good: in the old age the doctor was walking no less than 4 versts (4.24 km) a day.

His house was attended by M.Shchepkin, I.Aivazovsky, V.Zhukovsky... A.Pushkin who visited the Crimea in 1920 was probably treated by F.Milgauzen. The doctor treated many inhabitants of Simferopol free of charge.

In addition to the medical treatment, a scientist was engaged in meteorological research. In 1821 he founded the first meteorological station in the Crimea.

"Karolinovka" estate

"Salgirka" park

In the beginning of the 19th cent. Pyotr Simon Pallas, a famous naturalist, geographer, and traveler bought a plot of land outside the city, laid out a garden and built a house there. The estate was called "Karolinovka" in honor of the scientist's wife. Soon the estate was sold. It is P.Pallas that the Crimea is owed to as to the renaissance of vine growing and winemaking. The estate was restores in the 80-ies of the 20th cent.

Former boy's gymnasia

32 Karla Marksa St.

The following outstanding personalities studied in this modest building: I.Kurchatov - later a scientist-physicist, A.Spendiarov - an Armenian composer and conductor, I.Gasprinsky - an enlightener of the Crimean Tatar people, I.Aivazovsky - a painter of seascapes, etc. D.Mendeleyev, later a scientist-chemist, and a Karaite poet I.Kazas - a public figure, an enlightener, an uncle of an artist M.Kazas taught for some time in the gymnasia. A school is located in the building of the gymnasia now.

CHRISTIAN TEMPLES

The first Christian church of Simferopol was located in a usual Tatar house (modern 8 Oktyabrskaya St., still acting today), bought for those purposes in 1784. Catherine II who visited Simferopol was not pleased with a poor decoration. The Empress allocated money for building an Orthodox Temple. The cathedral named Aleksandro-Nevsky was constructed. True, the construction of the cathedral dragged on for many years. The cathedral was sanctified in 1829 and in 100 years it was exploded on instructions of Soviet authorities. A tank "T-34" is standing now on the site of the cathedral.

The most significant in terms of architecture among the Simferopol acting churches are as follows: Svyatotroitsky Cathedral (12 Odesskaya St.), Petropavlovsky Cathedral (16 Oktyabrskaya St.), Tryokhsvyatskaya Church (16 Gogolya St.), Church of the Seventh-day Adventists (3 Vorovskogo St.).

MONUMENTS TO THE OUSTANDING PEOPLE

A monument to Sanctifier Luka (in the world - V.Voino-Yasenetsky), the former archbishop of Simferopol and of the Crimea, Professor, Doctor of Medicine is located in Pushkinskaya Street.

A monument to A.Suvorov is erected behind the Hotel "Ukraina". In 1777 on this site there was a camp of the Russian troops under the command of the outstanding military leader.

An obelisk in honor of V.Dolgoruky is erected opposite the Victory Square.

There are many other monuments to historic personalities, scientists, cultural and art workers in Simferopol.

A.Suvorov

Simferopol is a city of museums. The richest Crimean collections of unique archeological findings, historic and ethnographic exhibits, works of art are gathered here.

Wealth of ethnocultures

Still in the 2nd cent. B.C., as a Roman historian Plinius-senior affirmed, there were more than 30 nationalities in the mountains of Tauris. The remains of the nations, used to be great ones, settled here as well as the new nations were formed, for example, the Crimean Tatars, the aboriginal inhabitants of the Crimea.

The Crimean Tatars wearing national clothes. Engraving (CEM)

The Slavs - Ukrainians, Russians, Belarusians, Bulgarians, Czechs constitute the most numerous group of the Crimean population. Many representatives of the Tatar ethnos deported still in 1944 on Stalin's instructions returned to the peninsula in the 90-es of the 20th cent.

The number of nationalities, forming the population of the Crimea today, reaches one hundred. They try to preserve the culture of their ancestors. Those who are interested in ethnography will like folklore festivals that are conducted annually in different corners of the Crimea. One can receive more information about them in the Ethnographical Museum or in the national societies.

The Crimean Republican Museum of Regional Studies

14 Gogolya St.
Tel.: 27-6347
8 a.m. - 5 p.m., except Tuesdays

The museum is located in the building of the former Gubernsky (Regional) Court, built in the 19th cent. in the neoclassical style. The museum was set up in 1921 by means of merge of the collections of the Museum of the Ancient Tauris Scientific Archive Commission and the Naturalist and Historic Museum of the Tauris Zemstvo (elective district council in pre-revolutionary Russia). The collection of the museum counts more than 100.000 copies. There are several permanent exhibitions in the halls: "Natural landscapes of the Crimea" where relics which age is more than 100 years are demonstrated; "The past of Tavrida" - here you can view the findings from the ancient tombs, articles of the family life, handmade goods of the Middle Ages masters; "The Crimea in the Great Patriotic War" - presents a heroic history of the peninsula in times of war. Real treasures are kept in the museum, for example, a unique collection of the Russian and Western European paintings devoted to Tauris.

A medal in commemoration of Catherine's II trip to Tavrida (CRMRS)

The Simferopol Art Museum

35 K.Libknekhta St.
Tel.: 27-5404
10 a.m. - 5 p.m., except Mondays

Since 1937 the art gallery is located in the building of the former Officers Assembly of the 51th Lithuanian regiment. Till then the museum was an Art Department of the Tavrida Central Museum. Pre-war collection has dispersed among the other collections. The employees of the museum had to collect the exhibits all over again, and now the museum contains about 6,000 paintings of the most talented masters of a paintbrush since the 16th cent.

"Swifts and roofs". S.Mamchich (SAM)

The Crimean Ethnographical Museum

18 Pushkina St.,
Tel.: 25-5223
9 a.m. - 4 p.m., except Tuesdays

A branch of the Crimean Republican Museum of Regional Studies was set up in 1992. An exposition is called "Mosaics of the Crimean Cultures". The articles of the family life of Crimean Tatars, Karaites, aboriginal inhabitants of the Crimea, Bulgarians, Russians, Ukrainians, Germans, and other peoples, forming the mixed population of the peninsula, are exhibited here.

Yalta - the capital of the South Coast

The significance of Yalta lies in its natural riches that gave it the glory of a first-rate resort...

G. Moskvich

YUZHNOBEREZHNOIE SHOSSE
pl. 60-letiia SSSR
ul. Kazantseva
ul. Repina
Proletarskaia ul.
ul. Krivoshty
Miskhorskaia ul.
ul. Naidenova
ul. Dzerzhinskogo
KIEVSKAIA UL.
MOSKOVSKAIA UL.
Derekoika (Bystraia)
Sadovaia ul.
ul. Chkalova
Rabochaia ul.
Orekhovaia ul.
Leningradskaia ul.
ul. Rudanskogo
SVERDLOVA
ul. Mukhina
Sovietskaia pl.
rynok
KARLA MARKSA
skver im. N.A. Nekrasova
pl. Lenina
ul. Khalturina
Volkova
Averkina
kholm Darsan
ul. Timiriazieva
Sievastopol'
ul. Lukomskogo
ul. Schorsa
ul. Volkova
SADOVAIA UL.
UL. KIROVA
skver im. N.N. Baturina
ul. Chekhova
Gorodskoi sad
Botkinskaia ul.
skvier im. M.I. Kalinina
naberezhnaia im. Lenina
ul. Marshaka
Sevastopol'
ul. Lomonosova
ul. Biriukova
Pushkinskaia ul.
ul. Gogolia
Pionerskaia ul.
Krasnoarmeiskaia ul.
ul. Bliukhera
ul. Gor'kogo
Tavricheskaia ul.
Balaklavskaia ul.
Volodarskogo
ul. Kommunarov
ul. Schepkina
ul. Dostoievskogo
ul. Stroitielei
ul. Sechenova
Sosnovaia ul.
Krasnoarmeiskaia ul.
Primorskii park im. Y.A. Gagarina
Yaltinskii zaliv
CHERNOE MORE
© SSPE "Kartographia"

History in a Few Lines

The IVth -Vth centuries B.C. *- Founding of the Yalita settlement by Greek colonists.*
The VIth century *- Establishing of the Byzantine Rule.*
The XIVth-XVth centuries *- Yalta becomes a Genoese colony Healita (Etalita).*
The XVth century *- The town leveled by an earthquake comes under the control of the Osman Empire.*
1812 *- Foundation of the Botanical Gardens in the village of Nikita.*

The St. John Chrysostom Bell Tower. Ancient engraving of the 19th century

1837 *- Yalta was nominated the capital of the uyezd (district).*
1848 *- Building of the road connecting Yalta and Sevastopol.*
November, 1920 *- The final establishment of the Soviet Power.*
November, 1941 - April, 1944 *- The city is occupied by the Nazi Germany forces.*
2002 *- There are 84,000 people living in this city-resort.*

Panorama of Yalta

The most popular resort on the southern shore looks like a vast amphitheatre in the antique style, when viewed from the sea. On the background the wooded mountains, Nikitsky mountain pasture in the north-east part, Yaltinska Chine (in the centre), and the Mohabi Mountain on the west form a huge semicirle (up to 1,400 м). The streets in the city go from the embankment upwards along the hills and foothills. A particularly effective view on Yalta is in the evening from a pleasure boat, when the city is shining with multicolored lights, which are gradually climbing up the dark mass of mountains all across the land.

This advantageous geographic situation promotes the formation of the Mediterranean climate in this region of the Crimea. The chine protects the city from cold northern winds, therefore the average temperature in February is +4°C. It is snowing on rare occasions in Yalta and the thin show layer lasts only during several hours, therefore you should be up as early as possible if you want to see palm trees covered with snow.

There is no wearisome heat in summer, since sea breezes ventilate the Yalta amphitheatre well. The average temperature of July is about +24°C. Sun is shining here for 2,250 hours a year, it is the same as in Nice. Sea is warmed up in shore of Yalta at a later time compared to Yevpatoriya or Feodosiya, but it is possible to bath for a month longer - till the middle of October.

The permanent population of the city counts about 88,000 people. During a holiday season the number of population increases: despite high prices, huge masses of visitors come to this place. However, many people go to the so-called Greater Yalta, including, in addition to Yalta, towns and settlements from Gurzuf in the east to Foros in the west - all comprising 72 kilometers!

It is not known when the settlement appeared on the place of which a wonderful resort is widespread. But it is obvious that the Greeks were its founders (Yalta or Yalita means "shore" in Greek). Formerly this area was inhabited by Tavrs, since peculiar burial places - stone chests" (6th-5th centuries B.C.) have been discovered on the slopes of the Polikurovsky Hill (north-eastern part of the city).

The first record about Yalta (12th century) was made by the Arabic geographer Al-Idrizi. The settlement was called Dzhalita. Since the 14th century Yalta under different names, such as Haulita, Etalita, etc. appeared in the peninsula. In the 15th century, life in Yalta was hardly glimmering, because Christians, which were hard suffering from the oppression on the part of the Turks, mainly inhabited this place.

After the Christians left the peninsula (1778) for the Sea of Azov coast, Yalta became almost deserted. In his work "Leisure Hours of the Crimean Judge..." P. Sumarokov noted that in 1800 in Yalta there were "13 peasants' houses of the Greek Balaklava battalion", all in all. In 1820-ies, about 300 people lived in the village, mainly the Crimean Tatars. In 1837, a road made of the gravel connected Yalta with Alushta and Simferopol, and in 1848 a road was constructed from Sevastopol to Yalta. The life in the town livened up at once, particularly due to the fact that the settlement was granted the status of a small town, and then the status of a uyezd (district) town. Still in the middle of the 19th century, due to research of the well-known researcher S. Botkin, who discovered the healing power of the local climate, Yalta became a fashionable resort. This doctor came to the Crimea during the Russo-Turskish War to work in the hospitals of Sevastopol and Bakhchisarai. He recommended to the Imperial House to purchase a summer estate in the eastern shore of the Crimea. In that way Romanovs appeared in Livadiya. Following the Tsar, the court circle, Tsar's relatives, and well-to-do manufacturers started to build summer residences and palaces there. The

The embankment in the morning

A view of Yalta from a pleasure boat

southern coast started to look better, since, in addition to splendid buildings, wonderful parks and gardens had been laid out on this land.

The rapid development of the city as a popular resort was interrupted after the October of 1917. The change of regimes in the process of the Civil War was accompanied by the terror and executions. After the Soviet Power was finally established in the Crimea, Yalta was given a new name - Krasnoarmeisk. Fortunately, the new name did not get accustomed. Summer residences and palaces had been nationalized and sanatoriums and holiday homes for workers and peasants had been arranged in many of them.

The first sanatorium "Dolossy" for the medical treatment of the working people was built in the vicinity of Yalta in 1928. In 1940, there were already 42 sanatoriums and holiday homes, which could accommodate 5,560 people. During the war, many health centres were destroyed, but the construction resorts developed rapidly in the post-war period.

How the City of Yalta Came into Being

Long ago, the Greek ships put out to sea from Constantinople. The mother country was in the need of new lands, where it would be possible to grow crops and pasture sheep.

The ships drifted for a long time, since it was not without reason that the ancients called this cold sea "Pontos Euxinos", which meant "inhospitable sea". Huge violent waves flooded the decks and tore the sails to pieces... The spontaneous forces made the ships to lose their way and lose sight of one another. The rovers strained themselves to breaking point, people became horror-stricken waiting for inevitable death among boundless leaden waves... The storm abated, but dark and cold fog surrounded unhappy the wretched ships. The great Homeros told about the end of the world, where on the border of the Hades, the dark possessions of the hyperboreys are widespread, which is the country of the outer darkness and severe cold. Was it possible that Gods took them exactly there?!

There was no food and water, and only waves and fog were endless. There was no hope to see the land some day.... But it was like a miracle! Once, at daybreak that broke up the shroud of fog, the sea-folk saw a wonderful green shore before them.

- "Yalos!" - a person on patrol cried out. Soon the ships moored to the shore of the wonderful country, which was called Taurida by them. There was enough place for everyone, the mythical hyperboreys appeared to be hospitable and industrious people. In their neighborhood, the Greeks founded their coastal settlement, which they called "Yalos", that meant "shore".

How one can get to Yalta? This question requires a lengthy answer, since there are roads leading to the capital of the south-eastern shore region. All depends on the point of the Crimea, from which you start your journey. But in any case, you come to one of the Yalta terminals.

BUS STATION

All buses arrive to this bus station from other cities of the Crimea and from all over Ukraine. The fare from Simferopol is eight hryvnias, and you will pay two hryvnias more in the inter-city taxis, but on the other hand, you will reduce in such a way your travel time. On the second floor of the bus station there is a rest house. The luggage office woks till 6 p.m., and the bus station - from 6 a.m. till 8.30 p.m.

TROLLEYBUS STATION

It is next to the bus terminal. In summer, the trolleybuses depart to Simferopol every 20 minutes. A single ticket is around 5 hryvnias, and luggage is at extra cost. During the high season (from June 15 till August 25) it is advisable to purchase tickets well in advance.

INTER-CITY TAXIES

The majority of the routes are formed near the bus terminal (from its southern side). From this place you may go to Alupka (route No. 27), Simeiz (No. 26), Foros (No. 28), Nikitsky Botanical Gardens (No. 29), and Partenit (No. 46).

From the market place, the inter-city taxies go to Gurzuf (No. 31), Nikita (No. 34). The fare in the inter-city taxies is 1-2 hryvnias depending on the distance.

MARINE PASSANGER TERMINAL

Each year above 5 million people arrive to this terminal. In addition to the routes to the ports of Ukraine, ships from Yalta go to the Balkan and Turkish shores. From the berth located on the Lenin Embankment boats go to all cities and towns of the Crimea. Sightseeing tours are organized to the points of interest in the southern shore region.

THE URBAN TRANSPORT

It is possible to go for a trip by a trolleybus. Route No. 3 ends outside the city in Masandra. The fare is 40 kopecks. The inter-city taxies carry out the rest of work on the conveyance of passengers. The usual taxi transportation is expensive.

The ropeway connects the Embankment and the Darsan Hill.

Addresses and telephones:

City Militia Department: *Tel.:* **32-2250**

Person on duty of the State Motor Licencing and Inspection Department: *Tel.:* **31-4622**

First-aid station *Tel.:* **32-5073**

Drugstores (directory inquiries) *Tel.:* **0-67**

Health-resort out-patient's clinic: *2-a Kirov Street* *Tel.:* **32-5992**

Post Office:
1 Lenin Street *Tel.:* **31-2073**

Travel bureau:
8 Chekhov Street *Tel.:* **32-6959**

Bank on Katerininskaya Street

"Privatbank":
19 Vasiliev Street *Tel.:* **32-2040**

"Kreditbank":
22 Gogol Street *Tel.:* **23-0387**

Bus Station *8 Moskovska St.*

Directory inquiries:
Suburban traffic: *Tel.:* **34-2075**
Intercity traffic: *Tel.:* **34-2092**

Trolleybus station
8 Moskovskaya St. *Tel.:* **32-7994**

Marine Passanger Terminal
5 Roosevelt St. *Tel.:* **32-7535**

City Berth
Lenina Embankment *Tel.:* **32-5622**

Advance Sale of Tickets
Railway
12 Sverdlova St. *Tel.:* **32-4347**

Aviation
8 Moskovskaya St. *Tel.:* **32-3732**

Central Market
24 Kievskaya St.

To be sure, Yalta is the Crimean city which has the largest number of hotels. Range of prices for dwelling varies greatly: from 25 hryvnias to 5,600 hryvnias per 24 hours.

"Oreanda". A view from sea

"Oreanda"

35/2 Lenin Embankment
Tel.: 39-0608, 32-8227

It is one of the most fashionable hotels in the city with114 hotel rooms.

Apartments consist of 3 rooms: a sitting room, study, and bedroom. Water in the hotel rooms complies with the European standard. A Jacuzzi having the effect of the Turkish baths will enable one to relax after a lengthy sightseeing tour. In the hotel rooms there are mini-safes for keeping precious jewelry. The price is 3,920-5,600 hryvnias in the high season. In winter, the prices drop by more than a half.

The suite consists of 2 rooms, the prices ranging from 2,744 to 3,080 hryvnias per 24 hours. Semi-luxurous hotel apartments are from 1,800-2,350 hryvnias, one-room apartment - from 950 hryvnias (single) to 1,680 hryavnias (double). Of course, prices can strike down, but provided there is demand, there is supply! Hotel rooms are furnished with electronic locks. The cost of a hotel room includes the following services: breakfast, visiting the beach, a swimming pool (there are two swimming pools in the "Oreanda" hotel, indoor and outdoor), gymnasium, and Turkish baths.

At the hotel there is bowling, casino, night club, and tennis-courts. Service price is the same both for the citizens of Ukraine and foreigners at the cafe and the restaurant of the "Oreanda" hotel. Such a democracy is not peculiar to many national institutions. Two rooms for negotiations are at the service of the delegations and businessmen.

The shortcomings are the following: the low-quality beach, although it is the trouble for the whole city of Yalta; the hotels are located in the crowded places, as a result there are blinker lights and rattling music all the night; the curiosity of many gapers goggling the whole day long through the railing at people splashing in the swimming-pool.

The payment can be effected by credit cards.

"Lito" (Summer)

Prymorsky Park
Tel.: 32-1011

The hotel and entertaining complex is located in the heart of a wonderful park on the seashore. The hotel is small - there 15 rooms all in all in it, two of them are of the highest category. All hotel rooms are double rooms. The price of the most expensive hotel room is about 2,200 hryvnias in the high season, an ordinary hotel double room is 770 hryvnias. A surcharge for a child (depending on the age, from 2 to 16) should be made from 60 to 90 hryvnias, and for a grown up person such a hotel room would cost 320 hryvnias per 24 hours.

Bowling club in the "Lito" (Summer) hotel

The first Yalta's bowling appeared in this hotel. Also, the "Lito" (Summer) proposes to its guests the billiards, a club, bar, restaurant, and playing room for children. A splendid banquet room can be a point of interest in this complex. It is located above the sea-level, at a height of 30 m. A picturesque view on the Yalta bay opens from this place.

The absence of its own beach is the shortcoming of this place.

Tourists' Recreational Complex "Palace"

8 Chekhova Street
Tel.: 23-0486

The Tourists' Recreational Complex has 37 hotel rooms, nine of them are double first-class rooms, and one - apartments. The price of living in a double room ranges from 265 to 425 hryvnias per man.

At the tourist hotel there are a car park, bar, cafe and restaurant; sauna is only in the apartments.

There is no beach since the hotel is located in the centre of the city. One more shortcoming consists in the fact that the credit cards are not accepted for payment.

"Vremena Goda" (Seasons)

23 Rudanskoho St.
Tel.: 32-6012

The complex includes the hotel, a restaurant, and a medical centre. The price for apartments makes up 1,650 hryvnias per 24 hours (2-3 persons), the suit is less expensive making up from 800 to 1,000 hryvnias. The price of a single room is 250 hryvnias per man and a double room is 360 hryvnias for two persons. A discount system starts after three days of living at the hotel. While a mother with a child under 12 years of age is accommodated in a double room, she pays the price of a single room. All the hotel rooms are with modern conveniences (douche, lavatory, telephone, refrigerator and air-conditioner). There is also a sauna, swimming pool with sweet water, children's room, and training hall. Here the persons interested can pass total medical examination.

The beach of this complex is out of the city in 15-minutes journey by the inter-city taxies.

"Yalta"

50 Drazhinskoho St.,
Tel.: 27-0260, 35-0218

This 17-storied giant, emerging from the greenery of the Massandra park towards the sea, has not been a single complex for a long time now. It is the hotel complex, which is the largest in the Crimea, accommodating about 2,500 tourists.

There are not many rooms of the "suit" category - about 30, a suit for two is 900 hryvnias in the high season. There is a large number of semi-luxury rooms at 380 hryvnias/24 hours per man. Very comfortable double rooms will cost 240 hryvnias per man. The lowest price of a double room of the first category is 168 hryvnias per man.

This accommodation price includes breakfast, hotel dues, cost of using the beach and swimming pool. All rooms in the "Yalta" hotel are with modern conveniences, but not all rooms are equipped with air conditioners.

The hotel complex is abounding in restaurants and cafes. One can choose the cookery to one's own taste.

It is possible to get to "Yalta's" own beach by the elevator, the complex building is rather high over the seashore.

Surcharge is necessary for using the sauna, masseur services, as well as for swimming in the swimming pool with dolphins (50 hryvnias per 5 minutes).

"Visa" and "Master Card" are accepted for payment..

In addition to the listed expensive hotels, there are less expensive hotels in Yalta.

"Yalta" hotel in the Massandra Park

The "Crimea"

1/6 Moskovskaya Street
Tel.: 27-1710, 32-6001

The price of a room varies from 140 to 300 hryvnias per 24 hours (for two persons). A single room without conveniences is 35 hryvnias and a double room - 60 hryvnias.

The "Venice" hotel is located in this building (Tel.: 32-6042), which is of the higher rate. The price of its rooms is from 300 to 600 hryvnias (breakfast including).

"Otdykh" (Recreation)

14 Drazhinskogo Street
Tel.: 35-3079

An ancient house with a romantic staircase and interesting designing. The hotel has 18 rooms, five of them are of the high category (the autonomous water supply, refrigerator, and TV set), the price is from 95 to 135 hryvnias per 24 hours; 13 rooms of the lower category, from 80 to 120 hryvnias (single, double, and rooms for three persons).

"Masandra"

46 Drazhinskogo Street
Tel.: 27-2401, 27-2427

There are 136 hotel rooms in it, 18 of them are equipped with air conditioners. All double rooms, the price is 220 hryvnias for two persons. It is located in the ancient part and has its own beach. In Yalta there are also some private hotels at the following addresses: 11 Pushkinskaya Street (Tel.: 32-1575), and 6 Katerininskaya Street, and others.

"Espanyola"

35-g Lenin Embankment
Tel.: 39-0631 from 11.00 a.m. till the last client

The schooner, in which a fish restaurant is located, has been built for shooting the "Treasure Island" film. Prices are rather expensive in this restaurant, but you get so much romanticism, in particular in the evening! For the shy clients there exist special rooms. The cabins are supplied with air conditioners. The price of a dinner is 100-150- hryvnias. A cup of coffee costs from 6 hryvnias, beer - from 10 hryvnias. The specialty of the house is the salmon under the sauce. Dishes of fish - from 40 hryvnias, of meat - from 30 hryvnias. Also dietetical and vegetarian dishes are served.

"White Lion"

31-a Lenin Embankment
Tel.: 32-7736 from 9.00 a.m. till the last client

The elite restaurant located in the white building under a

red roof, which is like a mini-palace. The price of a dinner is 100-150 hryvnias. The European cuisine. The specialty of the house - the sturgeon "White Lion" - 80 hryvnias, salad "Albino" (seafood with the cognak) - 38 hryvnias. There are dishes for the vegetarians. Fulfillment of the order takes from 20 to 50 minutes. While waiting for their food, the clients are listening to the "live music". Payment for this pleasure makes up 5 hryvnias for entry to this restaurant. It is possible to spend a nice time there.

At present, a restaurant is opened at the ship of Argonauts

"Zolote Runo" (The Golden Fleece)

8 Lenin Embankment
Tel. 32-8272
from 10.00 a.m. till the last client is served.

There is one more establishment on the ship, but it is connected with the antique Greece. Probably, Jason sold the Golden Fleece from the Kingdom of Colchis and opened a restaurant with the European cuisine and high prices. Price of a dinner is from 80 to 100 hryvnias (drinks are not included). Salads are the following: salad of vegetables - from 20 hryvnias, of fish - from 30 hryvnias, meat salad - from 50 hryvnias. Coffee - starting from 3 hryvnias. The restaurant is not designed for the clients-vegetarians or those preferring dietetical cuisine.

"Cactus"

7 Rousevelt Street
Tel. 32-1614
from 11.00 a.m. till 12.00 p.m.

It is one of the best restaurants in Yalta, located on the 1st floor of the marine pas-

senger terminal and having the Mexican and American cuisine. There is also the banquet room and separate cabins. Prices are high. Specialty of the house: calves' liver a la Caribbean - 52 hryvnias, steak "Matador" - 56 hryvnias, steak "The Bone" a la America - 99 hryvnias. Fish dishes - from 70 hryvnias, soups - from 20 hryvnias. And, of course, a genuine tequila! Tips - to client's discretion.

Here one may also find a casino and discotheque.

"Ostriv Skarbiv" (Treasure Island)

Lenin Embankment
Tel.: 32-1909 from 8.00 a.m. till 4.00 a.m.

An open-air restaurant on the seashore with an interior in the pirate schooner style. It offers a European cuisine, there are no dietary and vegetarian dishes. The price of dinner is close to 300 hryvnias. The order is served within half an hour. Specialty of the house - cocktail, 30 hryvnias. Fish soup "Buyabez" is 45 hryvnias. A "live" music is offered in the evenings. Tips are included into the price of food.

"Allegro"

48 Drazhinskogo Street
Tel.: 35-0600
from 9.00 a.m. till the last client.

An Italian restaurant in the Massandra Park. A pleasant surrounding with an aquarium, paintings, greenery and billiards. Specialty of the house is the following: beefsteak "Allegro" - 45 hryvnias, sword-fish - 67 hryvnias. Stuffed mutton trotters should be ordered five hours before the beginning of the evening party, price is 90 hryvnias per one kg. The banquet room has air conditioning, there is also a hall for nonsmokers. Live music in the evenings. Tips make up 10% of the order price.

"Peking"
50 Drazhinskogo Street
Tel.: 35-0002
twenty-four hours a day

The Chinese restaurant is located on the ground floor of the "Yalta" complex. The interior is made in the traditional yellow and red colors. Light Chinese music sets one's mind at rest and brings relaxation. A specialty of the house - duck a la Peking - should be ordered three hours in advance, the price is 228 hryvnias. For

dessert fried pineapples with honey are offered at 19 hryvnias. Tips make up 10% of the order price.

Restaurant "Gurman" ("Gourmet")
11 Lenina St, Yalta,
tel.(0654) 32-0306
11.00 - before posl. client

Sharm of a french province, stylized interior, european kitchen, live music. Here, there is all for pleasing pastime: inimitable atmosphere, comfortable conditions for rest, perfect service. This really is a worthy place for worthy people.(C. 196).

"Slavyansky"
25 Lenina Embankment
Tel.: 32-2100
from 9.00 a.m.
till 12.00 p.m.

The price of a dinner is 85 hryvnias. European cuisine. There is an open-air platform, two halls with air-conditioners. In the evenings live music is offered at three hryvnias per man. Tips are given on the client's discretion.

"Sribna Pidkova" (Silver Horseshoe)
Prymorsky Park
Tel.: 32-8698
on a twenty-four hours base

The cafe is stylized as a cowboy saloon. The American cuisine, price of a dinner averages 30 hryvnias. The specialty of the house is meat a la Texas - 12 hryvnias. Fish dishes cost around 20 hryvnias. Time of servicing the order is no more than 20 minutes. It is the favorite cafe of the Yalta youth. In the evenings a discotheque is held.

"Limpopo"
Prymorsky Park
Tel.: 32-3139 from 8.00 a.m. till the last client.

This disco-bar is located in the green zone of the city and it is like the aforementioned cafe. Prices are the same, and the menu is almost the same. In any case, the beefsteak "The Fierce Harry" and beefsteak "Arizona" evidently smell of the Wild West. One of the most popular city discotheques is also located here.

"Alan"
3 Ignatenko Street
Tel.: 32-7709 from 8.00 a.m. till 10.00 p.m.

The tea-room, where wonderful milk cocktails are prepared. The specialty of the house - "Alan" cocktail - is especially tasty. Its price is 3 hryvnias. Here one can take some pastries, juice, coffee and arrange a holiday for children. Children, as well as grown ups, will be delighted with the confectionery. Pastry or a piece of cake costs from two to four hryvnias.

"Siren" (The Lilac)
6 Roosevelt Street
from 8.00 a.m.
to 8.00 p.m.

It is a good canteen with a decent cuisine and pleasant interior. In any case, tables are covered with clean tablecloths, repairs were made, and what is the most important - the cooking is tasty! You pay about 10-12 hryvnias for a good dinner consisting of soup, meat with garnish, and fruit compote

with a patty. It is not so exquisite, but at the same time, it is not so expensive. Air-conditioning is provided.

The "Crimea"
3 Moskovskaya Street
from 8.00 a.m. to 8.00 p.m.

It is a classical dining-room. Almost all the visitors to the beach, who are non-official holiday-makers, try to get to this dining-room. The range of dishes is conventional: small meat-balls, ravioli, and cutlets. It should be noted that cooking is good there. Prices are low - about 10 hryvnias per dinner, but to say the truth, the portion is small. It is designed for the undemanding family people. During the rush hours, there may be a queue, but it moves rather quickly.

To find an entertainment to one's liking in Yalta is not a problem at all. All people, including intellectuals and adherents of an active way of life, as well as children and those preferring loneliness and peace, will be able to relax with pleasure and for their own good... There are wonderful parks, different side-shows, sail, amusement on beach, discotheques for youth, and respectable night clubs - all to your choice, dear guests!

It is possible to make a promenade on a pleasure yacht along the coast of Great Yalta

BEACHES

It is, perhaps, the weak point of Yalta. The sanatoria, holiday homes, and hotels occupied the beaches, which were good in the slightest degree. The beach, which was not much to look at, is at the Embankment, near the "Oreanda" beach. However, it is not the beach at all, but the place, where you can enter the dirty sea free of charge. Another city beach (it is free for the Yalta citizens) is in the eastern part of the city, near the Massandra beach. Visitors should pay for entry. The conveniences are doubtful, that is why it is better for visitors to use the Massandra beach, where the entrance fee is paid, but it is cleaner and more comfortable. In addition to the cabins, there is a douche with sweet water, paid toilet, rental chaise-longes, and a reasonably priced cafe.

PARKS

In Yalta there are many parks and squares. The most famous of them are the Prymorsky park named after Yury Gagarin and Massandra Park.

The Prymorsky Park starts from the "Oreanda" hotel on the Lenin Embankment. From the Maxim Gorky monument a wonderful palm alley will lead to the "Lito" (Summer) hotel, near which the bowling is located and where all wishing can spend their time knocking down the ninepins. In the park you will see various cafes and product booths. Walk along the shady alleys to admire the architectural peculiarities of the Yalta health centres located in this green part of the city.

The Massandra Park, laid out in the 40-ies of the 19th century on the instruction of the count M. Vorontsov, is in the opposite part of Yalta. In order to get to its territory, it is necessary to go up from the Embankment along the Drazhinskogo Street almost to the "Masandra" hotel. The park is laid out in the landscape style and counts about 200 types and species of trees and shrubbery, many of which have been brought to the Crimea from other parts of the world. In addition to "Yalta" and "Masandra" hotels, buildings of the Sechenov Institute are also located there. At this clinic there exists an inexpensive (compared to other Yalta hotels) and comfortable hotel.

In the Yalta dolphinarium

CHILDREN'S ENTERTAINMENT

"Polyana Kazok" (Meadow of Fairy Tales) is the most popular place where children strive to get. A unique open-air museum located two kilometers from Yalta. It is possible to get there by bus No.8 or by inter-city taxies going to Alupka. In the park-museum there are more than 300 sculptures of fairy-tale characters, such as Baba-Yaga (old witch) and Maugli, epic heroes and gnomes, Cheburashka and Doktor Ai-Bolit.

Next to the "Polyna Kazok" there is the Yalta

Sight-seeing tours toany corner of the Crimea

Zoo, where children can see a live tiger or funny monkey.

The side-shows are organized on the embankment: cars, bicycles, merry-go-rounds, inflatable boats, etc. There are also entertainments for little ones, as well as for grown-ups.

In the city cinema theatres the most crowd-pulling feature films and multi-performances are organized for children.

ENTERTAINMENT FOR GROWN-UPS

In summer, the concerts of the CIS "star" performers take place in Yalta. Usually, the visiting variety actors and singers perform in the "Yuvileiny" Concert Hall.

The admirers of the dramatic art are invited by the city A. Chekhov Theatre. The exhibition hall of the Artists Union of Ukraine offers paintings of the Crimean artists, sculptures, and items of arts and crafts.

At night, in addition to the promenade on a pleasure boat along the Yalta bay, one may take a stroll along the embankment shining with lights, or visit the night clubs, as well as a variety show and discotheque.

NIGHT CLUBS

The night club "Saturn" on the Sovyetskaya Square is the most accessible of them. In addition to the club and cinema theatre, there is also a bar-variety show.

The elite club "Tornado" offers a lazer show and dances from the sunset (from 9.00 p.m.) till the dawn (to the accompaniment of music of professional DJs).

The visitors are intrigued by the romantic name of the "Las Nubes" club, which means "Clouds" when translated from Spanish.

DISCOTHEQUES

In addition to the "Limpopo" and "Sribna Pidkova" (Silver Horseshoe), (see the Part "Food"), there are the discotheques in the city, such as "Bastion" in the Primorsky Park, "Druzhba" (Friendship) platform, and a disco-bar "Coral". The "Cactus" restaurant is visited by the peculiar public since the price of entry is 100 hryvnias.

"Polyana Kazok" *Tel.: 39-5203*
from 9.00 a.m. to 7.00 p.m., without days off

The Circus
31 Moskovskaya Street *Tel.:* **34-1900**

"Saturn" Cinema Theatre
Sovyetskaya Square *Tel.:* **32-3909**

Internet-Cafe
3 Katerininskaya Street

"Yuvileyny" Concert Hall *Tel.:* **32-6954**
2 Chornomorsky Lane

A. Chekhov Theatre *Tel.:* **32-2233**
11 Katerynynska Street

Exhibition Hall
2 Gogol Street *Tel.:* **32-7088**

NIGHT CLUBS:

"Tornado" *Tel.:* **32-2036**
11 Lenin Embankment

"Las Nubes"
3 Sverdlov Street

"Coral" (disco-bar)
29 Lomonosov Street *Tel.:* **31-8536**

Yalta in the evening. A view from the Massandra Park

The Crimean Mountaineering Club

The Yalta branch of the Crimean Mountaineering Club, which is the first tourist organization in the Crimea, was created in 1891. The board of the club was located in Odessa, the Yalta branch was headed by the well-known doctors V. Dmitriyev, F. Veber, and others. They developed the mountain routes and excursion-health paths. The task of the club was "... to carry out a scientific research in the

One should take a guide in case of going to climb a mountain

Tavrichesky Mountains and facilitate the stay of naturalists and artists going to the mountains with a scientific or artistic aim", as well as the preservation of rare plants and collection of materials on the geology, geography, history, zoology, and ethnology of the Crimea. Till 1915, 117 issues of "The Notes of the Crimean Mountaineering Club" have been published.

The holiday-makers in Yalta can independently see the most bright recreation sights of the southern coast. The Great Yalta is rich in wonderful palaces, ancient parks, and architectural monuments.

Distribute the time of your vacation so that it will enable your to make a trip to Livadiya and Alupka, walk along the Sunny Path, ascend the "Ai-Petri" Mountain and to the Resurrection Church on the Krasnaya (Red) Cliff. You will be able to make a plan of sightseeing tours after you read about out-of-city tours. Yalta is a young city, notwithstanding the fact that the first record about it appeared in the times immemorial. The settlement of these places started only in the second half of the 19th century. When the Senate in 1838 declared Yalta a city, there was only one street - Yelizavetinskaya, not counting the Embankment. In the new-formed city there were 30 houses and 224 citizens...

The city museums of Yalta are not so rich in the unique exhibits, as Feodosiya or Sevastopol, but the Yalta citizens can be proud of numerous memorial houses, in which

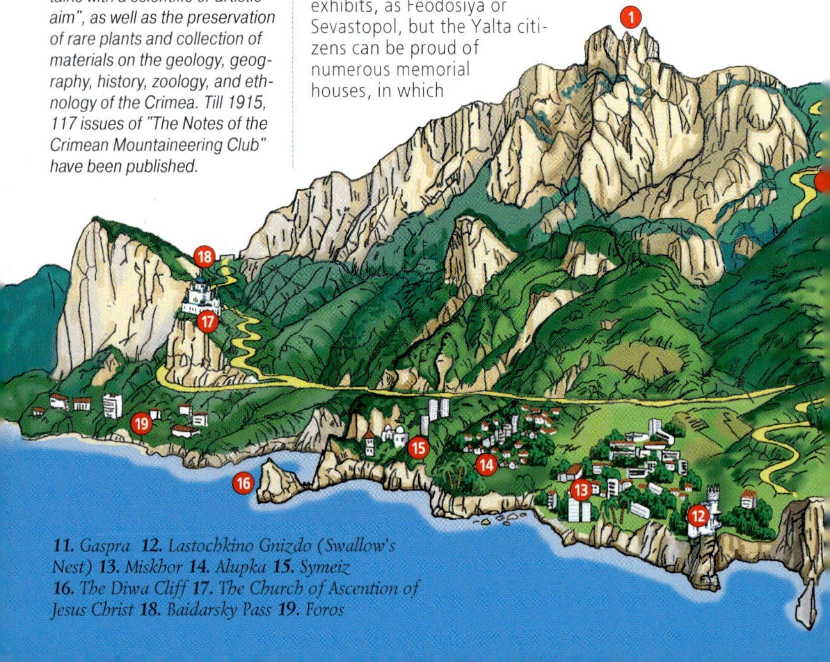

11. Gaspra 12. Lastochkino Gnizdo (Swallow's Nest) 13. Miskhor 14. Alupka 15. Symeiz 16. The Diwa Cliff 17. The Church of Ascention of Jesus Christ 18. Baidarsky Pass 19. Foros

the museums of well-known figures in the sphere of culture and art are opened at present. The Ignatenko Street (the former Yelizavetinskaya Street) is a kind of a recreation sight in the modern city. It can serve a live illustration of the old city building up, since it is narrow, crooked and is densely built up with houses.

On the Naberezhnaya Street there was a single building of the custom house 165 years ago. And the street itself was nothing else than simply a seashore line. By the way, an old mosque building was used for the custom house. Soon, along the Naberezhnaya Street the chestnut trees have been planted, and the street got a new name - Bulvarnaya Street. Small ships moored directly to the shore. At present on this street (the modern Roosevelt Street) the marine passenger terminal is located. The present Lenin Embankment was built considerably later.

The building of the former "Rossiya" hotel (13 Lenin Embankment), built in 1875, is the point of interest in Yalta. It was the most luxury hotel in the city. The troupe of the Moscow Artistic Theatre stayed in this hotel in April 1900.

In the former summer residence "Omur" (32 Kirov Street), belonging to K. Ivailovskaya, A. Chekhov, L. Tolstoy, and M. Gorky lived in their time.

The building - the former palace of the Bukhara Emir, located in the park zone, is interesting in the architectural sense. This house was built by the design of the Tarasovs brothers in 1903. At present, this building houses the library of the "Yalta" sanatorium.

The world known Crimean wines are the result of the scientific research of employees of the well-known Scientific-Research Institute of Wine-Making and Wine "Magarach". The Magarach vineyards and the Ninitsky Botanical Gardens were founded in 1812, and they exist as a single whole.

One of the oldest film studios in the country is located on the Polikurov Hill. At present it is called the "Yalta Film".

Uchan-Su

The excursion office often combines the ascending on the rope-way from Miskhor to the Ai-Petri peak and descending from the mountain by the serpentine. The Greeks called it the "Creamsto Nero" ("Flowing Water"). The Uchan-Su waters

fall from the 98-height by two terraces. The sight of the waterfall is particularly impressing in the early spring, during the period of snow melting. A powerful flow falls down the cliff with a din and breaks into millions of spray. The picture is framed with century-old pine-trees, which stubbornly climb up the cliffy spurs, towards the sky blue. In summer, only some streams fall down the cliff.

1. *The jags of Ai-Petri* **2.** *The Waterflow Uchan-Su*
3. *A road to the Great Canyon* **4.** *Ayu-Dag*
5. *Adalara Mountains* **6.** *Gurzuf* **7.** *Nikitsky Botanical Gardens*
8. *Massandra* **9.** *Yalta* **10.** *Livadiya*

Portraits of F. Vasilyeva and I. Kramskoy

After the southern shore of the Crimea became a fashionable resort, not only notable courtiers and rich dignitaries started to come here. Many writers, artists, and scientists left their bright traces in the history of the city.

In 1871, **Feodor Vasilyev**, master of the lyrical landscape came to Yalta. In this city he created his best works, such as "A Road in the Crimea", "Breakers", and others. Unfortunately, the artist lived a short life: he died being 23 years of age. Buried on the Polikur Cemetery.

Anton Chekhov also spent his last years in Yalta. The writer had the tuberculosis and could not afford himself to go away to Europe for treatment. In 1898, his illness made the writer to settle for a permanent residence in the Crimea. In the village of Autka near Yalta a house was built, where A. Chekhov had settled with his mother and sister Maria. At present, it houses the "Bila Dacha" (White Dacha) museum.

In order to enable the ill writer to see the staging of his plays, such as "Chaika" (Seagull) and "Dyadya Vanya" (Uncle Vanya), the troupe of the Moscow Artistic Theatre headed by K. Stanislavsky and V. Nemirovich-Danchenko, came to Yalta in summer of 1898. Here, in Autka, in the Church of St. Theodore Tiro, the wedding ceremony of Anton Chekhov and the actress Olga Knipper took place.

In Yalta, A. Chekhov wrote such plays, as "Tri Sestry" (Three Sisters) and "Vishnyovy Sad" (Cherry Orchard), as well as nine stories, among them, a well-known "Dama s Sobachkoi" (A Lady with a Doggy). The action of this story is partially developing in Yalta.

On the writer's initiative, the first antituberculous sanatorium had been opened for the poor.

The name of the Ukrainian poetess **Lesya Ukrainka** is also connected with Yalta. Here she wrote her first play "Iphigenia in Taurida", as well as the poems that were included into the cycle "Krymskiye Otzvuki" (The Crimean Reminiscences). A museum is opened in the house, where Lesya Ukrainka stayed in 1907-1908.

The poet **Stepan Rudansky** was the first city doctor, who graduated from the Medical and Surgical Academy in Petersburg in 1861, and got an appointment to Yalta. He did much for equipping the city with modern services and utilities. A memorial plaque is established on a house in the Ignatenko Street, where S. Rudansky lived.

The Chekhov's family: writer's mother, sister Maria, wife Olga, and Anton Pavlovich

The cinema factory, where the first national films were shot, was opened in Yalta due to Aleksandr Khanzhonkov.

The Armenian composer **Aleksander Spendiarov** graduated from the gymnasia in Simferopol. Since 1901 he lived in Yalta, where he wrote the majority of his works, such as "The Fisherman and the Fairy", "Three Palms", etc. His house was always opened for guests, such as composers, artists, and writers.

A well-known doctor **Vladimir Dmitriyev** came to Yalta on the recommendation of S. Botkin, who discovered that his colleague had the tuberculosis. V. Dmitriyev lived in the Crimea for 37 years. He studied treatment by the grapes, sea bathing, and other balneal factors. He created the first weather station in Yalta, developed the pedestrian routes to the different regions of the Crimea. He was buried on the Polikurov Cemetery. One of the streets in the city bears his name.

An unusual monument was erected by the romantic poet **Vladimir Lugovskoi.** He bequeathed to brick up his heart in the cliff in the park of the Writers' Recreation and Rest Centre. At present, this cliff is called the Luhovskoi's Cliff.

In 1867, an American journalist S. Clemens, the future writer **Mark Twain**, visited the city of Yalta.

The names of many well-known people are connected with Yalta. It was many times visited by L. Tolstoy, A. Kuprin, M. Schepkin, I. Levitan, S. Rakhmaninov, I. Kozlovsky, V. Korolenko, S. Marshak, and others.

Historical and Literary Museum

5-a Pushkinska Street
from 10.00 a.m. till 6.00 p.m., except for Monday and Thuesday. Tel.: 32-3065

The museum occupies two halls on the 1st floor of the building. The entry to each hall should be paid separately (2 hryvnias). In the archeological section the antique ceramics is exhibited, found during the archeological excavations in the vicinity of Yalta. In the second hall the photos and documents are exhibited pertaining to the public and cultural life of the district city of the 19th and the beginning of the 20th centuries.

City-Museum of A. P. Chekhov

112 Kirov Street
from 10.00 a.m. till 5.00 p.m., except for Monday and Tuesday. Tel.: 32-5042

In 1898, A.Cheknov bought a deserted plot of land in the village of Verkhnyaya Autka. In a year, a house was built by the original project of the architect L. Shapovalov. The name "Belaya Dacha" was fixed after this house, its doors were wide open for friends and acquaintances. Maxim Gorky was a frequent guest with A. P. Chekhov.

This unique doggy greeted guests of A. Chekhov. In the twilight it looked like a live doggy...

Lesia Ukrainka Museum

8 Katerininskaya Street
from 8.00 a.m. till 6.00 p.m., except for Monday and Tuesday Tel.: 32-5525

The former mansion of the merchant woman Lishchinskaya houses two museums: the ground floor is occupied by the Museum of the Pre-Revolutionary culture of Yalta, and on the first floor the museum exposition of the outstanding Ukrainian poetess is located. Here Lesya Ukrainka rented the rooms during her stay in Yalta for treatment. On the wooden balcony she took a rest during summer evenings and had a talk with her guests.

The House-Museum of Lesya Ukrainka. Architect P. Terebenev

At the museum on the ground floor, things characteristic of the life in Yalta at the beginning of the 20th century, such as a piano, gramophone and furniture are exhibited. Here there is also a sofa from the Rayevsky's estate, on which, probably, A. Pushkin took a rest, a desk from "Yasnaya Polyana" at which, probably, L. Tolstoy wrote the parts of his novel "Khadzhi Murat".

The House-Museum of N. Biryukov

1-a Krasnoarmeiskaya Street
from 10.00 a.m. till 6.00 p.m., except from Monday Tel.: 32-3676

The memorial museum of the writer was opened due to the activities of his wife Anna Ilyinichna. The fate of N.Biryukov is like the fate of N.Ostrovsky. A dangerous illness, which chained the writer till the end of his days to the wheelchair, did not hamper him from creative activities and active and interesting life.

"Belaya Dacha" Inhabitants

Anton Pavlovich brought his family to Yalta, including his mother and sister Maria Pavlovna. His sister was his guardian angel not only during his life, but also after his death. Due to her courage, a house of the great prose writer and playwright has been preserved. Maria Pavlovna was collecting letters of her brother, his manuscripts and personal belongings. In 1921, A. Chekhov Museum was organized in the house. When Yalta was occupied by the German troops, the following events took place on "Belaya Dacha". On the order of the commandant, the Museum should have become a flat for the German officers. But when they came to settle, Maria Pavlovna showed her inflexibility: nobody would live in the study of Anton Pavlovich! It is strange, but she succeeded in convincing the Wehrmacht officers in it. Some volumes of the writer's works translated into German became one of the arguments. Moreover, when the officer, who settled in the ground floor, was leaving Yalta, he gave a kind of a writ of protection to A. Chekhov Museum: on the house gate a document was posted up informing that the house is a private property of the German baron. Nobody else could dare to encroach upon the "property" of the German officer...

Till her very death, Maria Pavlovna remained a permanent director of the "Belaya Dacha".

The Roman-Catholic Church

St. Maria's Church
10 Chekhov Street
Tel.: 32-6400

Evangelical-Lutheran Church. Previously, the German church was located here, belonging to the German community of the city.

Oleksandr Nevsky's Cathedral
2 Sadovaya Street
Tel.: 32-1616

This beautiful cathedral was erected in 1903, under the guidance of the well-known Yalta architect N. Krasnov, who designed many palaces on the southern cost of the Crimea.

St. Theodore Tiron's Church
7 Shelomeyev Street
Tel.: 31-2777

In the church, which formerly was located in the village of Autka (at present, this district of Yalta is called

Chekhovo), the wedding ceremony of Anton Chekhov and Olga Knipper took place.

Roman-Catholic Church
25 Pushkinskaya Street
Tel.: 32-4039

In the building, constructed by the design of N. Krasnov, the Roman-Catholic parish is located in the Church of the Immaculate Conception of the Blessed Virgin. Also, the concerts of the organ and chamber music take place here.

St. John Chrysostom's Cathedral
The Polikurov Hill

The church and the bell-tower were built in 1832-1837. It was the first stone building of the city. During the war years, the cathedral was destroyed, only a high bell-tower was preserved, which was entered into the sea sailing directions as a guiding line for ships. At present, the church was reconstructed.

St. Nicholas' and Aleksandra's the Martyr Cathedral
25 Polikurovskaya Street
Tel.: 35-0043

A festive gold dome of the church is well seen on the background of the Massandra Park greenery. The name of the Russian Tsarina Aleksandra Feodorovna is included into the name of the cathedral.

The Armenian Church
3 Zagorodnaya Street
Tel.: 32-3075

A wonderful church, which resembled the St. Ripsime Cathedral in Echmiadzin (Armenia), was a result of creative cooperation of an architect Gabriel Ter-Mikaelian and a talented Armenian graphic artist and theatrical artist

Vardges Sureniants. The decorative elements of this church were made by the sketches of this artist (he was also the author of paintings in the interior and the altar). V. Sureniants was buried in this cathedral near the church walls, the church paintings were the last work of this well-known painter.

The Yalta Church was made to the order of the Baku oilman Pogos Ter-Gukasian in memory of his daughter, who passed away untimely and was buried in the family burial-vault at the basement of the building.

V. Sureniants

In addition to the original relieves, ornaments and stone "lace" of the decor, it is worth noting a wonderful staircase of 100 steps leading to the cathedral located on the hill.

A fragment of the cupola paintings

The building of the Armenian Church was many times used by the cinematographers. The episodes from the films, such as "St. Yorgen's Holiday", "The Shield and the Sword", "The Gadfly", and others were shot in this place.

The recently renewed public worship is accompanied by excellent organ music and wonderful singing.

Palace of Aleksander III

Inside the palace some details of the original interior had been preserved

M. Mesmakher

The corner of the park in the palace

The settlement is located in the nort-heastern part of Yalta, just next to the city boundaries. City trolleybus No. 3 goes to Masandra.

The city emerged in the first half of the 18th century. On its territory the remains of the antique settlement and a medieval monastery of the later period have been discovered.

In the Upper Masandra, one of the former imperial palaces - palace of Aleksander III - is located. Built on the wooded mountain slope, it seems a tiny palace due to its small size and rich decoration.

In the 30-ies of the 19th century, Massandra was the possession of the count M. Vorontsov. On the place of an old house, the count's heir decided to build a palace, having entrusted the design to the French architect M. Bushar. The construction was stopped due to the death of the owner of the estate. The work started 10 years later, when the land was purchased by the Appanage Department from S. Vorontsov's heirs. The Emperor Aleksander III wished that the palace became one more summer residence of the Tsar's family. The Petersburg's architect M. Mesmakher developed a new design. He left the main composition untouched, which was fulfilled in the romantic style, having decorated it with the decorative elements. It was an apt decision to use the yellow flooring tile in the elevation of the building, as well as carving on the gray stone, and original roofing slate. The contrasting colors and baroque elements in the exterior solution made the palace to look festive like in a fairy-tale.

The death of Aleksander III put off the end of work, particularly since his heir, Nikolai II, was going to build the palace for his family in some other place, the Massandra estate became out of use. Finally, it was decided to make a travel palace there - the Emperor was interested in creating the centre of the Crimean vineyard in Massandra and was going to come here to see to work by himself. In addition, the palace served as the game-home for the House of Romanovs. Hence, the interior decoration was rather modest, there were no administrative buildings, except for watch-house, or other buildings were not envisaged at all. The Tsar's family never remained to spend a night there - after a short rest and dinner all went to their favorite place - to Livadiya...

After the palace was nationalized, from the year 1929 till the beginning of the Great Patrioc War, the sanatorium for consumptives was located in this place.

After the war, the palace became a state summer residence. The USSR party figures came here to have a rest, as well as their foreign guests. In 1991, the Massandra Palace became a branch of the Alupka Palace and Park reserve, and since June 1, 1992, it was serivicing as a museum.

Excursion in front of the old winery building

Massandra is known to the whole world due to its unique wines, produced on the sunny southern coast. The Massandra winery includes some wineries, the best wine-makers of the Crimea work here.

The idea to turn the Taurida into the wine-making region belonged to the Prince G. Potemkin. He started to order the vine from abroad. On the southern cost of the Crimean peninsula, this business was continued by M. Vorontsov. Since 1823, more than four million of the best French, Rhine, Spanish and Greek vines were planted there. It was necessary to decide the issue of the wine-processing, production, and storing of the wine on an industrial scale.

In 1888, the Appanage Department proposed to S. Vorontsov's heirs, who continued the business of their father, to sell the wine-making economy and received their consent. Aleksander III was interested in the development of the Crimean wine-making.

In 1891, it was proposed to Prince L. Golitsyn, who till that time was busy with his own wine-making in the estate "Novy Svet" and in the village Tokluk near Sudak, to manage all wine-making economy in the Appanage Economy. His wines received gold medals, and at the world exhibition in Paris (1898) he was the Vice-Chairman of the expert Committee of the wine competition. The Prince Golitsyn was called the "king of experts". The Russian wines became a real sensation at the exhibition, since till that time, Russia was never considered to be a wine-making country...

In 1894, the construction of the Main Massandra wine cellar started. In time, seven huge tunnels were located under the ground.

At present, in Massandra there is the main plant of the production association producing the vintage dessert and strong wines. Many of them were marked with gold medals at the international exhibitions. The proud of the "Masandra" is the "Muskat white of the Red Stone" (21 gold medals and two Grand Prix Cups), white muskat "Livadiya" (super-cup Grand Prix), "Pinot-Gri", "Ai-Danil" (10 gold medals), "The Seventh Heaven of Golitsyn" (having tasted it, Lev Sergeyevich stated that he felt like in the seventh heavens), "Aleatiko", "Ayu-Dag" (the favorite wine of the Empress Aleksandra Feodorovna), sherry, Madeira, and others.

In the cellars of the winery a priceless collection of wines is preserved, counting more than one million bottles of selected wines of different brands and age. The oldest wine - Spanish sherry "De la Frontera" of the harvest of 1775. The collection wines of "Masandra" often have a venerable age from 50 to 200 years!

During the wine-tasting

They succeeded to save this collection in the years of the Great Patriotic War. Partly it was taken to some other place, and partly it was hided in the secret cellars and bricked up.

During the Gorbachev's campaign for sobriety, the elite wineyards of the Crimea have been saved due to the selflessness of the workers at this enterprise.

It is possible to make a tour of the winery, which ends in the tasting room (25 hryvnias).

In the wine cellar

In front of the pavilion the cactus garden is arranged on the background of which the tourists like to take photos

A small settlement to the east of Yalta is known for the unique botanical gardens located here, which was founded in 1812.

An order on the organization of this oldest scientific-research institution of the Crimea was signed on July 10, 1811, and an outstanding scientist-botanist Khristian Khristianovich Steven was appointed its director.

In 1807, an Academician first came to the peninsula for a business trip, and in three years he settled in the Crimea. Soon the Governor of the Novorosiysk region suggested to the scientist to become the director of the research botanical gardens. Under the direction of C. Steven the first planting of the fruit and ornamental trees have been carried out. In seven years, there were 240 species of plants, and 175,000 of trees from all the continents of the world grew there. The scientist wrote the first special work dedicated to the flora of the peninsula.

At present, the Nikitsky Botanical Gardens and their branches occupy about 1,000 hectares of land. The employees of this establishment carry out a great selective work, the collection of roses accounts for 2000 species! It would take several hours in order to go around the alleys and paths and see the unusual beauty of flowers, exotic trees, and fantastical shrubbery.

On the territory of the Botanical Gardens, beverages and any other products are much more expensive than outside its territory. A half-liter bottle of simple water will cost 3-4 hryvnias. The tourists travelling by cars should know that parking at the gate of the Gardens would cost much - four hryvnias per hour of parking. Taking into account that the entry is 10 hryvnias, the family excursion to the Botanical Gardens would not be cheap. It is possible to save on the parking and come to Yalta by an inter-city taxi No. 34 (the fare is one-two hryvnias), and you should provide yourself with mineral water well in advance in the ordinary shop. For money you saved in such a way, you can visit the tasting room of the Nikintsky Gardens, where the best wines of the well-known brand "Maharach" will be proposed. You will also taste the jams made of rare fruits growing on the territory of the Gardens. It is possible to buy the goods you like, but the prices are "beyond the means".

Among the palms growing in the Nikitsky Gardens there are also the banana palms. Unfortunately, they do not bear fruits there

The Cedar or Pine-Tree

In the Nikintsky Botanical Gardens several species of the cedar are growing - cedar of Lebanon, Atlassky, etc. One interesting story is related to the cedars...
The father of the Russian fleet, Tsar Petr I, studied the experience of shipbuilding in Holland. Local masters told him about the advantages of the cedar wood. Going to create his own shipyards, Petr ordered to find the cedar in the forests of the Motherland. But, alas, this tree is a heat-loving plant, and it was not growing in the imperial latitude. But the subjects could not disobey the Tsar, and for this reason they had found the Siberian pine-tree, a tree with similar characteristics, in the taiga. Without hesitation, the Tsar Petr ordered to name the pine-tree the cedar. Since that time on, cedars grow in the Siberia, which bear fruit - cones with tasty sabadilla-nuts. Indeed, cones do not grow on the true cedar...

Tasting of the "Magarach" production. Wines and exotic dishes of the persimmon, Zisyphus jujuba, and olives growing in the Botanical Gardens

Ponds with gold fishes are decorated with lotuses

Flourishing Yukka

1. The central entry
2. A tasting room
3. Administrative building
4. Trade House
5. Production-experimental department
6. Exhibition hall
7. "Health World" Shop
8. "Keif-Tane" Cafe
9. Colonnade cafe
10. "Tsvetochnoye" (Floral) cafe
11. "Floral" shop
12. Rosarium
13. Exhibition plot of chrysanthema

The main building

Palms alley

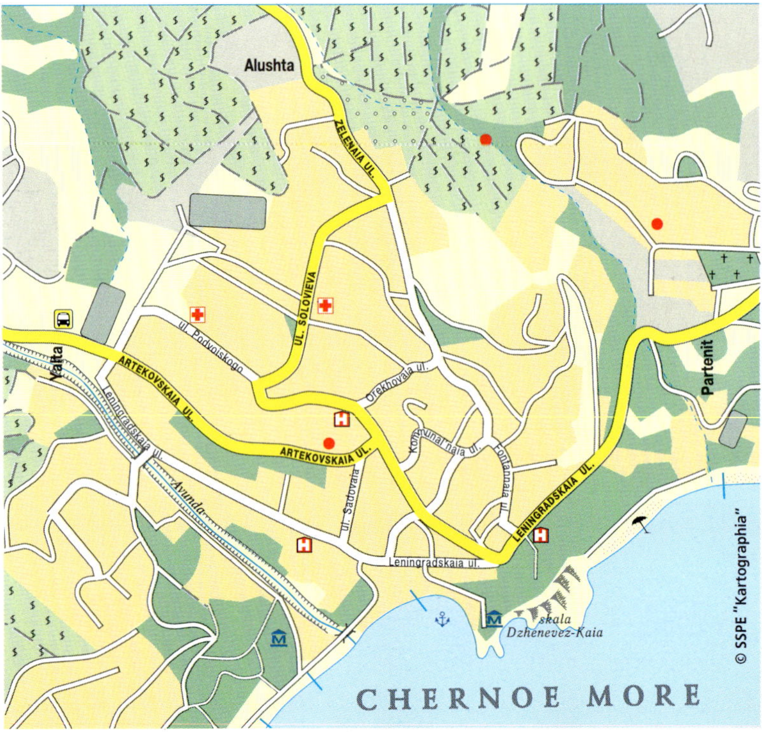

The modern Gurzuf (urban-type community) is an eastern countryside of Greater Yalta. In this town about 12,000 people live. The distance to Yalta by the motor road is 11 kilometers. Gurzuf is surrounded by the largest Crimean mountains, and the height of its four peaks are more than 1,500 meters. Even if they are not the Himalayas, they look impressive, it seems that they are emerging straight from the sea, and on their slopes the houses of the town stick to the mountains, like the birds' nestles.
It is possible to come to Gurzuf from Simferopol by the trolleybus or inter-city taxies - the bus stop is called "Gurzuf" on the Simferopol highway. It is possible to go down to the town on foot. From Yalta the inter-city taxies go to the central part of Gurzuf, this way is more comfortable. Also, from Yalta it is possible to get to Gurzuf by sea.

Hotels

"Adallary" *Tel.:* 36-4459
37 Leningradskaya Street

"Bogemia" *Tel..* 36-3802
9 Leningradskaya Street

"Skalnaya" (Rocky) *Tel.:* 36-3633
29 Leningradskaya Street

"Chaika" (Sea Gull)
15 Nikitina Street *Tel.:* 36-3177

WHERE TO STAY?

In the town there are several hotels, including the private hotels. If you did not succeed to settle in the hotels "Adallary", "Skalnaya", "Sea Gull", or "Bohemia", or you did not like the prices (it should be noted that they are very high), it is possible to choose the dwelling in the private sector, and it will cost much cheaper.

WHERE IS IT POSSIBLE TO HAVE A SNACK?

The restaurants are located on the seashore and along the main street of Gurzuf - Leningradskaya Street. Some cafes are located on the cutters lifted above the water. The tables are located on the decks under the tents. Prices are moderate. Along the seashore, fried fish is always sold, which has just been caught.

A view of Gurzuf, the Ayu-Dag and Genoese Cliff

Archeologists had discovered that people settled in the Gurzuf valley some five thousand years ago. During the archeological excavations on the Genoese Cliff the remains of the ceramic plates and dishes used by the ancient people were found. Later, in the 9th century B.C. - 3rd century A.D., the Tavrs lived here. On the pass Gurzuf Saddle the researchers had recently discovered their sanctuary. It turned out that it was the place where the wild animals were offered in sacrifice. Also there were instruments, implements, coins, and among them there were many rare coins, for instance, Chersonese stater of 95 B.C., with an image of the goddess Virgo, also the Roman and Bosporus coins, and statues of the antique gods.

Why was it here, in such a place, which is difficult to access that the Tavrs organized their sanctuary? Perhaps, because from the highest (1,388 мeters) pass of the Crimean mountains all the approaches to the sacred place and priceless relics could be hided in time in case of the enemies' attack.

The scientists did not succeed in discovering the presence of the Greeks in the vicinity of Gurzuf, but the Romans visited this place. The Crimea was included into the sphere of interests of the eastern part of the Roman Empire - Byzantium. It was the Byzantine Emperor Justinian I who ordered to built the fortification in the Horzuvity (in the 6th century it was the name of the place, on which the modern Gurzuf is located at present). By the way, the name of the city has not been deciphered till this time. Only the transformations are known: Horzuvity, Yurzuf, Gurzuf...

The fortress was erected on the Janevez-Kaya (the Genoeze Cliff - translated from the Tatar). It extends to the sea from three sides by the precipices. From this places all the bays of the seashore were well seen. It was not without reason that the fortress existed for more than 900 years. At first, it was a Byzantine fortification. In the 8th century, the Khazars ruined it. Two centuries elapsed before the local feudal lords reconstructed the buildings. In the 13th century, Gurzuf was included into the Feodoro principality, and from the middle of the 14th century it belonged to the so-called "Captain Gothia". Since this time, the Genoeses became the local masters, who in 1475 retreated under the pressure of the Turks. The Ottoman forces ruined the fortress and it was not reconstructed since that time. At present, the Artek hotel "Skalnaya" is located on this place.

After joining of the Crimea to Russia, the lands of the Gurzuf valley belonged to the Emperor's treasury. At the start of the 19th century, the duke Arman de Rishelieu, who was one of the founders of Odessa, built a house here. The well-known duke visited Gurzuf only two times, but he willingly placed his estates at the disposal of his acquaintances. In his house in 1820, A. Pushkin lived for three weeks.

The count Mikhail Vorontsov was one more owner of the estate. In the estate "Ai-Danil" he built the first wine-cellar in the Crimea. In 1840, the owner of the estate changed again, the senator Ivan Fundukley became its owner. He developed the wine-making started by M. Vorontsov, and he was engaged in charity. I. Fundukley's heirs sold the estate to Petr Gubonin, who turned the provincial Gurzuf into a wonderful resort.

The beach in Gurzuf

"Suuk-Su" Resort. Photo of the 19th century

Cliffs-Brothers

Young princes Petr and Georgy lived on the Medved-Mountain in a castle. They had their tutor - an old man Nimfolis. When the time came for him to leave his pupils, the sorcerer brought two boxes: one - with a rod, before which the sea gives way, and another - with silver wings, able to carry away to the clouds. "Use my gifts in order to increase your knowledge, but not to your selfish ends", said the old man and disappeared.
The brothers came to know the secrets of the sea gulf and secrets of the skies. But they heard about two beauties from the faraway country. Having ruined the city, they took the sisters to their castle. But the proud girls treated the brothers with contempt. How to melt ice in the sisters' hearts? And the brothers decided to strike them with the Nimfolis' gifts. Having tied the wings to the horse, they all set into the chariot and headed for the sun. Suddenly, a voice became heard ordering them to go back. The sisters began to laugh and called the brothers the cowards.
Next day the twins decided to show the secrets of the sea gulf to the girls. But as soon as they fell down, Nimfolis came to Petr:
- You came here having impure intentions. Go back or you will die!
But Petr disobeyed this order, fearing to provoke derision. There was a peal of thunder, and a thunderbolt killed four of them. The bodies of brothers and sisters turned into two white rocks in the Gurzuf Bay - Adalary ("brothers" when translated from the Tatar language).

In 1881, the industrialist P. Gubonin purchased the Gurzuf estate. This industrialist being 56 years of age, decided to organize a fashionable resort in this place. He extended his estate, built seven hotels and a restaurant, surrounded by a splendid park. At present, two sanatoria, the Military Sanatorium and "Pushkino" sanatorium are occupying this territory. The former Gubonin's hotels house the living quarters, and in the former restaurant a dining room is located.

It is worth going to the territory of the Military Sanatorium not only with the purpose to admire the marvelous buildings, as though trimmed with lace, but in order to see the beautiful fountains in the park. Unfortunately, only two fountains have been preserved out of five fountains built by Gubonin. They are "Rakhil" and "Night". The latter is a copy of the work by the German sculptor Berger.

The name of the Russian entrepreneur V. Berezin is also related to Gurzuf. He organized a resort establishment in his estate "Suuk-Su". At present, one of the "Artek" buildings "Lazurny" (Sky-Blue) is located here.

By the way, the "Artek" centre for children is also a point of interest. It is located on the seven-kilometer seashore from Gurzuf to Ayu-Dag. The "Artek" centre consists of 10 camps and is able to accommodate 5,000 children per shift. It is a real children's republic.

In the 20ies of the 19th century, the Frenchwoman Jeanne de Lamote lived on the present territory of the "Artek". In the lower part of the tract "The Devil's House" was located, in which the heroine of A. Duma's works lived.

The "Night" fountain in front of the former Gubonin's hotel

A. Pushkin's Museum

Tel.: 36-3876
from 10.00 a.m. till 5.00 p.m., except for Money and Tuesday

When in 1820, young A. Pushkin was travelling with the Rayevskys along the Caucasus and the Crimea, they spent several weeks in Gurzuf. The Duke Rishelieu proposed him to stay in his home. In a letter to his brother, A. Pushkin tells how happy he was in those days. The young poet fell in love with the younger daughter of the general Rayevsky - Maria, who later became the wife of the Decembrist S. Volkonsky and followed her husband to the Siberia.

At the museum, there are things testifying about the poet's stay in the Duke's house: a writing-desk at which A. Pushkin probably wrote his letters, books and paintings depicting Gurzuf of those times.

It is possible to visit a museum with a tour, since the territory of the "Pushkin" Sanatorium has been closed for "unorganized" tourists.

K. Korovin Artists' Recreation and Rest Centre

The Artists' Recreation and Rest Centre is located in the old part of the town. One of its buildings is located in the former "Salambo" summer residence, which formerly belonged to the well-known painter.

When in 1910, the Bolshoi Theatre staged A. Arends balley based on G. Flober's novel of the same name, the artist was proposed to make sceneries to this performance. K. Korovin was carried away by the fulfillment of this order to such an extent, that he even called his summer residence "Salambo".

He often stayed here in the course of seven years till 1917. The guests visited the artist, among them were such figures as M. Gorky, I. Repin, A. Kuprin, V. Surikov and F. Shalyapin. He painted the portrait of the well-known singer in his summer residence.

The "Vecherok" (Evening) cafe is located not far from the Korovin's summer residence. At the entrance, a small fountain was built. Nobody remembers when it was built, but they maintain that A. Pushkin drank from that fountain during his stay in Gurzuf.

A. Chekhov's Museum

22 Chekhov Street
Tel. 36-3005 from 10.00 a.m. till 6.00 p.m.

A. Chekhov purchased his summer residence in Gurzuf in 1900. Anton Pavlovych wrote his sister: "I bought a plot of land on the seashore with a beach and a cliff near the landing place and a park in Gurzuf". A. Chekhov was also the owner of a cozy bay, where a boat could moor. At present, the subsidiary of A. Chekhov's Yalta House-Museum is located in this building. It is possible to get into the bay after making a one-hryvnia payment to the custodian for the whole-day stay on the mini-beach. .

A.Mitskyewicz, V.Zhukovsky and A.Solzhenitsyn visited Gurzuf. The ship of Afanasy Nikitin entered Gurzuf on the way back from the trip "across three seas"...

Shaliapyn's Cliff

It is located on the front of the isles Adalary (White Stones). There is the following story about it. The well-known opera singer Feodor Shalyapin liked to visit Gurzuf. He took the fancy of the picturesque cliff advanced into the sea. The singer dreamt of building a "palace of the arts" on this cliff, but the landowner O. Solovyova had no wish to sell the cliff. Once during the summer evening Feodor Ivanovich sang some heartfelt romances on his friends' requests. Either, this evening was surprisingly good, or F. Shalyapin's performance was particularly moving, but the proprietress, being deeply touched by his singing, suddenly for all present took a decision to sell the cliff to him. But soon the revolution took place, and the singer's intentions were not fated to come true.

F. Shalyapin and A. Kuprin

A. Chekhov's house

If you decided to go for a walk along the Tsar's Path, you will come across Oreanda. A road goes past some alps, such as Krestovy, Ai-Nikola, Khachla-Kayasy, as well as past the sanatoria the "Lower Oreanda", "Gold Beach", "Mountain", "Sail", boarding houses, and the "Kichkine" tourist centre...

The path starts from the Livadiya Palace. Approximately in 1.5 km it is possible to see the pergola-rotunda. That is what remained from the large Emperor's palace built in 1852 by the design of the architect A. Stakensneider.

Oreanda (translated from the Greek - "rocky"), like Livadiya, was presented by Catherine II to the Greeks. In 1825, the lands passed into the ownership of the Russian tsars. On the design of the architect F. Elson, the "house with a tower" was erected, as well as a greenhouse and administrative buildings. In 1837, the Emperor Nikolai I presented the Oreanda to his august wife Aleksandra Feodorovna. The Empress was delighted with this gift, and since she had been noted for a weak health it was decided to build the summer residence in this place.

Aleksandra Feodorovna and Nikolai I

The German architect K. Shinkel, based on the plans of the area, made designs of an exceptionally wonderful villa, but due to the expensiveness of the future construction (the work was estimated at 1,000,000 silver rubles), the project was turned down. The architect A. Shtakensnider reduced the site area by 4.5 times and he chose another place for a house...

The year when the construction was completed, the family of Nikolai I had a rest in the Crimea for one and a half month. They liked a splendid park, picturesque suburbs,the and wonderful house and had no wish to leave this place. Alas, it was not for a long time, that Aleksandra Feodorovna enjoyed this gift: Nikolai I died after three years, and the widow had never visited the Crimea.

In 1881, the palace burnt down. In several years the Church of the Protection of the Blessed Virgin was erected on this place. The cathedral, existing till nowadays, was constructed in the traditions of the Caucasian-Byzantium architecture. Unfortunately, the wall paintings made in the studios of A. Salviati were not preserved. Only in the cupolas, pendentives, and partially on the western wall it is possible to see the remains of the wonderful interior decoration.

The elite sanatorium "Lower Oreanda" was built on the place of the palace, in the settlement there are also several health-centres, in which formerly the higher party and state figures had their rest.

General Secretary of the CC of the CPSU Leonid Brezhnev often spent his vacations in Oreanda

Golden Beach

Once upon a time, a wicked and greedy Turkish Amet-aga ruled the Yalta neighborhood. It was not a trouble at all for him to rob the subject. His wife Khodzhava and son Deli-Balta by name (Furious Axe) were noted for even worst characters. The population of the seaboard was becoming more and more poor, and Khodzhava's trunks were growing larger and larger...
But the time came for the Turks to leave the Crimean land. Amet-aga loaded the ship with the loot and sailed away. Suddenly a hurricane began: the ship was tossed about by the wind and waves like a nut-

shell. The ship was carried out to the Oreanda and thrown to the coastal mountains: it broke to pieces, and the wicked Khodzhava, the greedy ruler, and their pitiless son went to the bottom like the stones. When the Oreanda citizens approached the shore they saw that the beach is sown with gold coins, jewelry, and beautiful silver ware. All the seashore area was glittering with gold...
They say that till nowadays after a heavy gale the remains of that treasure are washed ashore, and for this reason this beach is called the Golden Beach.

The western coast of Yalta - Livadiya ("meadow" when translated from the Greek) was granted by Catherine II to the Greeeks of the Balaklava battalion. Soon the lands became the ownership of their commanding officer, the colonel F. Revelioti.

When Yalta turned into a place of summer rest for noble families, the Polish magnate Lev Pototski purchased Livadiya. In 1834, the manor house and administrative buildings were built and a wonderful park was laid out with exotic plants brought from different parts of the land.

Yard in the Livadiya Palace

In 1861, the Appanage Department purchased the Pototsky's estate for the Tsar's family. The architect I. Monigetti reconstructed the lordly estate; the Pototsky's house began to be called the Grand Palace (as distinct from the newly built Small Palace, or, as it was called, Chocolate Palace). The estate counted about 70 buildings, in the buildings the features of the eastern style, fashionable at that time, could be seen.

After Livadiya by the right of succession became the ownership of the Russian Emperor Nikolai II, it was decided to build a new palace, since the old one did not comply with the spirit of the age. Architector N. Krasnov was entrusted with the task of the construction of the new buildings, and it was completed in 1911. After the revolution, a sanatorium was opened in the Tsar's residence.

In February of 1945, a well-known Yalta Conference of the leaders of three allied states of the anti-Hitler coalition took place, consisting of Yosif Stalin (USSR), Franklin Delano Roosevelt (USA) and Winston Churchill (Great Britain). The setting of those days had been preserved, including the round table for negotiations and armchairs for the leaders of the state. The American delegation was accommodated in the Livadiya Palace. The President F. Roosevelt liked Livadiya to such an extent that he, while joking, expressed his wish to buy the estate. At present this palace houses the museum. Business hours are from 10.00 a.m. till 5.00 p.m., tel. 31-5579. The way from Yalta will take 15 minutes by an inter-city taxi. The promenade along the sea from the Primorsky Park will take about one hour.

Livadiaya. Photo of the 19th century

The Last Emperor and the Ballet Dancer

What kind of a man was the one whom addressed as "Your Emperor's Majesty"? Nikolai II was a good father and husband, but by no means he was a terrible autocrat. Very likely he would be happier in case he avoided the crown. But the laws of succession to the throne were strict.

When the future Tsar was a Tsarevitch, his father, Aleksander III brought the heir to the final performance of the choreographic school. Niki made acquaintance with a young balley dancer Matilda Krzesinska. The love affair started between the young people some time later.

Love of the successor to the throne promises many pleasant things, among them gifts, carriages, and mansions... It is possible to be his muse, mistress, friend, but it is never possible to become his wife! Niki was honest with Malechka (he called Matilda by this name), he confessed that among all the princesses, who were proposed to him as a wife, he preferred Alisa von Hessen: "There is a very strange phenomena, which I have noticed in myself: I have thought that two feelings, two loves simultaneously are combined in the soul".

Matilda Krzesinska

Before the wedding ceremony the last meeting of Nikolai II and Matilda Krzesinska took place. After that, Niki had never met with Malechka in private.

Livadiya Park

The palace looks like a fantastic white cloud on the background of the park greenery. The most wonderful park on the southern seashore is laid out around the house, and the caressing sea is splashing below...

In 1904, design and construction of the new tsar's palace was entrusted with N. Krasnov. The architect attempted to create a house full of sun, greenery, air and sea. The new palace was designated for taking a rest in the family circle, so there were not so many premises for show in the building. The palace is made in the style of the Italian Renaissance, of an artificial Inkerman stone. The building of the palace has 166 separate premises, one large courtyard and three little yards.

A refined building was equipped according to the latest technical achievements, including electricity, lifts and a telephone communication. Nikolai II took pleasure in using the automobile and the "Kodak" camera. In 1911, the first full-length film "Defense of Sevastopol" by V. Honcharov and A. Khanzhonkov was demonstrated in the Livadiya Palace.

It is striking that the palace was erected in the process of only 17 months! The Emperor was delighted with this fact: "We cannot find the words to express our delight and pleasure to have such a house built in the way we wanted it to be. Achitector Krasnov is a wonderful fine fellow..."

Everyone, who visited the study of Nikolai II, could pay attention that it is possible to breathe very easily in this room. Large windows are located in such a way that the fresh air constantly circulates in the premises without creating a draught.

The tracery railing closes the entry into the splendid Italian yard with the fountain and palms.

The table of negotiations of the participants in the Yalta Conference

The library

The beginning of the Sun Path

Address of the museum:
Settlement of Livadiya
Tel.: 31-5581 ⌚ from 10.00 a.m. till 5.00 p.m., except for Wednesday

The Robber and the Water-Nymph

Once upon a time, a beauty Arzy lived in Miskhor. She was slender, lissome and had bright black eyes, which gave no rest to many people. She often went to the fountain to have a rest near its fresh streams.
The greedy merchant Ali-Baba was Arzy's neighbor. He looked out for beautiful girls in the neighboring villages, kidnapped and sold them to the harems of rich men.
Ali-Baba had forthought to kidnap Arzy. But suddenly the news spread: Arzy is going to become married! The merchant became depressed...
But the villain had a piece of luck. The day before the wedding the girl came to the fountain to say goodbye, since she was going to become married to a guy from the faraway parts. There the trader was on the watch for her.
Ali sold the unhappy girl to the Sultan's harem. She felt miserable among the luxury of the palace. In some time, she gave birth to a boy, but Arzy could not love the Sultan. Having taken her child, she ascended to the seraglio's wall and plunged into the sea. That evening the Miskhor citizens saw for the first time on the seashore the grievous water-nymph with a child...

In the medieval ages on the Cape Ai-Todor (St. Theodore) a monastery was located, for this reason the cape was also called Monastyrsky. Above, on the Aurora's Cliff, there is the miniature castle, which has become an emblem of the southern coast. It is "Lastochkino gnezdo", built in 1912 by the architect A. Sherwood for the German entrepreneur Baron von Steingel. At present, an Italian restaurant is located there.

"Lastochkino gnezdo"

In the 1st century A. D., the Roman legionaries built the fortress on the Cape Ai-Todor. Since the end of the 19th century, the remains of this fortress started to be called Kharaks (meaning in the Greek language "fortifying"). Till this time, the archeologists continue to gather the nuggets of information on the history of this defensive construction. The former palace, the Kharaks estate, erected in 1907 on the design of N. Krasnov, is one of the buildings of the "Dnepr" sanatorium.

Gaspra settlement originated from a small village of 37 farmsteads (the 19th century), although the record about it appeared earlier (the 8th century). At present, in this resort settlement 12,000 people are living. In 1836, the architect F. Alson constructed in Gaspra a palace for the Prince A. Golitsyn. At the beginning of the 20th century, Lev Tolstoy had a rest here; at that time this estate was the property of the Countess Panina. At present, it is a building No. 1 of the "Yasnaya Polyana" sanatorium.

The next settlement located to the west is Miskhor decorated with wonderful parks of the 18th century. The "Dulber" Palace is one of the most beautiful. Prince P. Romanov constructed it at the end of the 19th century. It is made in the Moresque style and could serve an illustration to the fairy tales of the "One Thousand and One Night" series. During the years of the Civil War, members of the Emperor's family were held in custody there, and they managed to emigrate in 1920.

In 1930-ies the villages of Miskhor and Koreiz were united into one resort economy, there the best sanatoria and rest homes of the southern coast are located.

Majestic and mysterious Ai-Petri Mountain towers above the palaces and parks (1,234 meters). Its teeth are like a ruined palace. The best way to ascend it is by a rope-way. The lower station is in Miskhor, the cost of rising is 10 hryvnias. It is possible to go to Ai-Petri by an automobile.

"Dulber". Architect N.Krasnov

In Koreiz, the former Yusupov's palace built at the beginning of the 20th century by the architect H. Krasnov is located. In 1945, during the Yalta Conference, the Soviet delegation headed by Y. Stalin stayed there. At present, the historical palace is handed over to the Administration of the President of Ukraine.

ALUPKA

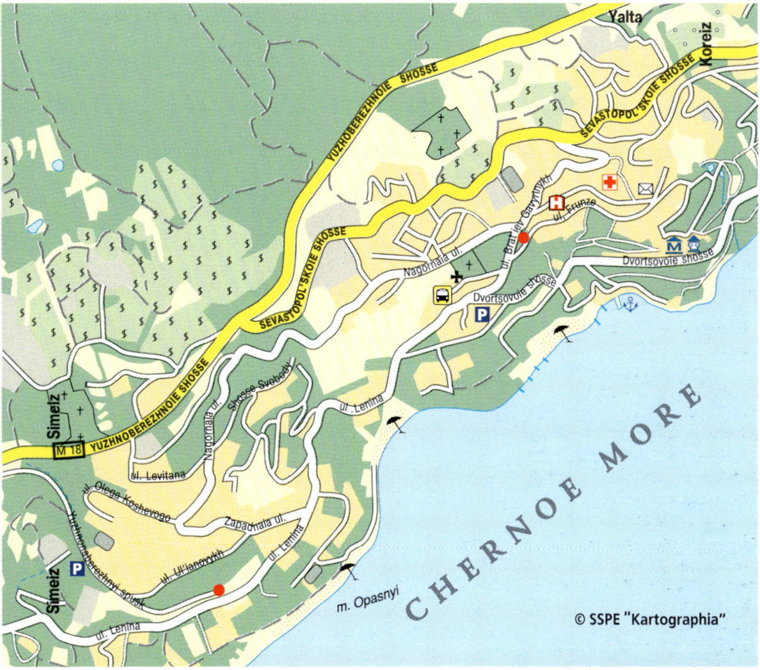

A small town counting 10,000 citizens is located on the steep costal slopes of the Main Chine. The air here is particularly fresh and pleasant due to the pines growing in the mountains above Alupka, hence the local sanatoriums are specializing in curing the diseases of the respiratory tract.

The town emerged in the 6th-5th centuries B. C. The name Alupka is, perhaps, of Greek origin: in the local forests foxes were found (translated from the Greek - "alepu"). In the 14th century the Genoese military port Lupiko was located in this place. Later on its place the Tatar village emerged. In the 18th century,.Grigory Potemkin became the owner of this part of the southern coast. Then in Alupka the Vorontsovs settled down. The count Vorontsov constructed a luxurious palace near the sea, which was surrounded by a wonderful park.

The name of the well-known artist Arkhip Kuindzhi , who was the pupil of I. Aivazovsky and the teacher of K.Bohayevsky, is connected with Alupka. A memorial plaque is put on the gate of the house where he lived.

In Alupka, there are several hotels, the best of which are "Alupka" (in the vicinity of the Vorontsov's palace) and "Samara" (not far from the bus terminal). Citizens of the town let their flats and rooms to the visitors. Prices here are lower than in Yalta, and the place is more attractive: air temperature is higher than in Yalta, but since the town is buried in verdure, heat is easy to endure.

The autumn is very beautiful in Alupka, the blooming roses in the beginning of December are not a rarity here.

The inter-city taxi No. 27 will get you to the centre of Alupka.

Alupka: a view from the sea

Telephones

House Intermediary Bureau *Tel.:* 72-1190
26 Brothers Gavrins Street

"Alupka" Hotel *Tel.:* 72-2297
8 Frunze Street

Bus Terminal
4 Lenin Street *Tel.:* 72-2190

Ticket Office *Tel.:* 72-2451
30 Rosa Luxemburg Street

Life-Saving Station *Tel.:* 98-676

Tour to the Vorontsovs' Palace in Alupka is, perhaps, the most popular one on the southern coast of the Crimea.

Interiors of the Vorontsov's palace

The palace was created in the Tudor style, combining the romanticism of the medieval knightly palace and the luxury of an English private residence. The Count Mikhail Vorontsov was the hero of 1812, and he spent his childhood in England, where his father was the envoy. Being 19 years old, Mikhail took part in the Russo-Turkish War, then he fought with Napoleon, having displayed personal bravery in the battles at Smolensk, Borodino, etc. When he was 41, Vorontsov was appointed the governor-general of the Novorosiysk Region.

The Count entrusted the English architect E. Blore and his assistant V. Hunt with making a design of the palace. The serfs, brought by M. Vorontsov from his north estates, and hired workers took part in the construction, which was a progressive solution of the problem in those times. The talented gardener K. Kebakh was engaged in laying out the park. He created the terraces ascending from the sea to the southern front and made in the Mauritian style. The white marble staircase guarded by the stone lions is the decoration of the ensemble. The vaulted arch with majolica balconies is decorated with the Arabic character, which inscribes the following aphorism: "There is no winner except for Allah".

The builders from the field-engineering battalion of colonel Shipilov made paths and alleys among the stones. For the construction of the Upper Park tons of stones were removed and the chernozem was brought. The most popular among the park fountains is "Maria" fountain, which is a copy of the fountain in Bakhchisarai.

The bricklayers, cabinet-makers, modelers, and embroideresses worked on the decoration of the interiors - Blue, Chintz, and Chinese rooms and the Winter Garden with wonderful sculptures. The museum was opened in 1921.

Many things from the interior decoration were not preserved. The Princess Maria, the heiress of the Vorontsovs went to Italy in 1882, and took the most valuable things with her.

Battlements on the Ai-Petri peak

In 1945, during the Yalta Conference, the English delegation was located in the palace. W. Churchill noted that he felt himself here like in his Motherland.

After the war, the former Vorontsovs' estate was a state summer residence in the course of ten years. The museum renewed its work in 1956.

From the Yalta bus terminal, the inter-city taxi No. 26 will bring you to the Alupka Palace. In order to get into the museum in summer, it is necessary to stay in a long queue. The price of the entry ticket is 6 hryvnias.

The Upper Park

Address of the museum:
10 Dvortsovy Highway
Tel.: 72-2372
from 10.00 a.m. till 5.00 p.m., except for Monday, Friday

The Blue Gulf

The last part of the story about Greater Yalta is dedicated to the locality from Simeiz to Foros. Such a short acquaintance cannot, respondent, as it may be, have the "blank spots". Particularly it is worth going to the southern coast in order to become convinced that it is impossible to convey the fascination of the Crimea by words!

Simeiz settlement (from Greek - "mark") is located 5 kilometers to the west of Alupka. It is widespread at the spurs of the Cat Mountain, which is one of the most picturesque mountains in the Main Chine. Here the fortification of the Tavrs was located, in the vicinity of the settlement the archeologists discovered the largest Tavrs' necropolis in the Crimea. The outskirts of Simeiz are also decorated with such cliffs as Diva, Swan Wing and Panea Mountain. On the latter cliff, Byzantine monastery was located.

Next to the Diva Cliff (by its shape it resembles a woman with flowing hair, who is coming out of the sea), formerly there was the Monk - the pointed cliff, which was like the hermit in the calotte. It fell under the blows of the waves, and only piling up of the stones remained in its memory.

In the 19th-20th centuries, the notable dignitaries and rich industrialists built their summer residences there. In the 20-ies of the 20th century, many estates were handed over to sanatoria and rest homes. The villas "Dream" and "Ksenia" were especially interesting. The latter was built in 1911, by the design of the architect N. Krasnov, at present, it is known as a "house with ghosts".

In Simeiz there was an observatory, where in 1959, for the first time, the depiction of the Moon underside was received. The telescope on the Koshka (Cat) Mountain was established at the end of the 19th century by I. Maltsev, the owner of the Simeiz, and presented to the Pulkov observatory. At present, the observatory moved to the settlement Nauchny (Scientific), but the antenna remained in memory of the research held there.

Next to Simeiz, there is the Blue Gulf with a wonderful aquapark, where the whole day would pass in entertainment.

In Melas, the palace of L. Petrovsky is located (19th century). At present, the "Melas" sanatorium belongs to the Ministry of Internal Affairs of Ukraine and is closed for the tours.

Above the Opolsnevy there is the Biuk-Isar Mountain, on the peak of which a threatening fortification of the Feodorites rose in the period of the early medieval years. The Ifigenia Cliff in the Beregove settlement is named so due to the myth about a stay of the Greek priestess in Taurida. They maintain that here the Tavrs Cathedral of the Virgin goddess was located. Next to the Beregove settlement, there is the pass Shaitan-Merdven (Devil's Staircase). It was used for passing from the Crimea Mountain to the southern coast.

Villa "Ksenia"

To the West of the Ai-Yuri (or Dragon) there is the resort settlement Foros. Over it, on the high Red Cliff, the Church of the Ascension of the Christ looks like it lives in the cloud-land. It was built in 1892, by the Academician-achitect N. Chagin to the order of the industrialist A. Kuznetsov. The Cathedral was erected in honor of saving Aleksander III on his way back from the Crimea: the train by which the Tsar's family was going, was wrecked near Kharkov.

In the middle of the 20th century, a restaurant was opened in the cathedral; they say that Nikita Khrushchev visited it. Then the construction was neglected, and the paintings were lost in the fire. Raisa Gorbacheva took up for the reconstruction of the cathedral in 1987.

Above the church, on the Baidar Pass in 1884, the Baidar Gates were erected (architect K. Ashliman). From them a wonderful view on the valley opens.

Near the eastern outskirts of Foros, the state summer residence the "Zaria" (Dawn) is located, where in the course of the putsch in August 1991, Mikhail Gorbachev, the first and the last President of the USSR, was under the house arrest. At present, this summer residence became the residence of the President of Ukraine.

The "Tesseli" ("Silence"), is the former general N.Rayevsky's estate. In 1932, it was granted to Maxim Gorky. At present, the trade representative office of the Republic of Tatarstan in the Crimea rents this summer residence.

Alushta - the centre of tourism

My second motherland, a secluded land of Alushta...

S. Sergeyev-Tsenskiy

Simferopol'
Sudak
SUDAKSKOIE SHOSSE
SIMFEROPOL'SKOIE SHOSSE
SUDAKSKAIA UL.
SIMFEROPOL'SKAIA UL.
Demerdzhi
ul. Lenina
Krasnoarmeiskaia ul.
peshekhodnyi tonnel'
Pereko pskaia ul.
ul. Turistov
Park kul'tury i otdykha
rynok
Partizanskaia ul.
Sovetskaia pl.
ul. Lenina
ul. 15-go Aprelia
Primorskii park
Ulu-Uzen'
SIMFEROPOL'SKAIA UL.
IL'ICHEVKA
rynok
Vinogradnaia ul.
ul. Gor'kogo
Oktiabr'skaia ul.
Ulu - Uzen'
ul. Gor'kogo
YALTINSKOIE SHOSSE
Oktiabrskaia ul.
Naberezhnaia ul.
CHERNOE MORE
RABOCHIY UGOLOK
Komsomol'skaia ul.
Komsomol'skaia pl.
© SSPE "Kartographia"
YALTINSKOIE SHOSSE
Chel'menchi
Naberezhnaia ul.
Yalta

History in a few lines

The 6th cent. - *the first record of Alushta.*

1239 - *the town is destroyed by the Mongols-Tatars.*

The 80-ies of the 14th cent. - *the beginning of the Genoese dominion. The town is called Lusta.*

1475 - *Alushta forms a part of Sudak Kadylyk.*

July, 1774 - *the Turkish troops landed on the shore near Alushta.*

1802 - *Alushta was given an official status of the town.*

1838 - *Alushta Volost (small rural district) formed a part of Yalta Uyezd (district).*

Alushta. Engraving of the 19th cent.

1920 - *establishment of the Soviet power.*

1923 - *nationalization of dachas of the Professors' corner. Opening of the first health centre.*

1934 - *opening of the biggest tourist centre in the Crimea.*

October, 1941 - April, 1944 - *Alushta is occupied by the Hitler's troops.*

1955 - *twelve health centres are operational on the Alushta shore.*

2002 - *there are 35,000 inhabitants in Alushta that celebrated its one-hundredth jubilee.*

Alushta against a background of Demergi

The area of Alushta is the closest Crimean resort locality from Simferopol. In addition to numerous health centres, those who arrived here are attracted by the suburbs of the city, relatively low prices for lodging and meals as well as by good fishing.

The city symbolically celebrated its one-hundredth anniversary in May 2002 but in reality Alushta is much older. Prokopy Cimmerian, a Byzantine historian, wrote about it as long ago as in the 6th cent. In his famous work "About constructions", describing the construction boomed in the peninsula, he mentioned about the fortress Aluston erected at that time.

During the invasion of the Mongols-Tatars the town was destroyed and it only revived when the Genoese restored the fortress and significantly enlarged its territory.

After the Turks conquered the Crimea, the town formed a part of Sudak Kadylyk, remaining a Christian settlement under it. The Genoese fortress fell under siege and has never been restored. They started building houses out of the leftovers of the fortress. Alushta was liberated from the dominion of the Turks sultan in the course of the Russian-Turkish war but soon the combat actions broke out here again: Turkish troops (7,000 soldiers) landed in the area of the Alushta shore. The army of 2,850 soldiers counteracted the landed troops. A grenadier battalion under the command of lieutenant colonel M. Golenishchev-Kutuzov formed a part of the army. The Turkish suffered a defeat but near the village of Shumy a future Field Marshal was badly wounded. While building the road Simferopol - Alushta in the 20-ies of the 19th cent., a monument to Kutuzov was erected on the spot where the soldiers were washing the wound of their commander. Kutuzov lost his eye in that battle.

In the 70-ies of the 19th century large-scale wine making private production facilities were set up around Alushta. After putting into operation a railway the city turned into a climatic resort: in the beginning of 1914 there were 4 hotels here.

For the health-resort visitors the area of Greater Alushta (so called coast from the settlement of Partenit to the village of Privetnoye (Affable) has a number of advantages in comparison with the luxurious Yalta. First, it will be much cheaper to have a rest here, secondly, it is not that hot in summer. It is explained by the fact that the mountains in the valley of Alushta retreated further from the shore and north winds better blow through the area.

An average temperature in summer is +23,8°C, in winter +3°C. There are no great climatic advances in the daytime, therefore Alushta coast can be recommended for the people with cardio-vascular diseases.

Addresses, telephones numbers

City Police Department Tel.30-238

Traffic Police Duty-Officer Tel.30-438

Ambulance station Tel.30-503

Drugstore (central)
13 Partizanskaya St. Tel. 31-229

Water-rescue station Tel.30-241

City Inquiry Service Tel.33-474

Central Post Office
15 Lenina St. Tel.30-404

Telegraph
15 Lenina St. Tel.31-122

Privatbant
50 Oktyabrskaya St. Tel.50-889

Railway booking-office
39 15th of April St. Tel.30-332

Air booking-office
9-a Gorkogo St. Tel.31-510

Advance bus booking-office
1 Simferopolskaya St. Tel.32-296

Order of taxi-cabs Tel.30-417

Behind the Angarsky mountain-pass the highway, dodging, forms a long descend, in the end of which a resort town called Alushta is located. One can come here by the highway from Simferopol or by sea from Yalta.

Angarsky mountain-pass on the Simferopol highway. A trolleybus goes from Alushta to the capital of the autonomy

Auto-terminal
1 Simferopolskaya St.
Tel. 52-586

Coaches from Simferopol to Alushta are leaving from the "Kurortnaya" ("Resort") coach station, which is located in the square near the railway terminal (see ##). The trip will take you no more than half an hour, trip fee - about UAH 5 . If you do not feel like going by coach, use the services of route taxis, leaving for Alushta or Yalta from the Simferopol trolley-bus station. The cost of a ticket for a route taxi is UAH 8 but it will bring you faster to the Alushta auto-terminal located not far from the entrance into the city near the central city loop.

Route buses are also going to Alushta from the central airport in Simferopol.

Coaches are leaving for the villages and settlements of Greater Alushta from the Alushta auto-terminal.

Trolleybus station
4 Gorkogo St.
Tel. 31-241

Those who are willing to make a trip along one of the most beautiful mountainous roads of the Crimea without being in a hurry will choose for sure a trip by trolleybus. An inter-city trolleybus # 51 is leaving each 10 - 20 minutes from the trolley-bus station in Simferopol (located in the same square in front of the railway terminal building). Trip time - 1 hour and 35 minutes, trip fee - UAH 1.55. If you arrived by air, you can go to Alushta directly from the airport by trolleybus # 64. Trip time - 2 hours. The final stop in the Alushta auto-terminal is located in the centre of the city not far from the seafront. trolleybuses ## 52, 55 going to Yalta stop on the central loop near the entrance into Alushta. The trolleybus # 53 will bring you from Alushta to Yalta.

Marine passenger terminal
6 Lenina St.
Tel. 31-147

Sea transportation in Alushta is of basically local character. Sea trip and excursion motor boats leave from the moorings in the front-sea, but, frankly speaking, rather irregularly.

City transport

There are four buses, three trolleybuses, route and ordinary taxies are among the kinds of the city transport. The trolleybus # 1 leaves for the village of Verkhnyaya Kutuzovka from the trolleybus station, the trolleybus # 2 will bring you to the Professor's Corner, the trolleybus # 3 - to the village of Zaprudnoye.

Bus routes ##1, 3 start at the marine passenger terminal and lead to the eastern part of the city, the bus # 2 will bring you to the settlement of Mirniy, the bus # 4 will bring you from the market place to the 60th anniversary of the USSR street in the northern suburb of Alushta.

There are few hotels in the classic meaning of the word. A majority of them are a mixture of a boarding house and a tourist centre. Let us mention the best of them.

"Alushta"
50 Oktyabrskaya St.
Tel. 55-278

A tall building is located in front of the coach station building. There are 120 rooms in the hotel including 4 suites. Double rooms with conveniences are not expensive - about UAH 50 per night, but running hot water supply depends on the city schedule, and, in addition, it would be desirable to refurbish the rooms. Additional conveniences are not available. A parking-place the vehicles is located across the street (UAH 3 per 24 hours). It will take you 15 minutes to reach a beach.

"Spartak"
9 Perekopskaya St.
Tel. 31-220

There are 250 rooms in the sports hotel including 4 suites. Air-conditioning is not available, but instead a running water supply is autonomous. The hotel has its own beach, sauna, tennis courts, and a fitness centre. There are a canteen, a bar and parking-place in the hotel.

"Chaika" ("A sea gull")
11 Krasnoarmeiskaya St.
Tel. 30-586

Lodging in the rooms with conveniences in the tourist and health centre is from UAH 80 to 100 per night per person, meals included. In addition to the standard rooms there are summer-houses without any conveniences - about UAH 50 per night per person, meals included. The centre has its own beach, a bar, a billiard, and a tennis courts.

"Raï" on the seashore

"Voskhod" ("Sunrise")
11 Oktyabrskaya St.
Tel. 31-540

There are 172 rooms in the tourist centre. A parking-place for vehicles is not available. The centre has its own beach, a cafe, a sauna, a swimming pool, a billiard, sports yards, and a library. Meals - in accordance with your desire.

Privately owned hotels are often located in the new beautiful houses

"Rai" ("Paradise")
4 Naberezhnaya St.
Tel. 31-230, 31-128

A two-storey mansion with a garage for 6 cars is located on the seashore. There are 10 double rooms in the mini-hotel from UAH 160 to 180 per night. Meals - UAH 50 per day per person. There are air-conditioners, all modern conveniences, an open swimming pool, an own beach, and a billiards. The guests of the "Rai" hotel are provided with medical care on the basis of the "Kiev" boarding house. A child can be provided with an additional place. There is a flexible discount system depending on the age of a child.

"Alushta" Hotel

"Krasny mak" ("Red poppy")
15 Lenina St.
Tel. 33-422

The hotel is located in the park zone of a centre of Alushta, at the distance of 100 m from the sea. The rooms are notable for the original design: bed-curtains above the bed or an imitation of a zebra skin, fireplaces, draping, and exquisite furniture. There is a sauna (UAH 50 per hour), rooms to have a rest, an excellent restaurant with European and Oriental cuisine. The cost of staying in the hotel is from UAH 200 to 550 per room.

Apartment renting intermediary office
7 Lenina St. Tel. 33-212

A choice of privately owned dwelling to be let to the holiday-makers is of different kinds - from a modest room to apartments with all modern conveniences. The prices are also different as well as the level of comfort, but on the other hand, everyone can choose a dwelling adequate to his taste and his wallet.

The restaurant

"Morskoy" ("Sea-like")
16 Naberezhnaya St. *Tel.* **34-452**
10 a.m. - 11 p.m.

"Vodolei" ("Water-carrier")
24 Naberezhnaya St. *Tel.* **30-409**
8 a.m. - mid-night

"Moskva" ("Moscow")
8 Gorkogo St. *Tel.* **31-008**
11 a.m. - 11 p.m.

"Krymchanka" ("A Girl-Crimean")
5 Lenina St. *Tel.* **33-265**
Open 24 hours

"Vstrecha" ("Encounter")
2 Lenina St. *Tel.* **58-098**
Open 24 hours

"Taverna" ("Tavern")
3 Lenina St. *Tel.* **31-185**
Open 24 hours

"Volna" ("Wave")
1 Lenina St. *Tel.* **30-539**
Open 24 hours

"Letniy Sad" ("A Summer Garden")
1 Lenina St. *Tel.* **31-598**
8 a.m. - 10 p.m.

"Panda"
23 15th of April St *Tel.* **30-412**
9 a.m. - 11 p.m.

"Pautinka"
("A Piece of Spider's Web")
21 V. Khromykh St. *Tel.* **31-071**
10 a.m. - mid-night

Chinese restaurant "Pekin"

The cost of the meals depends on the category of the entity, taking into account that meals can turn to be tasteful in an ordinary cafe with modest interior decorations and traditional menu without special pretentious cookery novelties...

"Pekin"
2 Parkovaya St.
Tel. 30-566
10 a.m. - 11 p.m.

The restaurant at the seafront is stylized under the Chinese pagoda. Cuisine - traditional Chinese, prices - traditionally high, numerous dishes (a duck peking style, fish) are to be ordered beforehand. The cost of the dinner is varied from UAH 100 to UAH 500 .

"Underworld"
6 Gorkogo St.
Tel. 35-000
9 a.m. - 6 a.m.

The restaurant is located near the trolley-bus station, its interior decoration is done in the form of the cave halls. Cuisine is mixed: Ukrainian, European, and Mexican ones. Cooks are proud of the flesh of sturgeon called "Sea czar" (UAH 42) and chicken Mexican style with tropical fruits in a foil (UAH38). The rest of the dishes are cheaper, a modest dinner - about 40 UAH. One will be served within five minutes, complicated dished will be served within half an hour. One can not only have dinner here but can have a good time as well.

"Vesioly Roger" ("Cheerful Roger")
13 Lenina St.
Tel. 30-459
Open 24 hours

European and Georgian cuisine are available in the cafe; a firm style cocktail "Cheerful Roger" - of course with rum. There are many seafood dishes in the menu. The cost of the dinner is about UAH 30. One will be served within 5 - 20 minutes. There are two halls and separate cabins in the cafe. Tips - 10%.

"Ostrov sokrovishch" ("Treasure Island")
13 Lenina St.
Tel. 58-105
Open 24 hours

There is another "pirate" cafe, a little more expensive, in the building where the "Cheerful Roger" cafe is located. Dinner in the "Treasure Island" costs about UAH 50. Firm style seafood salad with the same name costs UAH 20. One will be served within half an hour, tips - 10%.

"Medvezhy Ugol" ("God-forsaken Place")
11 Lenina St.
Tel. 33-369
Open 24 hours

A sympathetic cafe is not located in the suburbs of the city, as one could think out of its name, but, in fact, in the seafront. European cuisine, low prices. Firm style dishes are as follows: liver bear style - UAH 7 , sturgeon Spanish style - UAH 13. One will be served within 5 - 25 minutes.

Diet canteen
25 V. Khromykh St.
8 a.m. - 8 p.m.

The canteen is located in the centre of the city, not far from All the Saints Church. Low prices, wide choice of traditional dishes: porridges, cutlets, small meat-balls... they cook decently here, the canteen is an appropriate place for daily family dinners.

Alushta's entertainments are traditional for a resort city: beach enjoyments ("bananas", water hills, catamarans), cinemas, excursions, walks in the parks, casino, billiard, bars...

On the city beach of Alushta

BEACHES

Beaches of Alushta contain dark sand mixed with pebbles (tiny stones) and bigger ones - boulders. Water near the shore is transparent.

Well, the beach of the Children's Creative Work Centre could be considered the best one in the city. It is located at the park zone broken out around the former N. Stakheyev's dacha. It is pleasant to spend the time of the full blaze of the sun on the shadowy lawns. Children's auto-drum is also located here.

EXCURSIONS

Many excursion routes start in Alushta - to Sevastopol, Bakhchisarai, to the palaces of Greater Yalta, to Sudak, and also to the caves and protected areas in the Crimean mountains. Depending on the length of the routes the prices of excursions vary from UAH 20 to 45. Find it out if the cost of the entrance tickets to a museum or to the territory of the reserve is included to be ready for the potential surprises.

Tables of the excursion bureau are located along the seafront and in the adjacent streets. So, in Lenin street not far from the Museum of Regional Studies one can order a driving tour to the mountains in a sport utility vehicle. (Leonid Brezhnev was a pioneer of this kind of rest, he was fond of going along the Crimean mountainous roads). One can drive up to the top of the Demergi Mountain. Payment is executed on an hourly basis, one full day of driving is about UAH 800.

Sea trips are especially popular in summer, for example, to Sudak or Karadag dolphin arboretum. An excursion lasts 10 hours. It includes a tour round the Genoese fortress and the tour round the former biological research station located at the foot of Karadag.

NIGHT ENTERTAINMENTS

Those who prefer to spend an evening to the beer can attend a bar called "Fortress". In the entertainment facility "Paradise" in Partenit you are offered striptease, bar, billiard, watching movies. Alushta cinemas are often used for the night discotheques.

Popular singers from the Commonwealth of Independent States (CIS) are on the continuous concert tours in the Crimea in summer. Concerts take place on the city stages and in the movie and concert halls of the big health centres.

"Krym-trophy" invites to make a trip to the mountains

Addresses and telephones:

City House of Culture
8 V. Khromykh St. Tel. 30-603
City Concert Hall
1 Krasnoflotskaya St. Tel. 30-681
Side-shows
5 Gorkogo St. Tel. 33-234
"Krepost" (beer-bar) ("Fortress")
13 Lenina St.
"Paradise" (Partenit)
1 Solnechnaya St. Tel. 45-664

Cinemas:

"Priboy" ("Surf")
1 Glazkritskogo St. Tel. 30-378
"Chaika" ("A sea gull")
17 Lenina St. Tel. 30-757
"Shtorm" ("Storm")
7 Gorkogo St. Tel. 31-105
"Yuzhny" ("Southern")
24 Lenina St. Tel. 35-050

There are several memorial estates in Alushta, which acquaint the tourists with the life of the famous inhabitants of the city.

A gallery of Beketov's mansion

The Museum of Natural History

42 Partisanskaya St.
Tel. 35-033
10 a.m. - 6 p.m., except Monadys

There are more than 1,500 exhibits in the biggest Nature Reserve Museum, i.e., the Crimean one. There are stuffed birds and animals, 8 remarkable dioramas representing all the corners of the Crimean nature, rich collections of insects, herbaria, collections on minerals, etc. One can be listed for the excursion round the nature reserve (fee - UAH 50).

Near by, in the dendrological zoo, there are open-air cages with wild animals - moufflons, roes, bores, and foxes. There are gooses, ducks, and swans in the small ponds.

A mufflon is looking out for the visitors of the dendrological zoo

Swan islands in the northern part of the autonomy, in the Karkinit harbor shore, is the branch of the nature reserve.

The Literary and Memorial Estate of S.N. Sergeyev-Tsensky

5 Sergeyeva-Tsenskogo St.
Tel. 30-664
9 a.m. - 5 p.m., except Sundays, Mondays

It is easy to reach the house in the Orlinaya (Eagle) Mountain where the writer had been living for almost half century. One should go by the trolleybus # 2 to a stop "Memorial Estate of S.N. Sergeyev-Tsensky" and climb the staircase leading up to the hill. A garden with flower beds and vineyards is laid out round a small one-storey building.

The writer wrote epic novels "The Transfiguration of Russia" and "Sevastopol Drudgery" in Alushta.

Sergey Nikolayevich was buried near the house.

The Memorial Estate of N.A. Beketov

4 Komsomolskaya St.
Tel. 35-043
10 a.m. - 5 p.m., except Sundays, Mondays

The Russian Drama Theatre in Simferopol and several buildings in Alushta were built by the designs of the outstanding Ukrainian architect Aleksei Nikolayevich Beketov.

An age-old mansion built by a talented architect, served as a dacha to the Beketovs for many years. A tracery wooden veranda imparting a smart Oriental color to the building is especially beautiful. There are personal belongings of an Academician, his paintings, sketches, archive photos in the museum halls. Several rooms are occupied by an exposition of the modern Crimean artists.

The Historical and Regional Studies Museum

8 Lenina St.
Tel. 30-270
10 a.m. - 5 p.m., except Sundays

A branch of the Crimean Museum of Regional Studies. Among several thousand exhibits there are antique amphoras, family life objects of the Crimean Tatars, documents of the war years, photos of old Alushta.

A bath-tub of the Feodorites for a christening ceremony (AHRSM)

The Museum of I.S. Shmelev

2 Naberezhnaya St.
Tel. 30-570
10 a.m. - 5 p.m., except Sundays, Mondays

A writer Ivan Sergeyevich Shmelev lived in 1918 - 1922 in the house that earlier belonged to the Beketovs. The events of those rebellious years are described by him in his book "The sun of the dead" written after his emigration to France.

This region of the Crimea was a centre of Gothic Eparchy, a centre of Crimean Orthodoxy. The ruins of the numerous temples, chapels, and monasteries serve as an evidence of it.

A temple of the Middle Ages fortress Funa

According to a legend, Andrei Pervozvanny himself brought a God's word to Tavrida. Having passed through the whole Crimea, an Apostle lived for some time in Chersonese. Throughout the entire St. Andrei's journey, Christian communities were set up, temples were erected, sacred springs were coming into being.

Feodor Stratilat and All the Crimean Saints Church, built in 1842 by an architect K. Eshliman by the design of an architect G. Torichelli from Odessa, became the most significant Orthodox temple of Alushta. It resembles a village English church with Gothic elements. In 1962 the temple was closed, a bell-tower was demolished. The building was attached to the club of constructors. They built an extension in the form of a glass pavilion for dances. In 1988 the believers were allowed of restoring the church.

Feodor Stratilat temple was located on the slopes of the Demerdzhi Mountain, in the Middle Ages fortress Funa. A historian and engineer A. Bertje-Delagard restored an ancient church on the basis of the remains of the foundation and the walls.

Several temples, monasteries, and necropolises dated back to the 10th - 16th century were found out in the Ayu-Dag Mountain. It is an evidence of dense settling the mountain by the Christians in the Middle Ages. A temple of St. Konstantin and St. Yelena is supposed to have been located on the top of the Bear-Mountain. A Byzantine Emperor (the capital was called Constantinopol after him) was putting into life the principles of humanism and loyalty to different beliefs. He was canonized and declared a model of a Christian despite the fact that he was only christened just before he passed away. There was a monastery-lighthouse in the Ayu-Dag Mountain as well.

Kosmodamyanovsky Monastery is located at the distance of 20 km from Alushta in the hollow among the Crimean Mountains. According to a legend, doctors-healers Kosma and Damian who lived in Rome in the end of the 3rd century were exiled to Tavrida. Due to their passionate prayers a magic healing spring emerged in the Crimean forest. Soon a chapel made of stone was built on this spot. It was named after the saint healers. In the second half of the 19th century a monastery was set up here. Later its constructions were demolished. A preserved chapel was transformed into a summer temple. People are coming here to get some healing water, which gains a special power on the 14th of July on the day of the saint Kosma and Damian.

A temple named after Feodor Stratilat and All the Crimean Saints

Saint Feodor

Saint Feodor is worshiped in the Crimea. Numerous churches named after Feodor Stratilat, Saint Feodor Tiron, a name of the cape Ai-Todor, serve as an evidence of it.

Traditionally heirs of the Romanovs throne married princesses from the reigning houses of Europe. And as far as the princesses were of Catholic belief, in accordance with the rules of the Russian succession to the throne, prior to the wedding ceremony they were to accept Christianity. While being christened a princess traditionally got a patronymic Fedorovna, by means of what a future Empress received a protection from Saint Feodor.

St. Feodor Stratilat. Mosaic works were made by the artists S. Markin and A.Gubsky.

Feodor Stratilat (i.e., "a military leader") suffered for the belief in the 4th cent. under the Rome Emperor Likiny. Being a brave worrier, Feodor Stratilat broke the golden statues of the Barbarian gods and disseminated the pieces of gold to the poor people. For that reason he was tortured and crucified. But in the night time an Angel of the God healed the courageous Christian. The guards who came in the morning to pick up a dead body of the sufferer saw him safe and sound and believed in Christ. Then an Emperor ordered to cut off his head. Thanks to the Greeks they learnt about Saint Feodor in Tavrida .

Feodora - a girl-worrior

Feodora, a czarina of Sugdeya was beautiful. Still being a girl a czar's daughter was brought up as a future ruler. Irakly and Konstantin, her twin-cousins, were brought up in the czar's Palace together with her. Feodora was never inferior to the young men in learning or in the military arts. Brothers fell in love with the young czarina, but she gave a vow of celibacy to preserve her freedom forever and to devote all her efforts to the labor for the sake of the state. Konstantin resigned himself with the choice of the girl and became her loyal and reliable assistant. Having failed to persuade czarina to marry him, ambitious Irakly decided to force her to change her mind.
The Genoese were eager to conquer Sugdeya at that time. Irakly came to the Consul of Caffa and suggested helping to seize the town in exchange of a czarina. Treachery helped him to open the gate and let in the invaders into his native town. Feodora, Konstantin, and the worriers managed to take cover on the Castel Mountain in the properly fortified citadel on its top. The Genoese decided to siege the fortress. But Irakly could not bear waiting to catch the girl. He penetrated into the fortress through a secret passage. Having met a brother there a scoundrel killed him and then opened the gate of the fortress. Having seen that Konstantin is killed and understood that Irakly was guilty in his death, czarina killed the betrayer with her sword and rushed herself in the very midst of the enemies. The defenders of the fortress and their proud czarina perished in that horrible battle.
In that night the slopes of the Castel Mountain were stained with the flows of blood. Today brown lichen in the southwest slope of the mountain reminds about the death of the courageous worriers of Sugdeya.

It is historically established that Alushta is inferior to many Crimean cities in the number of sights, but instead Alushta is notable for a modest charm of a quiet resort town.

One can see all the approaches to the city from the Castel Mountain

ROUND TOWER

In the 6th century the Byzantines erected a fortress Aluston. In the 14th cent the Genoese changed the external look of the fortress: in addition to a citadel there was a fortification with three towers. Only two of them remained until now.

The first one - Ashaga-Kule (Lower Tower) served as a southern edge of the fortification. One can come up to the tower along the 15th of April Street. It is a pity but a powerful fortification did not preserve an appropriate magnificent look - all kinds of extensions, attached to its foot like birds' nests, diminish its historical "significance". One can see the remains of the second one - Orta-Kule (Middle Tower) - in Volodarskogo street.

Round-shape tower

FORTIFICATIONS IN THE CASTEL MOUNTAIN

The mountain (439 m) in the southern suburb of Alushta is a monument of nature. The remains of the fortifications on its top witness that somewhere there was a fortress here. The name "Castel" came from the Greek word "castellum" that means "a fortress, a fortification". It is supposed to be the last fort of the Fedorites - inhabitants of the Kingdom Feodoro (the Mountainous Crimea). Alas, but it is impossible to view the remains of the fortifications - they are located in the closed zone.

DACHA "GOLUBKA" ("A LITTLE FEMALE PIGEON")

The building of the city library in 20 Lenina street earlier belonged to General A. Golubov. In 1894 a future Emperor Nikolai II met here his fiancee Alice Gessen-Darmshtadt. A fiance and a fiancee went to Livadiya to Alexander III who was seriously ill to get a blessing for their marriage. A memorial board attached to the building tells about it.

Iosif Stalin stayed here as well in 1945 when going to participate in the Yalta Conference.

STAKHEYEV'S DACHA

A merchant Nikolai Dmitriyevich Stakheyev funded the construction of the seafront , profitable houses, laying out vineyards in Alushta. In the 80-ies of the 19th cent. a beautiful villa was constructed in the Primorsky (near sea) park. A famous artist I. Shishkin stayed here. The owner of the house was Shishkin's nephew. The Centre of the Children's Creative Work is located in this building now. There is a shadowy park round the house where it is pleasant to have a rest when the sun is in a full blaze.

MALPOST

In the 80-ies of the 19th century a regular communication between Alushta and Simferopol was established by means of the so-called malposts (post-office carriages). The visitors ordered seats in the carriages of the post-office stations. The cost of the trip from Simferopol to Alushta by malpost in 1910 was 3 roubles, trip time - 7-8 hours.

PROFESSORS' CORNER

A historical resort area is located in the southwest suburb of Alushta. One can walk here from the centre of the city along the seafront.

In the 80-ies of the 19th cent. outstanding scientists and cultural figures build their dachas here: Professor N.Golovkinsky, Rector of the Odessa University, Professor of Medicine A.Golubev, and others.

A beach in the Professors' Corner

They started to call the picturesque suburb of the town Professors' Corner. Gardens and parks were laid out round the dachas - the shore acquired a well-groomed and civilized view. This is a beautiful place for bathing - tiny pebbles, flat bottom and clear water. Later this locality was densely covered with dachas. Villas "Anna" and "Marina", located in the seafront (now they are the buildings of the health centre "A Sea Corner"), are considered to be architectural monuments. Linden's dacha is famous for the fact that the first health centre of Alushta was set up in it.

In 1923 dachas of the Professors' Corner were nationalized. A holiday home of the Crimean Council of Trade Unions was set up on its basis.

About Alushta with love

This corner of the Crimea has always attracted poets and artists. Polish poet A.Mitskevich, travelling throughout the Crimea in 1825, mentioned that Alushta is one the most beautiful places of the peninsula. Inspired by the beauty of the nature, the a poet devoted several sonnets to Alushta.
A.Griboyedov, author of the comedy "Grief out of mind" visited the Crimea the same year. He climbed Chatyrdag twice and was amazed with the panorama opened from the top of the mountain.
The Ukrainian writer M.Kotsyubynskiy spent about 4 months in this area. In 1896 he was a member of an expedition on struggle with filloksera (grape's disease). Short stories "On the stone", "In the shaitan's nets", and "Into the sinful world" were written on the basis of his Crimean impressions.
M.Gorky visited Alushta twice. First time - having a walking tour throughout the country in 1921, and second time - in 1928 when he has already become a famous writer.
In autumn of 1906 A.Kuprin was a guest of S.Sergeyev-Tsensky. K.Paustovsky visited Alushta the same time. Names of V.Zhukovsky and V.Bryusov, V.Vishnevsky and B.Lavrenyov, a polar investigator I.Papanin are connected with the city.

It is pleasant to spend siesta hours under the huge plane-tree near the Seafront

The path to the East - from Alushta to Sudak - is running across the resort virgin lands. Villages and settlements, subordinated to the City Council, - Semidvorye, Solnechnogorskoye, Malorechenskoye, Rybachye, Privetnoye - are located like a chain along the coast.

The Guaskos' brothers

There is a lonely half-demolished tower in the far edge of the Kanackskaya valley, at the rocky shore of the sea, on the cape Agira. Choban-Kule - Shepherd's Tower - as the local people used to call it. It is all that is left from the formidable castle of the feudal lords of the Guaskos' who terrified all the area round the castle.
So-called "case of the Guaskos' brothers" is kept in the archives of Genoa - a correspondence of Christoforo di Negro, last Consul of Soldaya (Sudak) and Antonio di Kabela, Consul of Caffa.
The Guaskos' brothers illegally captured Soldaya's villages of Scuti and Tasili where they established their own regulations: introduces additional taxes, openly robbed the inhabitants of the villages, and also administered justice, tortured and killed the people. For those purposes they installed a gibbet and pillories in the village.
The Consul of Soldaya sent his people to get fired the instruments of tortures, trying to make overbearing feudal lords listen to reason and to stop arbitrary rule. But the people of di Negro were met by an armed detachment - the Guaskos' were not going to obey the orders of the Consul of Soldaya and declared that they were only subordinated to the Consul of Caffa. Di Negro made a complaint to Caffa about the self-will of the Genoese feudal lords, but the Guaskos' bribed di Kabela, and the latter recommended Di Negro not to disturb the brothers. Alas, an indignant Consul of Soldaya did not obtain justice in Genoa either...

Choban-Kule Tower on the Cape Agira

The west of Big Alushta is an agricultural region and the favorite place of making holidays for the so-called "wild" (unorganized) tourists. In the Middle Ages this part of the coast was densely populated that caused, alas, the liquidation of the local forests. Therefore the authors of the tourist guides of the beginning of the 20th century did not recommend travelling along the eastern part of the southern coast of the Crimea - desert, dull, with bad roads. Since then the situation has changed to the better, but you will not meet here any palaces, luxurious villas, and beautiful parks. The only "eastern" excursion for the holiday-makers of Alushta - is a trip to the water-fall Dzhur-Dzhur (see p. # as to the independent trip to that natural monument). When buying a ticket (UAH 20) find it out if the cost of visiting the water-fall itself is included, as far as it is located on the territory of the natural reserve, the entrance to which is paid - UAH 3 .

According to one of the legends, the water-fall Dzhur-Dzhur was called formerly Ai-Andry after an Apostle Andrei Pervozvanny

On the glade, where the excursion buses park, one can have a snack and some tea made out of the ecologically clean herbs of the Crimea. Tea pickings are sold here as well.

The water-fall Dzhur-Dzhur (in the very name of it one can hear a purl of the water-falling streams) is formed by the river Eastern Ulu-Uzenm, running along the picturesque gorge Khapkal, at the distance of two kilometers from the village of Generalskoye. Height of the water-fall is only 15 m, but instead it is the most full watered one in the Crimea, and, it does not dry up even in the most drought-afflicted years. If you go up-stream for about a kilometer, you can see several wonderful cascades. It is always chilly and dull at the water-fall. Thick brushwood and mossy stones surrounding the water-fall and against them the silver purling streams - what a decoration for shooting fairy-tale movies! But be very careful with the slippery stones.

Moving further on the way to Sudak, pay attention to the beauty of the surrounding locality. A robe of the highway either approaches the sea or runs away into the mountains speckled with the shadows from playing of the sun and clouds.

A village of Provetnoye (former - Scuti) brings up the rear of Greater Alushta. In the medieval epoch a patrimonial castle of the Guaskos' brothers was located here. In the near by ravine a pottery was located. About twenty kilns and a great deal of broken ceramics were found here.

A village of Lazurnoje is now located on the site of Castel-Primorsky estate. The path is running to it along the seashore past a boarding house "Morskoi Bereg" ("A seashore"), a health camp "Orlyonok" ("A Little Eagle"), and a holiday home "Lazurnoye" ("Sky-blue"). These sites are connected with the names of the Doctor of Medicine N.Suslova and Professor N.Golovkinsky. A former rector of the Odessa University, who had been engaged in hydro-geological research of the Crimea, lived here his last years. A watter-fall on the Uzen-Bash River is named after Professor N.Golovkinsky. An original monument to a famous scientist was erecter in 1900 not far from his house in Lazurnoye by the Tauris Zemstvo (elective district council in pre-revolutionary Russia).

The Rayevskys' House "Karasan" in the moresque style

To reach the tourist centre "Karabakh" - a former estate of P.Keppen, an outstanding investigator of the Crimea, one should go westward along the shore. It is easier to get there by a route taxi from the settlement of Maly Mayak (A small light-house). In the territory of the tourist centre one can view a cypress grove and a family burial vault of the Keppens.

Do not miss a picturesque conglomeration of the rocks - Kuchuk-Lambatsky Chaos, which is considered a natural monument.

Further your path is running to the cape Plaka (A flat stone). This cape is not very tall (40 m) but it is protruded far into the sea. A settlement of Lampas (in Greek - "a lamp, a light-house) is supposed to have been located here. The archeologists discovered the remains of the medieval fortifications on the cape. In the ancient park, laid out as long ago as in the 19th cent., against the greenery one can clearly see a red roof of the house, styling under a tiny castle. It is a former Palace of the Princes Gagarins, built in 1907. Nowadays it is one of the buildings of the health centre "Utyos" ("Cliff").

An estate of the Tauris Governor A.Borozdin was located on the site of the estate almost 100 years prior to the building of the castle. Borozdin's daughter Mariya was the wife of a Decembrist Iosiph Podjio. Having used his ties, A.Borozdin obtained an imprisonment of his son-in-law into a solitary cell to prevent his daughter accompanying the exiled into the Siberia. For eight years Iosiph was unable to let his people know about him. Having lost her last hope, Mariya got married for the second time, and only after that the Decembrist was condemned to penal servitude.

A footpath will bring you to the former house of the Rayevskys. The name "Karasan" was given to the house by Rayevsky-junior as a good memory of his staying in the Persian Province Khorasan. The owner the the estate was the Pushkin's friend. His sister, Mariya Rayevskaya, with whom a poet fell in love once, was a wife of a Decembrist S.Volkonsky. She followed her husband who was condemned to penal servitude despite strong desire of her relatives to prevent it. A unique grove of the Italian pines is located near the Palace.

The first female - medical doctor

Nadezhda Suslova (after marriage - Golubeva) was born in a peasant family. It did not prevent her from finishing a private boarding-school, passing examinations without attending classes in the gymnasia, and entering Medical and Surgical Gymnasia in Saint-Petersburg. It was forbidden to the females to receive higher education in Russia at that time, therefore she had to finish her education in Switzerland. Nadezhda Petrovna became the first Russian female - medical doctor, a Doctor of Medicine. In 1893 she moved to the suburbs of Alushta along with her husband - Professor A.Golubev. She provided medical services to the local population free of chage, was engaged in charity activities: with her own money she founded a free school for the village children, promoted the opening of a gymnasia and a city hospital in Alushta. She wrote several philosophic books. She was buried in the village of Lazurnoye on the top of the hill surrounded with cypresses and vineyards.

The former Palace of the Princes Gagarins

The beach of Partenit, the cape Kuchuk-Ayu, and the cape Plaka

A castle of disgrace

Not only trading ships were in a hurry floating to Partenit, but rich dignitaries were also rushing here in search of entertainments. There was a pompous castle on one of the mountains: rich interior decorations, a beautiful garden, and fountains where there was wine instead of water. 200 girls-slaves, brought here from throughout the Crimea, were waiting for the arrival of a seignior. Annually, in the beginning of the summer a ship with the strangers moored to the shore and merry-making started in the castle to be over by autumn. Then the master ordered to bring the captives to the room of execution where the miserable girls were beheaded. The local people called the horrible house "a castle of disgrace".
Once the servants stole the nuns from Sugdeya and Chersonese. Rumors about it reached the Bishop. He came into the castle, but was thrown into the dungeon. In the morning the master freed the Bishop and swore on the Bible that there were no nuns in the castle. The Bishop believed the treacherous villain, but soon a rock with the castle fell through the earth. A flame shot up from the huge hole and got burnt out everyhting around, so not a trace remains from the Devil's castle and his master.

A resort settlement at the eastern slopes of the Bear-Mountain has an extremely ancient history. The people settled here as long ago as in the epoch of the late Stone Age. Partenit (in Greek - "a virgin") as a civilized settlement is known since the 8th century. The geographical location of the settlement was suitable in the best possible way for the being a trade centre of the southern coastal settlements. It is not in vein that it was called a "huge market place" of Partenit.

Partenit was a centre of the Gothic Eparchy; a famous Bishop Ioan Gothic was born here. He headed an anti Khazars insurrection. After the insurrection was suppressed in 787 the Bishop had to move into Asia Minor where he soon passed away. According to a legend, his remains were by miracle transferred to Partenit and were buried in the Peter's and Paul's Temple erected by the Saint Bishop. A basilica of the Saint Apostles was discovered in the 19th century during the construction of a road. Archeologist N.Repnikov was engaged in the investigations of the temple. There were discovered remains of the mosaic floors, remains of the foundations, fragments of the walls, and also a tomb. It is this tomb that is supposed to be a burial of Ioan Gothic. However the tomb turned out to be empty. Perhaps it was a kenotaf - a symbolic burial of a man who died in a foreign land. Foundations of a basilica are preserved now.

Many legends are connected with Partenit: a famous myth about Iphigenia, a legend about a petrified giant bear that turned into the Ayu-Dag Mountain, etc. There were a lot of different events for the milleniums of the historical development, and those events gave ground for the legends.

A modern town does not look like a medieval huge market place at all: tall buildings of the health centres and residential apartment houses, beautiful parks and a seafront with good amenities, numerous bars stores and restaurants... In summer the inhabitants of Partenit let their apartment to the holiday-makers. A bigger part of the Partenit valley belongs to the military health centre "Krym". One can penetrate into its territory by means of passes or entrance tickets. The cost of staying on the comfortable beach of the health centre is UAH 5 per hour. One can buy a season ticket, it will be much cheaper.

There is a boating station in front of the small cape Kuchuk-Ayu (A little bear), near by - a small beach of the settlement (entrance - UAH 2).

If you are staying in Partenit do not miss an opportunity to climb the Ayu-Dag Mountain. The territory of the mountain belongs to the natural reserve, it means that one can only attend it with an organized excursion. The place of getting together of the participants of the excursion is canteen # 2 of the health centre "Krym".

The valley of Alushta is guarded by one the most wonderful peaks of the Crimean mountains - Demerdzhi. The nature created on its slopes the fairy tale forms of weathering: here one can find the Ghost Valley, the Head of Catherine (or may be Mariya or a Worrier - depending on what legend you are trusting more).

On the slopes of Demerdzhi: a cow and grapes

An excursion to Demerdzhi belongs to the most popular ones. You can start directly from Alushta (it will cost you approximately UAH 20), but there is another option as well: you are coming to the village of Luchistoye by route bus (on this road they were shooting the famous movie "A Caucasion female-captive"). Walk further along the highway from the final bus stop. The village of Luchistoye is located just at the foot of the mountain. Soon a footpath will turn to the right from the highway to the rocky hill.

You will find on your way a horse club "A golden horseshoe". Have a horse ride to the top of Demerdzhi or simply take a picture being on the horseback.

Further your way is passing by the ruins of the medieval fortress Funa (in Greek - "smoky"). Earlier the mountain itself was called the same way, probably because of the frequent thick mists shrouding the peak. The fortress was erected by the Feodorites on the trade way from Aluston to the steppe of the Crimea. Here one can view a partially preserved St. Feodor Stratilat's temple. Don't be surprised if suddenly a man shows up affirming that you have to pay UAH 3 for viewing the ruins and taking pictures against them. We did not have an opportunity to double-check if this fact is legitimate. But blackberries and hips are everywhere around - absolutely free.

A walk round Demerdzhi

At the foot of the mountain there is a chaotic agglomeration of boulders that buried under them a part of the village of Demerdzhi. In 1894 a mountain land-slip took place, as a result of it the village had to be shifted - now it is the village of Luchistoye.

On the southeast slope there is a famous Ghost Valley with stone columns, towers, mushrooms, etc. It is an impressive show in the evening, in the mysterious mist.

On the top of Demerdzhi the winds created a human's bust - from the highway it looks like a female head with a crown on it - they call it the head of the Catherine II. A beautiful view of the suburbs of the valley of Alushta is opened from it.

Mariya and a blacksmith

The hordes of the invaders-nomads conquered Tauris. One of the detachments settled itself on the Funa Mountain. At the very misty top of the mountain they built a huge smithy where a horrible black-beard blacksmith hammered weapons for the invaders. The blacksmith needed assistants that were brought by the worriers from the villages around. Adult men died of the unbearable labor, and the blacksmith demanded more and more new slaves...

The elders decided to ask the strangers to leave them alone, but a blacksmith threw the envoys into the fire. Then the beautiful Mariya came to talk to a cruel villain. She wanted to soften his stone heart, but the blacksmith only laughed in response to her entreaties.

- "I will not go away, and you will stay here with me", he cried, and when Mariya pushed him off in anger, he grasped a sword and pierced the miserable girl with it.

The ancient mountain could not bear it, shot up flame swallowed the blacksmith and the smithy. Villain's assistants turned into stone statues on the slopes. After that they began to call the mountain Demerdzhi, i.e., a blacksmith-mountain.

In the Ghost Valley

In the Cave Emine-Bair-Khosar

One remembers for a long time cne's trip to Chatyrdag. You should certainly climb the top of the mountain - Eklizi-Burun. A unique panorama of the Crimean peninsula is open from here - in fine weather when looking from this point the line of the horizon moves off at the distance of approximately 100 km. You will see the Sea of Azov and the valleys of the Northern Crimea, Yevpatoriya harbor and the hills of Sevastopol, valley of Bakhchisarai, landscapes of the South Coast and the boundless blue of the Black Sea.

But, anyway, attending caves is the main objective of the excursion. Excursion groups schedule the attending time beforehand, but the "wild" (unorganized) tourists will have to stay in the line for the entrance tickets and then to wait more for the beginning of the excursion at the entrance. It takes from one hour and a half to two hours and a half.

The price of the entrance ticket is from 6 to UAH 18 depending on the number of the halls to be attended. The Tiger's Passage, the Hall of the Fairy Tales, and the Fall Through Hall are open for attending. A complete excursion lasts for about one hour and a half. The temperature of the air underground is practically stable throughout the year - it is about +8°C, so your snickers, trousers, and a field jacket will not be in vain. One can rent a field jacket at the entrance for UAH 3 - 4.

The cave Emine-Bair-Khosar was equipped for the excursions not long ago. It is located in three stages; Upper and Lower Bair, passages and galleries of the Middle Bair. The cave is inhabited: owls and bats live here. There is a well - downfall above the main hall. Speleologists found the bones of the animals that fell down and died here. A paleontological exposition is set up in one of the compartments of the cave.

Inside the cave you will see flowers and waterfalls, underground lakes and tracery galleries-passages, whimsical figures of the animals and fantastic creatures. A guide will tell you a lot of interesting stories, will tell what miracles can be made from stones by ordinary water. In fact what is a stalactite, that huge stone icicle hanging from the ceiling of a dull cave? Drops of water with the minerals dissolved in them were trickling down for hundreds of thousands years and were falling on a small protuberance. And a stalagmite, being created by falling drops of water, was growing up to meet a stalactite. When they meet, a stalagmite will be created. But it will happen not very soon because stone columns and icicles grow only several millimeters per century. Therefore be careful with the interior of the caves - think of the future attendees and do not make angry the master of the underground cave. Certainly, it is a fairy tale that there is a Spirit in each cave that protects its calmness, but, you know, a fairy tale is a lie, but it contains a hint...

Chatyrdag is rich in caves - there are about 150 caves that are open. Only two of them are equipped for attending: there are passages, staircases, permanent lighting .

You can take several pictures for the good memory of the underground kingdom. The cost of taking pictures is UAH 6. One can buy ready pictures, video films and souvenirs at the booking offices.

Miracles of the Marble Cave - one of the most beautiful caves in the world

Near the fortress walls of Sudak

Peace and quiet, caressing sea, velvety sand and greenery of vineyards, wide open space and distance are the components that creates the mood of friendliness and mildness of Sudak that attracts people here...

S.Yelpatyevsky

■ Sudak is a seaside resort of the southeast Crimea. The climate is mild here; it is similar to the south coastal one. The summer is dry, the winter is rather severe. The temperature in July-August rises up to +38°C, and in February it drops to -20°C. But the winter is short, and it is breezes that save from the obsessive heat in summer. The sea gets warmed thoroughly early. The bathing season - the longest in the Crimea opens in the beginning of June (temperature of the water is +18,7°C) and lasts till mid-October (+17°C).

The researchers suppose that the Alans founded Sudak in the 3rd century, though the ancient people selected these localities much earlier. In the suburbs of the city the archeologists discovered the tools of the people of the Stone Age. This region attracted the Tauri as well - several Tauri settlements dated back to the 1st Millenium B.C. were found between the Megan Cape and the Karaoul-Oba Mountain. In addition to quite peaceful trades - cattle breeding and farming - the Tauri did not scruple to be engaged in petty piracy, robbing the Greek ships passing by. The inhabitants of the Bosporus even had to erect their own fortress on the western spurs of the Karaoul-Oba Mountain to protect the ships from the pirates' attacks.

A settlement of Sugdak (Sugdeya) appeared on the site of the modern beach of the settlement of Uyutnoye at the foot of the Krepostnaya (Fortress) Mountain. The Alans is an Iranian language tribe, ancestors of the modern Ossets, showed up in the Crimea in the 2nd - 3rd centuries. "Sugda" is translated from the Iranian language as "chaste, saint". Some researchers think that Sudak was the main port of the Alans. The records of Sudak in the written sources appeared in the 8th century.

During the Byzantine dominion the first fortifications of the Sudak's fortress on the northern slope of the Krepostnaya

History in a few lines

212 - *Sugdeya was founded by the Alans.*
The 6th century - *construction works started to erect the fortress.*
The 8th century - *Sudak forms a part of the Byzantine dominions in the Crimea.*
The 9th century - *a Khazar military fore-post is located here.*
The 11th century - *beginning of the violent growth of the city, that was under the rule of the Polovtsians at that time.*
The 13th century - *Sudak becomes the biggest Venetian trading station.*
1221 - *the Turks-Seldzhucks attacked the city.*
January 27, 1223 - *the first raid of the Mongols-Tatars.*
June 1365 - *the Genoese seized the city and the vicinity.*
June 1475 - *the Turks-Osmanians seized the city.*
The end of the 18th century - *the Sudak's valley first belongs to G.Potyomkin and then to the representatives of the Russian nobility.*
1920 - *establishment of the Soviet power.*
November 1, 1941 - April 13, 1944 - *the period of Hitler's troops occupation.*
1979 - *Sudak receives a formal status of the city.*
2002 - *there are 18,000 thousand inhabitants in Sudak.*

(Fortress) Mountain were laid out. In the middle of the 7th century when the Khazars showed up in the Crimea, a representative of the Khazar power settled in Sudak. In the 8th century the Byzantine population of Sugdeya increased significantly because of the wave of the iconoclasts that had to escape from the centre of the empire. They founded churches and monasteries in the vicinity of the Alepkhor River valley.

The first evidence of the connections between the Kievan Princedom and Surozh (the way the Rus people called Sudak) was found by the researchers in the "Hagiography of Stephan Surozhsky" (9th century), the biography of a famous bishop of Sugdeya. One of the Rus Princes, who made a plundering raid from Chersonese to the Bosporus at the beginning of the 9th century, attacked the rich city. After a nine-day siege Sudak has fallen and was sacked bulkily by the prince's armed forces. However in the future Kievan Rus and Surozh maintained solid trading relations. Merchants were coming here from all over the world. Many neighboring rulers could not let the glory of the richest city have a minute's peace. In the beginning of the 13th century Sudak was seized by the Turks-Seldzhucks that were expelled by the Mongols-Tatars. The raids had been going on for one hundred years. The power on the city was undermined, and soon the Caffian Genoese seized the weakened Sudak. The Consul of Soldaya (the way the Genoese called Sudak) was subordinated to the Consul of Caffa. Having got an annual contribution, the Tatars did not interfere with the commerce. The independence of the Genoese colonies was lost after the Turks had seized the Crimean Khanate.

His Highness Prince G.Potyomkin made an attempt of Sudak's revival. Gardens were planted and vineyards were laid out, but after the prince's death the affairs were going down the hill. In the second half of the 19th century there was the only street in the town, the rest of the territory was split into the dachas plots. But steadily the intensive construction works started in Sudak.

After the cruel struggle for the establishment of the Soviet power in the Sudak's valley there were set up several sovkhozes (State farms) on the basis of the former estates.

The memory of the Great Patriotic is reflected in the names of the Sudak's streets - Tankistov (Tankmen) street, Desantnikov (Paratroopers) street, 14th of April Street (the date of the liberation of Sudak from the Hitler's troops).

Since the 60-ies of the 20th century Sudak has been developing as a resort city. This city has a great resort future.

A view on Sudak from the Krepostnaya (Fortress) Mountain

Addresses and telephones:

City Police Department
10 Partisanskaya St. *Tel.* **21-344**

Traffic Police Duty-Officer *Tel.* **33-214**
1-a Feodosiya shosse (Feodosiya highway)

Ambulance station *Tel.* **21-347**

Drugstore (on duty)
36 Lenina St. *Tel.* **21-252**

Water-rescue station *Tel.* **21-167**
1 Naberezhnaya St. (Seafront)

Central Post Office
82 Lenina St. *Tel.* **21-646**

Trunk-call office
34 Oktyabrskaya *Tel.* **21-932**

Railroad booking-office *Tel.* **21-903**
8 Pochtovaya St. (Post Office)

Air booking-office
17 Partisanskaya St. *Tel.* **21-837**

Excursion office
79-a Lenina St. *Tel.* **21-486**

Privatbank
85 Lenina St. *Tel.* **22-535**

Apartment renting intermediary office
71 Lenina St. *Tel.* **21-678**

Low prices for lodging and meals attract the tourists to Sudak. In addition to the private individuals that let their rooms there are two hotels in the city.

TOK "Horizont" ("Horizon")

8 Turistskoye shosse (Tourists Highway)
Tel. 22-179

The tourist and health centre is located in the suburb "Uyutnoye" just opposite the Sudak's fortress. It will take you 15-20 minutes to walk to the sea beach located at the foot of the Krepostnaya (Fortress) Mountain. A small park with sports yards is located round the building. In the lobby of the hotel one can order an excursion to any corner of the Crimea. The cost of a room with conveniences and meals is about UAH 250 per night.

"Surozh"

75 Lenina St.
Tel. 21-241

The hotel is located in the centre of the city near the park zone and a marketplace. It is 10-15 minutes walking from here to the beach. Water supply depends on the schedule of the city water supply enterprise operations. There is no sauna, swimming pool, etc. The cost of the room of the highest category is about UAH 200 (meals inclusive). The cost of lodging in a room without conveniences is UAH 60 per night (meals inclusive).

There are roads from Alushta, Simferopol, and Feodosiya to Sudak. One can reach the city by sea as well.

BUS SERVICE

1 Alushtinskaya St.
Tel. 21-506

Feodosiya, the closest resort-city with the railroad service, is located at the distance of 60 km from Sudak. The tourists that came by train to Feodosiya can reach Sudak by coach rather quickly. It is longer to go here from Simferopol as far as it is located at the distance of 106 km.

SEA SERVICE

Sea moorages of the Sudak's bay are located at the Seafront. From the centre of the city one can reach them along Morskaya Street and Cypress Alley via the park. Motor boats from the seaside cities of the Crimea are coming here. Voyages along the Karadag and the beautiful bays of the settlement of Novy Svet (New World) as well as to Feodosiya are also arranged here.

Low prices for lodging and meals attract the tourists to Sudak. In addition to the private individuals that let their rooms there are two hotels in the city.

Sudak's highway

A park in Sudak. One feels solitary and cozy here

What can attract a tourist to Sudak in addition to the magnificent ruins of the fortress and the landscapes pleasant for the eyes? Of course, it is a great deal of tasteful and cheap fruits.

There are perfect vineyards, the best pears and apples in the Sudak's valley and its vicinity. There are enough cafes and canteens in the city but attending a Sudak's marketplace can bring enjoyment to the gourmets.

Bars and cafes are concentrated along Lenina Street, Cypress Alley, and the Seafront. A choice of dishes is basically traditional: Oriental cuisine is represented by shurpa, pilaf, lagman, shashlik (pieces of mutton roasted on a spit); European cuisine - by beef stakes and fish dishes; Ukrainian cuisine - by borsch and vareniks (curd or fruit dumplings); Russian cuisine - by pelmeni (Siberian meat dumplings); Tatar cuisine - by chebureks (kind of meat pasty eaten in the Crimea and the Caucasus), etc.

Cafes in Sudak do not differ significantly from each other as to their interior decorations and prices. The cost of lunch in average is UAH 10. Of course, each entity offers its firm dishes. For example, cafe **"Lavanda"** offers a chop with eggplants, cafe **"Agat"** offers pilaf on a special recipe. The time of cooking dishes is from 10 to 40 minutes. In summer many entities are operational 24 hours.

A choice of simple entertainment in Sudak is not big. The main entertainment is to attend the beach stretching for 2 km from the Alchak Cape to the Krepostnaya (Fortress) Mountain. The bottom of the Sudak's bay is flat, gently sloping, without any unpleasant surprises. The beach contains petty pebbles and sand, the width of the coast strip is from 6 m to 30 m. A secluded small beach is located in the settlement of Uyutnoye. One can get there going along a footpath, by-passing the fortress from the west side, passing by the Portovaya (Port) Tower. A small nudist beach is located in a small bay of the Kiz-Kule-Burun Cape.

A Seafront with the adjacent parks of the health centres is the central place of entertainment. There is a boating station in the Seafront where one can hire various swimming means. In the evening there are discotheques in the dance pavilions of the health centres.

There are enthralling shows in the territory of the fortress: fancy-dress performances with fencing and knights' tournaments.

The inhabitants of Sudak and the guests of the city are having a good time in the city-park where there is a stadium, discotheques, and numerous cafes. The local people like to have walks up to the Fireinaya Hill, earlier "Fireika", that used to be a favorite place of festive gatherings on public holidays.

Addresses and telephones:

Agat" ("Agate")
(cafe and discotheque)
Cypress Alley *Tel.* **21-602**

"Chaika" ("A sea gull")
72 Lenina St. *Tel.* **21-865**

"Grand-pries"
6 Vinogradnaya St. *Tel.* **32-272**

"Consul"
89 Lenina St.

"Oasis"
Cypress Alley

Amazing pilaf

"Baron Munhgauzen"
Cypress Alley

"Allegro"
Cypress Alley

"Lavanda" ("Lavender")
4 Gagarina St. *Tel.* **31-622**

There are perfect vineyards in the suburbs

Toplovsky nunnery

The Toplovsky nunnery of St. Paraskeva is located not far from the settlement of Topolevka. It is founded near a healing spring. Its history is as follows.
In 1825 in Kiziltash ravine between Sudak and the settlement of Shchebetovka, in one of the caves where there was a healing spring, a Tatar shepherd discovered a God's Mother icon. Since then they were holding services in the cave. In 1830 Konstantina-associate settled here. When Innokenty, a member of higher orders of clergy, founded a monastery in the ravine, a nun left for the spring of St.Paraskeva. Soon the Toplovsky nunnery was founded here. Now the nunnery has a big territory. Thousands of pilgrims as well as those who are eager to be healed in the waters of the sacred spring are coming here. Excursions to the Toplovsky nunnery of St. Paraskeva are arranged from many Crimean cities, including Sudak.

God's Mother Pokrova Temple

The foundations of the temple were laid out in 1819. Due to the Turkish dominion many Christian churches were demolished by that time and there was not enough room for all the parishioners in a small temple in the territory of the fortress. In addition, it was located far from the settlement. Therefore it was decided to erect a new church in Sudak. In 1912 the Emperor Nikolai II visited the settlement of Novy Svet (New World). He donated the necessary amount of money for the restoration of the church. In 1936 a pioneer club was located in it. Since the 90-ies of the 20th century the door of the temple is open again for the believers.

St. Paraskeva's Temple

A medieval Greek temple of St. Paraskeva was preserved in the settlement of Uyutnoye. A cemetery used to be located round it - it is an evidence of the fact that the church has been acting for a long time. Nowadays the building needs to be restored.

Lutheran church

The Lutheran church was built in 1887 for the believers of the German colony. A Gothic inscription above the entrance says: "Let it be peace on this site. God Savaoph ordered it."
In Soviet times the church was closed, a club and a cinema were located in it. Now an exhibition hall of the reserve "Sudak's fortress" is located in the building. In 2002 wax figures of the famous people were exhibited here: G.Potyomkin, Catherine II, M.Kutuzov, Roksolana, P.Vrangel, N.Makhno, and others.
Near the church behind an iron fence there is a small lapidary facility where the tombs from the graves of the outstanding Sudak's inhabitants have been gathered together.

Temple of Twelve Apostles

The temple is a vivid sample of the medieval architecture. It is located behind the Genoese fortress on the slope of the Palvani-Oba Mountain near the Portovaya Tower.
The travelers in the 19th century still could see on its walls a Secret Supper fresco with the pictures of Jesus and twelve apostles (was not preserved). The name of the church has been derived out of it. In the masonry of the Portovaya Tower there were found the blocks with the carved crosses. Probably the tombs from the church cemetery were used when building the church.

Temple of the Twelve Apostles on the Palvani-Oba Mountain was demolished twice. For the second time it was restored as an Armenian church

Peter Simeon Pallas

Peter Simeon Pallas a famous scientist, a researcher of the Crimean peninsula spent many years in Sudak. His first acquaintance with Sudak dates back to 1794. In a year two estates in the Crimea including a plot of land with a vineyard in Sudak were granted to the Academician. A former house of the scientist is located in 9 Desantnikov Street. Being engaged in the practical vine growing, the Academician attracted attention of the wine-makers to the aboriginal sorts of the Kozskaya Valley. Unique wines are made now from these sorts.

In 1804 P.Pallas founded at the public expense the first national specialized school of vine growing and winemaking. On instruction of the government the scientist had been a supervisor of this educational establishment for six years. The specialized school existed till 1847.

In 1807 a famous botanist **Khristian Khristianovich Steven**, who continued his senior colleague's activities on the investigation of the Crimean nature, visited the house of P.Pallas. Till the last days of his life K.Steven visited Sudak almost every year. In 1835 he married Mariya Gartsevich, an inhabitant of Sudak. K.Steven spent summers and autumns in his wife's estate, located in the Ai-Savskaya valley, and winters - in Simferopol. He gathered a huge herbarium (1,654 kinds of plants) of the Crimean flora. A former estate of the Stevens is located in 10 Alushtinskaya Street.

M.Voloshin, K.Bogayevsky, M.Latri, A.Tolstoy, N.Berdyayev and others used to attend more than once the house of the sisters **Alelaida and Evgeniya Gertsyk** in 39 Gagarina Street. Now the branch of the Yalta vocational training school is located here. The sisters Gertsyks are heiresses of a famous Polish and Lithuanian noble family. In 1910 in Petersburg the collected poems of Alelaida Gertsyk were published. Later in the 20-ies in Sudak she had to go through famine, hardship, and jail. Her emotional experiences became the basis for the creation of the collected poems "Cellar poems". Alelaida was discharged due to the collected poems. A dedication of the collected poems to a young investigator, who turned out to be a poetry lover, done at his request, became a key to be set free.

The name of **Aleksandr Afanasyevich Spendiarov** (his dacha was demolished during the war) is also connected with Sudak. The composer was working here with a special inspiration. His best opera "Almast" was created in Sudak. **Sophia Parnok**, a poetess and translator who lived in Sudak from 1917 to 1922, wrote the libretto for the opera.

Artists I.Aivazovsky, A.Fessler, E.Magdesian, N.Yaroshenko, M.Latri, M.Voloshin, K.Bogayevsky liked to paint the suburbs of Sudak.

These wonderful places attract attention of numerous scientists and cultural figures the same way now as it was in the past.

A wax figure of G.Potyomkin

German colony

After Russia had annexed the Crimea, many Tatars left the peninsula. To populate uninhabited lands (and not only the Crimean ones) Catherine II issued a manifesto, according to which the foreigners were invited to Russia to develop the uninhabited territories. The first experience of the colonization was unsuccessful - criminals, drunkards, and lazy persons turned out to be among the migrants. After the introduction of the additional rules (colonists were to have the habits of farming, cattle breeding or to have a trade), the things changed for the better. In 1805 a German colony of the migrants from Baden, Vurtemberg, and Zurich was set up in Sudak. It was located below the Genoese fortress. It was exactly the way the Germans called their settlement - die Festung (a fortress). Durable houses with neat gardens and yards were built here, the streets were well groomed. Due to that fact the colony differed positively from the small neighboring Tatar village. The descendants of the German colonists - artist Fredrick Gross, economist Nikolai Zibert, and others - left a striking trace in the history of the Crimea.

A Lutheran church in the settlement of Uyutnoye, a former German colony

The Girlish Tower

The tower on the top of the Krepostnaya (Fortress) Mountain is solitary and impregnable. It is called Kyz-Kule - the Girlish Tower. They say that an arkhont (a ruler) of Sugdeya had a beautiful daughter. Diophantus, a military leader of the great Mitridate IV of Yeupatore, fell in love with her. An arkhont promised that his daughter would marry a noble military leader, but there was an obstacle: the girl loved a simple shepherd, a deserving young man. To part the lovers, the arkhont sent the chosen one on a mission to Miletus and ordered

Ruins of the Girlish (Patrol) Tower

the servants to kill him on the way. Having found out that the beloved died, arkhont's daughter called on Diophantus to the top of the tower and said:

- Worthless people - you are and my father! You do not know what a heart and love mean. I will show it to you! Having said this the girl threw herself down...

However, there is another version. A fresco, on which there is a Catholic Madonna with her heart pierced with seven swords, was founded on the wall of one of the tower's rooms in the end of the 19th century. A home chapel was supposed to be located here.

But it is also possible that the name of the tower is distorted Khyz-Kule - a Patrol Tower.

Frankly speaking, without the Genoese fortress modern Sudak would be not interesting at all in terms of history - very few things left from its magnificence in the past. But the fortress could be a great compensation for the non-availability of the other historical monuments.

There were the fortifications on this site prior to the time when the Genoese showed up here. Archeologists affirm that the construction started prior to the 10th century. The plates on the fortress towers date back the beginning of the fortifications construction works to 1371. The last tower was erected in 1469. The urban population of Sudak at that time was about 15,000 inhabitants.

The museum (Tel. 210029, open from 9 a.m. to 9 p.m.) is located in the settlement of Uyutnoye. An excursion starts from the parking place where the excursion buses come. Here you can leave your car if you came to view the fortress independently (UAH 1,5 per hour; along the Tourist shosse (Tourist highway), to the left at the fortifications of the fortress). The tickets are sold in the booking-office at the entrance gate (UAH 4 for adults, UAH 5 - for using cameras).

A round-shape pre-bridge fortification - barbacan - has been restored in front of the main gate. They spanned the moat with a bridge at the fortifications, the moat was filled with water still in the 19th century. The guard was on duty at the bridge. In the night the bridge was lifted, and the gate, covered with the metal sheets, was lowered. The gate is located in between two towers. The western one is the tower of Yacobo Torcello (1382 or 1385), the eastern one is the tower of Bernabo di Franci di Pagano (1414). The plates are walled into the towers. There are inscriptions on the plates in Medieval Latin mentioning the date of the construction and the name of the Consul of the Soldaya fortress at the time of the construction. There is a coat of arms of Genoa, a coat of arms of the ruling doge, and a coat of arms of the Consul on the plates.

An excursion starts from the western tower and goes along the fortifications. The following tower has only been restores partially. There is a stone building erected under the Consul Pascual Djudich (1392). Not far from the fortifications there are

One can make a picture in the costumes of different epochs. The hire of a costume is UAH 5.

the remains of the stone buildings. There were the storage tanks for the water and a bit further -two barracks of the Kirilovsky regiment settled here after 1783. The barracks built on the instruction of G.Potyomkin. Here, in the fortress, there was a commandant's office, there were guards on the combat sites of the towers. The fortress is called Kirilovskaya on the maps of that time.

The fortifications lead to the Round Tower. It probably remained from Byzantine times. Near by, in the layer of the ground there were discovered the objects of the Tauris origin. Further you will see the towers of Lucini di Flisco Lavani (1409), Corrado Chicalo (1404), and a Nameless one.

To the other side of the gate there are five more buildings of different years. The fortifications of the lower tier of the fortress consist of a solid stone wall 2 m thick and 6-8 m high, reinforced with the combat towers. The wall and the towers ended with merlons behind which the defenders of the fortress were concealing themselves. On the bare top of the Krepostnaya (Fortress) Mountain there is the Girlish Tower.

The set of the second tier contains a Consul Castle connected by a wall with the Georgiyevskaya Tower. One can only penetrate inside via a lift-bridge on the level of the second floor. In addition to the residential rooms there was a small arms warehouse and a storage tank for the water in the donjeaun - the main tower of the castle. Along the wall connecting the donjeaun with the side tower there was a site for the shots. In the corner of the combat tower there was a secret passage to the footpath in the rock. From here by means of the rope ladder the defenders of the fortress could imperceptibly leave the tower under siege.

The Consul's Castle and the ancient mosque

The city blocks were located between the two tiers: residential houses, service premises, small arms warehouses, churches (there were several churches in the fortress). "A temple on the consoles" and a mosque remained until nowadays. The history of the latter is rather interesting. As a historian A.Bertje-Delagard supposed, the mosque was built in the 20-ies of the 13th century by the Turks-Seldjucks (there is an evidence that it only took them 14 days to build it!). Soon it was demolished. The mosque was restored and some time later it was redone into a Greek temple. The Genoese turned it into a Catholic Church, which is proved by an inscription above a mikhrab (a Moslem praying niche in the wall). Under the Turks there was a mosque here again. After 1783 - an Orthodox military church, a German Protestant church, a Catholic temple... Now the materials on history and archeology of Sudak and the Genoese fortress have been gathered in a former mosque. The fortress itself is a historical and architectural reserve, a branch of the St Sophia reserve in Kiev.

Cannons at the ruins of the Kirrilovsky barracks

The last consul

After the Turks had seized Caffa in the beginning of June 1475, they paid their warlike attention to Soldaya. The consul Khristoforo di Negro could escape to Genoa by sea without any problems, but he was an honest and courageous man, and therefore he decided to defend the fortress to the very end...
The responsibilities of a consul (a governor-general of a Genoese doge) were extensive and troublesome: he was a ruler of the city, and a commandant of the garrison of the fortress, and a judge in civil court cases. The consul had no any private land property, could not to be engaged in any other kinds of activities, and had no right to leave the fortress in the night-time. Di Negro was an excellent consul.
The fortifications that protected from the Tatar and other nomad tribes' raids lost their ground before the Turk artillery. The Genoese defended the fortress bravely, but the forces were unequal. Foodstuff was about to be over. When the enemy burst into the fortress, the survived worriers together with their consul concealed themselves in the city temple, but the Turks got fired the building...
Excavations made in 1928 confirmed that the last defenders of the fortress burnt alive in the church. Only several inhabitants of the city managed to use a secret passage and escape by sea from the citadel under siege.

The foundation of a basilica

A trip to Novy Svet (New World) will give you unforgettable impressions. The highway between Sudak and Novy Svet (New World) 7 km long runs through the most beautiful places of the eastern coast of the Crimea. These places used to be called "Paradiz" that means "a garden, paradise" in French.

It is worthwhile to have a walking tour round the suburbs of Novy Svet (New World). Excursion bureaus offer to visit several sights in the settlement - the museum of L.Golitsin, the champagne distillery "Novy Svet" and also to make a walking tour along the famous Golitsin's footpath.

Catherine II presented this valley surrounded with whimsical rocks to a French nobleman named de Galere, but soon he sold the gift. The locality changed the owners several times until Prince Lev Sergeyevich Golitsin bought the estate in 1878. He built a champagne distillery here. Soon they began to speak about the Russian champagne - it caused a real sensation. Golitsin's champagne was awarded with a Grand-pries at the Paris exhibition in 1900. To the honor of the wine-makers of the champagne distillery "Novy Svet" it should be mentioned that their champagne receives awards at the modern exhibitions now as well.

The tourists can get information about the creation of the excellent Crimean drink in the museum of winemaking (11 Shalyapina St., Tel. 32-921). In summer the museum is open from 9 a.m. to 3 p.m. seven days a week. In addition to the rich exposition telling about the activities of L.Golitsin and about the history of the champagne distillery, there is a wine-tasting hall in the building of the museum. An entrance ticket to the museum is UAH 2 , wine tasting - UAH 15 .

An excursion bureau of Sudak arranges excursions round the champagne distillery. One excursion per day is arranged for independent visiting - at 2 p.m. (from Tuesday to Friday). It is better to get registered in the list beforehand (Tel. 32-886, telephone for references - 32-891, between 8 a.m. - 12 a.m.). The participants of the tour are to be gathered together at the entrance gate of the champagne distillery 15 minutes prior to the beginning of the tour, the cost of the tour is UAH 25 .

Many things in Novy Svet are connected with the name of L.Golitsin. Golitsin's footpath is the following sight in terms of being popular after champagne. On prince's instruction the footpath was arranged along the shore. Having got a walk along the remarkable Novy Svet seafront, arranged on the shore of the Zelyonaya (Green) Bay, you can go on walking along this nice footpath, starting at the eastern slope of the Koba-Kaya Mountain. The entrance to the footpath is

Lev Sergeyevich Golitsin

Prince L.Golitsin is the father of the champagne winemaking. To set up the model winemaking farms Lev Sergeyevich spared neither strength nor time and money. His wine cellars, into the construction of which he involved remarkable scientists and first-class engineers, are quite operational now, despite the fact that so many years passed.

Having learnt the experiences of the European countries to be considered the best in terms of winemaking, he came to a conclusion that the national wines could be inferior to no foreign ones in anything. Having invested all his money into the development of the winemaking industry in the Crimea, the prince raised it to a much higher level: suddenly Russia became the country able to compete with France and Spain on the winemaking market. It was a miracle...

Despite the fact that Golitsin ruined himself, his heritage - the best Crimean wines - became the property of the future generations. It is interesting that in 1912 the prince presented to Nikolai II who was his guest at that time a really czar gift - his estate "Novy Svet"...

Golitsin's wine cellar where champagne was kept

paid - UAH 4 . The footpath, cut through in the rock and enclosed with a high parapet, brings us to the so-called Shalyapin's grotto. The prince used to arrange an excellent representative collection of vintage wines here. Even today one can see its niches.

St. Luca's Church

Above the remains of the stone terrace, where Prince L.Golitsin entertained his guests with the collection wines, resourceful entrepreneurs arranged a small attraction reminding so called "tarzanka". For UAH 10 those who are willing can fly over the stone boulders. In the depth of the grotto there is a well. The first cave monastery is supposed to have been located here in times of early Middle Ages. Under L.Golitsin one could see the remnants of the frescos on the walls of the grotto.

The footpath leads us further, and here we are in the Sinyaya (Dark Blue) Bay. Rocks yield the place to clayey loose crumb. It is slippery here, and one should be careful. There is no way through here when it is raining. Straight-ahead one can see the Kapchik Cape resembling a fossil pangolin. Having by-passed, it we are going down to the through grotto, via which you can walk from the Sinyaya (Dark Blue) Bay to the following one - Golubaya (Blue) Bay. Nudists selected the rocks near the grotto.

Treelike juniper - a relic plant of the Crimea

In the centre of the Golubaya (Blue) Bay there is the Tsar beach where Nikolai II was bathing when visiting Prince L.Golitsin. Nikolai II liked sea bathing and started the bathing season under the temperature of +15°C. It is impossible to reach the beach walking along the shore. One has to go back to the foot of the Kapchik Cape and, walking through the protected grove of treelike juniper, to reach a footpath leading to the sea. From the west the Golubaya (Blue) Bay is enclosed with the Karaoul-Oba Mountain.

The settlement of Novy Svet is small. In terms of the sights one can also visit a house built by Prince L.Golitsin for the guests coming to visit him. The house is located not far from the winemaking museum and is notable for the four towers with melrons. Now a store where one can buy champagne, a store of souvenirs, and an exhibition hall are located in it. Slantwise from the house across the street there is a small, like a toy, St. Luca's church.

For those travelling by their own cars, there is a big parking place at the entrance to the settlement (UAH 2 per hour).

Sinyaya (Dark Blue) Bay and Kapchik Cape

An Eagle and a Falcon

Koba-Kaya (Cave Mountain) has got a second name - Eagle Mountain. A huge Eagle used to live on the seashore. Everyone in the vicinity recognized him as a sovereign and bent heads at him. Being proud and masterful the Eagle did not allow anyone of approaching to him. But nobody dared to approach the sovereign because of the fear to be torn to pieces.

Falcon Mountain protects Novy Svet from the East side

Years passed. And a young Falcon showed up in this locality. The Falcon did not want to obey the horrible Eagle, and the cruel battle broke out. Who will win a victory? An Eagle is powerful, but already old, and a Falcon started to press its opponent to the sea. The wounded Eagle fell on the seashore, and the Falcon hanged over him - the way they remained in stone until now.

The road to the Solnechnaya (Sunny) Valley, notable for its vineyards and the largest number of the sunny days per year in the Crimea, runs through the picturesque eastern suburbs of Sudak.

St. Illiya's Temple and its priest

Devout Farther Pyotr was a priest in the old church of the village of Kozy. Parishioners loved their pastor - he was a person of ready sympathy, took care of the poor and cripples. His daughter helped him in these cares.
Suddenly the Turks burst into the village and a cruel battle broke out. Farther Pyotr has hidden the

women and kids in the secret place under the altar and left himself in the church. His daughter did not want to leave her father alone. Having burst into the church, the Turks killed both of them.
The priest was buried at the entrance to the St. Illiya's Temple. They installed a bench at his tombstone. The sick and cripples were coming here to pray and a miracle occurred more than once: a prayer at the tomb of a righteous man cured illnesses and wounds...
St. Illiya's Church was closed in 1939. In the 90-ies of the last century the restoration works were done. In 2000 the church was given back a marble font, a main relic of the temple. Now divine services are held here.

As a rule, an excursion combines visiting the Solnechnaya Valley (till 1945 - the village of Kozy) and the village of Mindalnoye where the wine distillery "Arkhaderesse" is located.
The Solnechnaya Valley is located at the distance of 4 km from the sea. Vineyards here with the aboriginal sorts preserved since Greek and the Genoese times - Ekim-Kara, Djevat-Kara, Kephessiya, Sary-Pandas - are well known all over the Crimea. The vineyard valley is surrounded by the picturesque chains and mountains: Parsuk-Kaya, Toklut-Syrt, Eltigen.
An ancient Greek St. Illiya's Church (10th - 14th centuries) is a sight of the Solnechnaya Valley. It is located on the top oh the hill over the central square of the village.
According to the descriptions of the travelers of the 19th century, one could see numerous archeological monuments in these localities - fortifications, burial grounds, and temples. The people settled in the valley of plenty since ancient times.
Having viewed the church, let us proceed further to the village of Mindalnoye. There are no more than ten houses in the village, but its main sight is the famous wine cellars of the "Solnechnaya Valley" distillery. The cellars were laid out in 1893-1895 that can be proved by the inscriptions on the walls. Having been engaged in champagne production, L.Golitsin was looking for the sites to plant the appropriate sorts of grape. He has chosen the secluded hills of the Kozskaya valley. As is generally known, in due course the prince ruined himself, and in order to save his business he sold 240 dessiatinas (measure of land = 2.7 acres) of his Tockluck estate to Prince K.Gorchakov, having become a steward in the estate. Vines and wind protection strips out of almond-trees were planted, wine cellars were constructed. In 1899 K.Gorchakov visited his estate "Arkhaderesse" for the first time. He was disappointed, got quarreled with L.Golitsin, and hired a different steward...
However the wine cellars are operational until now. They do not produce champagne here, but among the output of the distillery there are unique wines: "Chyorny Doctor" ("Black Doctor"), "Solnechnaya Valley" that were awarded with the prizes and gold medals.
If you came to the distillery independently and are willing to have an excursion, drop in at the store located at the entrance gate. An excursion without wine tasting costs UAH 7 . Please, call the Executive Board of the "Solnechnaya Valley" distillery beforehand and get information about the schedule of excursions (Tel. 25-230 or 25-233).

"Solnechnaya Valley" distillery

The golden sands of Feodosiya

Die Griechen bauten hier eine
Kolonie und nannten sie Feodossija,
was Gottesgabe bedeutet...

P. Surmakow

Dzhankoi
BLIZHNIIE KAMYSHI
KERCHENSKOIE SH
KERCHENSKOIE SHOSSE
UL. FED'KO
Geologicheskaia ul.
Baibuga
Baibuga
UL. CHKALOVA
Chernomorskaia nab.
Aivazovskaia
ul. Engel'sa
ul. Pervushina
ul. Stepaniana
ul. Shevchenko
ul. Garnaieva
ul. Garnaieva
Rechnaia ul.
KRYMSKAIA UL.
ul. Chkalova
ul. Marshala Yeremenko
UL. FED'KO
Komsomol'skii park
prosp. Lenina
Baranovskaia ul.
ul. Chkalova
ul. Aniunasa
ul. Aniunasa
SIMFEROPOL'SKOIE
SHOSSE
KRYMSKAIA UL.
Moskovskaia ul.
UL. FED'KO
g.Lysaia
ul. Chkalova
ul. Generala Gorbachova
Boievaia ul.
UL. KARLA MARKSA
UL. VOLODARSKOGO
Boievaia ul.
UL. SVERDLOVA
Pervomaiskaia ul.
Kyivskaia ul.
UL. POBEDY
prosp. Lenina
Galereinaia ul.
Sovetskaia ul.
ul. Voikova
ul. Panova
ul. Voikova
ul. Voikova
ul. Panova
ul. Nazukina
ul. Gor'kogo
ul. Desantnikov
ul. V. Korobkova
ul. Svobody
ul. Chekhova
ul. Timiriazeva
ul. Lenina
ul. Lenina
ul. Chekhova
Korabel'naia ul.
RABOCH
GORODO
CHERNOE MORE
Feodosiiskii zaliv
© SSPE "Kartographia"

History in a few lines

The VI century B.C. - *the foundation of Feodosiya by emigrants from Miletus. Soon it becomes a typical town-state.*
355 B.C. - *Feodosiya becomes a part of the Bosporus kingdom.*
107 B.C. - *after the neutralization of the Scythians' revolt under the leadership of Savmak against the Bosporus king Feodosiya switches under the Pontu's rule.*
The I century B.C. - *the establishment of the Roman domination.*
The IV century - *the destructive invasion of Huns.*
The V century - *emergence of the Alans' settlement of Ardabda ("Of seven Gods").*
The end of the VI century - *seizure of Feodosiya by Khazars.*
1239 - *domination of the Golden Horde.*
70-80 of the XIII century - *emigrants from Genoa found a settlement in the natural boundary of Cafa (in the Italian manner - Caffa), next to Feodosiya.*
The XIV century - *emergence of the Armenian settlement.*
June, 1475 - *Cafa is captured by a Turkish landing force. The town receives a new name - Kefe.*
The XIV-XVII centuries - *Kefe is the main slave market in the Crimea.*
1616, 1628, 1667 - *campaigns of Zaporozhian Cossacks against Kefe end in liberation of slaves-Christians.*
1783 - *after the annexation of the Crimea by Russian empire the town is given back it name of Feodosiya.*
1920 - *establishment of the Soviet power.*
November, 1941 - April 1944 - *the town is occupied by fascists.*
2002 - *about 79,000 people reside in the large health-resort centre of the Autonomous Republic of Crimea.*

A house - a ship. A. Grin's museum at Galereinaya

This town has preserved till these days its name given it on its birth. Of course, the Miletus Greeks founded their settlement in the VI century B.C. not on an uninhabited place: a settlement existed here before the appearance of enterprising emigrants from Asia Minor yet. But history holds back it, therefore we shall consider that Feodosiya (the "Given by God" if translated from Greek) arose at the shore of a vast bay by the spurs of a low mountain chain of Tete-Oba more than 25 centuries ago. The town has a highly advantages geographical situation: from one side - mountains, from the second side - the steppe, from the third one - the sea. All this forms a mild climate - transitional from a subtropical Mediterranean one to a temperate continental one. In summer the steppe intense heat is alleviated by sea breezes, and winter frosts are regulated by the sea, therefore in December - February the temperature often rises up to +15°C. The average summer temperature is about +30°C, but the atmosphere is congenial owing to the influence of dry winds decreasing the excessive humidity.

The sea in the Feodosiya bay is warm, the temperature of the water in summer is +23-25°C, sometimes it reaches +27°C. Occasionally there happens a sharp, during one day, cold snap conditioned by a phenomena of driving away the water when a strong continued wind from the land drives far away in the sea the warmed upper layer of water, and its place is occupied by deep-sea waters of temperature +10-12°C. Fortunately, such phenomena are of short duration and fairly rare. The sloping shores, the excellent fine sand, the caressing sun, the small depth of the sea by the edge of the shore, all of this makes Feodosiya extremely attractive for family rest.

Feodosiya and its environs are chosen by tourists wishing to save themselves from the bustle, crush, and high prices of the South Coast and preferring to combine sea bathing with strolls to historic places and picturesque landscapes and also with medical treatment. In addition, this ancient land is an excellent climatic and balneological health resort where, in addition to the sea and the sand, the mineral waters ("Feodosiyskaya" and "Narzan Krymsky") and the sulphide mud of the salt Adzhigolskoye lake located at a distance of 12 km from the town are natural medical factors.

After the railway Feodosiya-Dzhankoi was built in 1892 which has connected the town with industrial and agricultural districts of the country it has returned to life again. Excellent country-cottages, banks, hotels, new town blocks of buildings - the town resembled Mediterranean health resorts of Italy and France to the contemporaries.

THE RAILWAY

The railway is a peculiar sight of Feodosiya - to be precise, not the railway

The railway station by the sea

itself, but its disposition at the bay shore, practically at the beach. The railway station building is at the beginning of Gorkogo street being a natural continuation of the embankment. A through service connects Feodosiya with Kiev, Moscow, Kharkov, Dnepropetrovsk, Krivoi Rog.

The road to the sea goes across the railway bad

In summer time new additional routes are opened, the quantity of trains is increased, therefore one can come to Feodosiya and to leave it without any problems, if, of course, one has troubled beforehand about the tickets.

THE COACH COMMUNICATION

If you go from Simferopol, then from the railway station the coach for Feodosiya departs from the coach station of "Tsentralny" ("Central"). If you have arrived to the capital of the Autonomous Republic by plane, then to Feodosiya you will be delivered by a coach which departs from the coach station being opposite the air terminal.

Feodosiya is connected by the coach communications with the Crimean towns - Simferopol, Kerch, Sevastopol, Yalta, Alushta, Sudak, Shchelkin, etc., and also with Krasnodar, Gelendzhik, Novorossiysk, Kherson... Near voyages are carried out also from the town bus station situated at 13 Nazukina street.

THE SEA TRANSPORT

Tourists wishing to go for a sea voyage can take advantage of the port arrival and departure building services.

TOWN LINES

The bus represents the town transport in Feodosiya, but lately the minibuses successfully competed with the latter. Private cabmen wait for their clients by the stations and markets. Frequently they also acts as intermediary agents when solving the "apartment issue".

Addresses and telephones:

Municipal department of militia *tel. 32-571*

Officer on duty of the State Traffic Inspectorate *tel. 30-214*

Confidential service *tel. 31-339*

Emergency aid station *tel. 03*

Chemist's shop *(on duty)* *tel. 32-583*

Water-rescue station *tel. 30-462*

Mountain-rescue service *tel. 71-060*

Municipal information bureau *tel. 71-513*

Information bureau on international codes *tel. 32-250*

Acceptance of telegrams on credit *tel. 30-599*

Head post-office *tel. 31-485*
9 Galereinaya St. (the intertown trunk-call office is also there)

Intertown public telephone
2 Nazukina St. 13, K. Libknekhta

Bank "Privatbank"
1a Fedko St. *tel. 31-771*

Bank "Kreditbank"
179 Chkalova St. *tel. 73-168*

Bank "Ukrsotsbank"
12 Gorkogo St. *tel. 31-268*

Information bureau of the railway station *tel. 32-198*

Railway ticket office
5 Voikova St.

Air communications agency
5 Voikova St.

Information bureau *tel. 0-06*

Intertown coach station
28 Engelsa St. *tel. 73-400*
(one can get to it by bus No. 2 or No. 4)

Booking tickets *tel. 71-052*

Port arrival and departure building
13 Gorkogo St. *tel. 39-347*

Ordering a taxi *tel. 73-082*

There are no high class hotel in Feodosiya, but one can find a fairly good lodging. Here you will not find such a luxury as in Yalta, but, on the other hand, such prices also are not observed. If you together with your family are going to luxuriate on a lovely sand and also to be distracted from bustle, not spending fantastic sums on your rest, then you have come just to the very place you need.

"Astoriya"
9 Lenina St.
tel. 32-343

The best hotel of the town is situated practically by the sea. Its receptionist works round-the-clock. The

embankment, restaurants, cafes, the railway station are next to it.

This is a first class hotel for 300 lodgers. A place in a room de luxe costs UAH 83. A day in a room semi-de luxe is UAH 44. In the rooms of this class there is an autonomous water supply. In a room without conveniences - at a price of UAH 20 - there is no hot water, as it is generally known. Also at the hotel there are no air-conditioners, depositary storage vaults, but, on the other hand, there is a parking space, a restaurant, a sauna, and a massage room - naturally, at an extra charge. Credit cards, unfortunately, are not serviced.

At the Kerchenskoye highway two "Golden beaches" are located - the tourist centre (more expensive) and the motor camping-site (cheaper)

"Moryak" ("Sailor")
8 Lenina St. tel. 32-414

It is situated text to the "Astoriya". It has fewer rooms, but there is a system of air conditioning. In the rooms de luxe at the cost of UAH 180 a day water heaters are installed. Rooms of a lower category are accordingly cheaper. The construction of a sauna is planned.

You will have to leave your car at the town parking space as the hotel has no its own parking yet.

"Georgiyevskaya"
3 The 8th of March St.
tel. 30-141

A definite remoteness from the sea is compensated by a large set of conveniences. The building was repaired not long ago. True, installations of air-conditioners has essentially affected the cost of the rooms: a double room de luxe costs UAH 246 (with a breakfast).

"Vzlyot" ("Take-off")
33 Kalinina St.
tel. 71-133

At this hotel ((its name was "Uyut" (Cosiness") before) there are several rooms of the de luxe category, a little more of rooms semi-de luxe, about 30 fairly cheap rooms. Apply to the receptionist on the issue of the availability of vacant rooms. There are a cafe and a paid parking attached to the hotel.

THE APARTMENT BUREAU AND THE "PRIVATE TRADERS"

If there are no vacant places at the hotels of the town, don't despair; you know, most of the tourists visiting Feodosiya rent apartments from private persons. One can apply to the **apartment-intermediary bureau:** 74 Gvardeiskaya St., tel. 31-724. Nevertheless, the owners of the dwellings will find you themselves: at any station the new-comers are met by more than one dozen of persons wishing to let a room or an apartment. We recommend you both to bargain and to choose: inspect several versions without fail before agreeing in order not find himself in a sloppy hovel at a sizeable price. One can rent not a bad room during the high season at UAH 15-20 a day.

Not long ago several private hotels were opened in the town.

TOURIST CENTRES

Suitable conditions of residence for unpretentious persons and also for admirers of a genuine tourist way of life are offered by tourist centres located in the main beyond the precincts of the town along the Kerchenskoye highway. These are the motor camping-sites "Lazurny" and "Zolotoi plyazh" ("Golden beach").

Addresses and telephones:

Cafes, restaurants:

"Batterflyai"
17a Voikova St.,
12.00-24.00 tel. **30-925**

"Roza vetrov"
5 Voikova St.,
round-the-clock tel. **30-647**

"Tangolita" tel. **30-164**
2 Voikova St., 9.00-23.00

"Staraya krepost" ("Old fortress")
8 Kuybysheva St.,
8.00-24.00 tel. **35-107**

"Charochka u kumy"
36 K. Marksa St.,
9.00-2.00 tel. **30-535**

"Smak" ("Taste") *(coffee-house),*
11 Sverdlova St.,
round-the-clock tel. **32-085**

"Pitstseriya"
6 Viti Korobkova St.,
9.00-22.00 tel. **31-201**

"Rul" ("Helm") tel. **30-078**
13 Nazukina St., 9.00-23.00

"Talisman"
(wine-tasting hall)
19 Samarinoi St.,
11.00-23.00 tel. **37-946**

"Skazka" ("Tale")
15 Krymskaya St.,
8.00-23.00 tel. **76-341**

Cafe - dining-room
48 K. Marksa St.,
8.00-20.0 tel. **30-258**

Markets:

Central market
2 Nakhimova St.

Food market
10 Starshinova St.

Non-food market
25 Starshinova St.

The main pleasant peculiarity of the Feodosiya public catering is its accessibility with a relatively good quality. Here there are enough small cosy cafes where they will feed you with a tasty and inexpensive dinner. To those who like to sit at a restaurant we advise to visit the establishment attached to the hotel "Astoria", especially if you miss the Soviet times. For the admirers of the exotic cuisine it is worth to drop in the "Batterflyai" where they make Chinese dishes. The present-day restaurants are more democratic, you will not find among them a chic and, accordingly, a very expensive one.

The attention of the tourists who like to eat well will be attracted by a cafe with a playful name of "Charochka u kumy" ("A drink with the Godmother"). Its interior is stylized to resemble a Ukrainian tavern, it is decorated by a mock-up of a water-mill; the cuisine is, to be sure, a national one. The cost of a decent dinner is about UAH 30. You will have to wait a little (from 15 to 40 minutes depending of the complexity of the dish) while the order is fulfilled. Enjoy the music, the picturesque furniture, and a pleasant talk - to such cafes one comes with his friends.

Next to it is the "Domashnyaya kukhnya" ("Home cuisine") - a cafe of the same class, with a European cuisine, a small hall, and a lovely cosy small courtyard where it is so pleasant to sit on a summer day under the canopy of grapes.

And also here, in the town's central part, a cafe with a romantic name of "Roza vetrov" ("Wind-rose") is situated. The sea theme does not confine itself to the name: the menu bears the same spirit, for instance, a schnitzel by the recipe of Greek navigators or fish in Sicilian style wait for you. Prices are reasonable: from UAH 5 to UAH 20. A large hall can accommodate a considerable company. During the summer heat an air-conditioner operates.

Cafe "Charochka u kumy"

In the central part of Feodosiya there is a number of decent dinning-rooms where you can dine out quickly and inexpensively. Pay special attention to the baking - pies in Feodosiya are very tasty and fairly cheap!

Besides, at the tourists' disposal there are town shops and markets with a large selection of fresh products.

In August the markets strike the gourmets' imagination, all the more that the prices in Feodosiya are a little lower than at the South Coast

In a town with such a rich history and a wonderful climate everyone will be able to occupy his spare time to his taste. You like to dream taking a walk in shady lanes, don't you? You give preference to walking tours along cool museum halls, don't you? You don't like any entertainment, except for the beach ones, do you? You crave for driving the balls on the green cloth, don't you? In short, any whim for your money and even without it.

TOWN BEACHES

In Feodosiya the beaches are golden not only by the colour of the sand. In the first place, there are many of them - there is enough place for all comers. Those who consider that it is crowded at the town beaches (and they stretch along the whole sea-coast of the Feodosiya's bay, from the port up to the northern outskirts and further) can make themselves comfortable beyond the town boundaries where a town bus (the cost of the passage is 40 kop.) or minibuses run.

Who from the little ones will refuse to take a drive along the smart embankment on a colourful small train?

To go down the hillock costs UAH 5

The bathing season ordinarily continues from the end of May till October, because the sea is shallow and gets warmed quickly. The town beaches are equipped with hillocks, hiring stations, there are without fail rescue stations, lavatories, and changing-huts. In contradistinction to the South Coast ones, the Feodosiya's beaches are free of charge. If you are afraid of receiving surplus ultra-violet, a night bathing will do for you. It is romantic, and, besides, it is not necessary to stint himself in time being careful not to be burnt. But be careful with alcoholic drinks, it is not worth to combine swimming with libation.

CHILDREN'S AMUSEMENT

At the embankment and near the railway station building, in a shady public garden, there are for children swing-roundabouts, cafes, and trays with ice-cream and other sweets. By the building of the **"Krym"** ("Crimea") cinema young race-drivers can try their strength in driving a car. Also here, in the cinema, cartoon films and the latest films for children and adults are demonstrated. One can observe real fireworks of stars on the concert hall stage - In summer traditional tours of Ukrainian and foreign variety performers take place in towns of the Crimea.

The park by the railway station does best of all for a midday siesta. On its green lawns people by whole families and alone make themselves comfortable - citizens breathing peacefully and noisily on the ground embarrass nobody.

Addresses and telephones:

Cinema "Krym" ("Crimea")
1 Lenina Ave. *tel.* **30-988**
Concert hall "Zvyozdny" ("Starry")
5 Gorbachyova St. *tel.* **35-681**
Complex "Grinvich" ("Greenwich")
7a Galereinaya St. *tel.* **30-952**
Casino "Flamingo"
6 Kirova St. *tel.* **30-352**
Bar "Zolotoi Kiy" ("Golden cue")
2 Bazarny lane *tel.* **32-467**

NIGHT ENTERTAINMENT

The night town invites its visitors to clubs and casinos, to discotheques, to night bars. Dances, cocktails, billiards, show-programs, games of chance - we think that you will not be bored. The entertainment complex **"Grinvich"** ("Greenwich") is considered one of the best in the town. In addition to the roulette, Black Jack, American pool, and Russian billiards, there is here a bar with a wide choice of drinks and refreshments, a strip-tease-show is organized for connoisseurs.

The billiards on the embankment

The game business is also represented by the establishments "Flamingo", "Zolotoi kiy" ("Golden billiard cue"), and others.

Konstantin Bogayevsky was another famous artist whose name was related to Feodosiya. Having been born in the town of Aivazovsky, he managed not to be lost against the background of Aivazovsky, not to fall under his influence, but to find his own unique way in art. "I has been born and has lived all my life in Feodosiya, an ancient town with whose antiquity perhaps only

In Koktebel. 1905.
K. Bogayevsky

Rome and Athens can argue, a town surrounded by "sepulchres of nameless steppe tribes", in a wreath of Genoese towers, in the shade of arcades, among hills, deserted and scorched, and the sea, also deserted and severe". These are, unconditionally, words of a man who worshipped his native land. His landscapes, wonderful, mysterious, romantic, can be seen in the town picture-gallery. To our regret, there is no museum of this great singer of Feodosiya. After his tragic death - Konstantin Fyodorovich lost his life on 1943 during bombing - his heritage was practically plundered. The painter's wife, Zhozefina Durante, who came of Genoese consuls' descendants, a woman unpractical and weak, could neither defend the Bogayevsky's house, nor preserve his pictures...

The name of Ivan Aivazovsky is inseparably linked with Feodosiya. On July 29, 1817 in a family of an impoverished Armenian merchant a boy who was fated to become an unsurpassed master of a sea-scape was born. By his first works drawn in coal the future painter of sea-scapes has decorated the whitened walls of houses. The talented child had been taken notice of by the Feodosiya governor, A. Kaznacheyev who helped him to enter the Simferopol gymnasia and then - also the St. Petersburg Academy of Arts, where Nikolai I himself was interested in his works.

Aivazovsky was notable for his fantastic efficiency - about 6,000 canvases have been created by him! He could paint a picture during 2-3 hours and even flaunted it, making a peculiar show when before the very eyes of dumbfounded spectators a virginal cloth was transformed during an hour into a pictorial canvas. Ivan Konstantinovich was a real virtuoso, and, in addition, he had a phenomenal memory. He had quickly refused sketches as the work from life looked boring and faded while a drawing from memory had become vivid and bright. Aivazovsky made only superficial sketches, and already in his studio he painted from memory. "Considering a picture, I don't divert my attention from it not only by idle talk but even also by the view of outside objects... An obligatory term of my studio - plain walls covered neither by pictures, nor by sketches", - the maestro wrote.

In addition to his talent of a painter, nature has presented this Russian artist - a Turk by his origin and an Armenian by his upbringing - with a practical sharpness. His pictures were bought up in a moment. A correct marketing policy played not the last part in it: in the master's studio both exclusive canvases for rich men, and sea-scapes for a mass buyers, and souvenirs for people with an empty pocket were created.

With all his pragmatism, Aivazovsky was a benefactor of Feodosiya, strove for making it beautiful and modern. He had donated to the town a picture-gallery, built in 1845 at his expense, with all the pictures being in it.

Several years, from 1924 up to 1930, there lived here Aleksandr Grin. For six years at least half his works were written by the writer-romantic. It seams that the Feodosiya's land had a wholesome effect on a person's creative potential, because the best Grin's novels such as the "Golden chain", "She who runs over the waves", "A road to nowhere" have been written here...

Of course, in this remarkable town there lived and created many outstanding personalities, but in order to remember all of them an individual book has to be written.

A commercial talent

If you had no money, but wanted very much to receive something of the Aivazovsky's paintings, then you could purchase the artist's photograph where instead of a picture a small piece of cloth of size of a postage-stamp, with the famous initial of "A", was inserted in the frame.

The museum of local lore, history, and economy

11 Lenina Ave.
tel. 30-936

The Feodosiya museums are unique in their own way. Judge yourself: the museum of local lore, history, and economy (the former museum of antiquities) is the oldest museum of the Crimea. Unfortunately, the first building which opened its halls for viewing the exhibit on May 25, 1811 has not lasted out. Many effort for opening the museum was made by a writer and historian, S.Bronevsky, who was at that time the Feodosiya's governor. A.Pushkin mentioned him in the description of his (Pushkin's) three-day staying in ancient Cafa in August, 1820 - the poet stopped at the Bronevsky's house. In his letter to his brother Lev the poet tells about extensive knowledge of his host in the field of the Crimea history.

A fragment of the black-lacquer ceramics painting

At present this museum is located in an old house of the XIX century. In the museum halls one can see the exhibit related to various ages: ancient tools and antique vases, the Genoese plate for breaking ground and the Armenian cloister carved gates, old postcards of the beginning of the last century, and photographs of the Second World war heroes... A diorama where specimens of rare flora and fauna of the peninsula are collected is located in the department of nature. In the courtyard of the museum on a lasted out small piece of a medieval roadway a lapidary is situated. A ticket is UAH 2.

The I.Aivazovsky picture-gallery

2 Galereinaya St.
tel. 30-929

The famous artist arranged this gallery in 1880 in his own house leaving it by his will testament to his home town. Now here is one of the largest collections of sea-scapes painting in Europe. Besides the canvases of Aivazovsky himself, works of K.Bogayevsky, M.Voloshin, M.Latri, and of other masters are exhibited. Much has been done for preservation of the gallery and a painting studio for gifted children by its director, an artist N.Barsamov. A ticket to the museum and the photography are relatively expensive because the gallery is divided into separate halls every of which is repaid separately (UAH 3 for every ticket). In general, a family trip to the museum by a full program can cost a pretty penny...

The brig "Mercury" attacked by two Turkish vessels. I. Aivazovsky

The A.Grin's literary-memorial museum

10 Galereinaya St.
tel. 31-309

In the house where the writer lived in 1924-1929 a memorial museum was opened in 1970. Its interiors are stylized to resemble a ship. In the rooms-cabins decorated by a Moscow artist and architect S. Brodsky the Grin's prose romantic atmosphere is felt. Things which belonged to the creator of the "Scarlet sails" and the "Golden chain", pages of manuscripts, the first editions, etc. are collected here. The building front decorated by the panel "Brigantina" ("Brigantine") belongs to the objects forming the image of the town. An entrance ticket costs UAH 3, a photo - UAH 2.

The museum of hang-gliding

12 Kuybysheva St.
tel. 32-028

The museum exists from 1990. We have not succeeded to determine its working hours. It turned out that the museum of the domestic mini-aviation history works by the principle "call - and they will open the door for you". One is to call the director of the museum by the phone 7-64-70 and to come to an agreement on the time of the excursion. Perhaps, the order of visiting the museum will be soon changed, therefore both telephone numbers are offered.

From the days of old the town was decorated by churches, mosques, kenasas - because people of various religions settled here. Settled and built their temples.

The Vvedenskaya church golden crosses

The St. Sarkis (St. Sergy) temple

11 Timiryazeva St.

Armenians appeared in the Crimea in the XI century. Their community in Feodosiya was fairly numerous - In the XV century there were 45 Armenian churches in Cafa.

The St. Sarkis church was built in the XIV century by the Italian sculptor Biodzholi. This is a typical example of the classical Armenian architecture of the early Middle Ages. Next to the church there is a belfry built later.

The temple has lasted out well, especially interesting the khachkars are - small marble plates with an imprint of a cross (the translation of a khachkar is a "holy cross") walled into the walls of the church and dedicated to some momentous events or concrete persons.

In the courtyard of the temple the I. Aivazovsky grave is. In this church the famous artist was baptized, here he got married, and also here the burial service was read in May, 1900. Later above the burial vault where the artist's body lies they erected a marble sarcophagus. The Aivazovsky's second wife, Anna Nikitichna, who died in 1944, has been buried also here.

The Mufti-Dzhami mosque

The Mufti-Dzhami mosque

the corner of Karaimskaya and Lenina streets

During the period of the Turkish rule a great number of Moslem temples were built in Cafa. The Mufti-Dzhami mosque has lasted out till now. True, it was rebuilt more than once, and after the annexation of the Crimea by Russia an Armenian-Catholic church settled here. The temple was constructed between 1623 and 1639. Now the mosque has again become an acting one, you see, the Moslem community of the town totals several thousand people.

Vvedenskaya church

11 Krasnoarmeiskaya St.

The antique Greek church was dedicated to the presentation of the Virgin in the temple. The construction is dated from the VIII-IX centuries. In the Soviet time a gymnasium was in the building of the oldest architectural monument. Now the church is an acting one, the temple belongs to the Ukrainian Orthodox Church. The priest, archpriest Father Aleksandr, has painted its interior by himself.

The Svyato-Yekaterininskaya Church

95 Fedko St.

The church built at the beginning of the last century is a striking example of Russian cult architecture. The smart turquoise-white building is richly decorated by architectural details: pillars, pilasters, small arches, stone patterns, etc.

The Kazansky Cathedral

52 Karla Marksa St.

The temple in honour of the Kazanskaya God's Mother icon was erected in 1907. Its history is like that. In 1887 the St. Petersburg Kazansky Cathedral churchwarden presented the Toplovsky Svyato-Paraskeviyevsky cloister with his country-cottage "Cafa" in Feodosiya on condition that on this territory a church would be arranged.

The Feodosiya citizens have endowed the Kazansky temple with the plot of land adjoining it. In 1890 the Toplovskaya cloister received as a gift the precious icon of Kazanskaya God's Mother - a copy of an ancient Scripture.

In 1891 a small temple in honour of great-martyr and healer Panteleimon was founded. Fifteen years later a stone cathedral in honour of God's Mother's Kazanskaya icon was erected instead of the wooden church.

After the October coup the temple was ransacked. For a long time to come the temple stood empty, but in 1943 it was opened again for carrying out services which continued all the subsequent years right up to now.

In 50-ties - 60-ties the Simferopol and Crimean archbishop, sanctifier Luka (Voino-Yasenetsky) participated in the cathedral renovation, carried out here a service - the festive liturgy.

The memory of the God's Mother's Kazanskaya icon is celebrated on July 21 and November 4.

The Svyato-Yekaterininskaya Church

The holy valley

In the Karantin, beyond the Genoa fortress eastern wall, there spreads out a small valley closely built over by medieval temples which have lasted out well up to the present time. The temple of Georgiy the Victorious stands out among them - the strict lines of walls of the fortress kind in combination with the belfry graceful dome simbolize an indissoluble connection of people's earthly and spiritual essence. The churches of Ioann-Theologian and Ioann-Forerunner and the temple of the first martyr, archdeacon Stefan are also here.

The town's visiting card - the Saint Konstantin's tower

According to Mr. I. Sarkisov-Serazini, who compiled Feodosiya guide-books at the end of the XIX - the beginning of the XX centuries, most artists and engravers drawing the town identified the local scenery with the Saint Konstantin's tower during its pre-port period. And it

is no mere chance that on lithographs and drawings of the forties-fifties the Konstantinovskaya tower ancient walls contours come forward to the foreground. And up to now it determines the town's relief which we remember. The Turkish bastion joining it is used by enterprising Feodosiyans sometimes as a dance pavilion, sometimes for a bar.

After the Genoese emigrants had bought the territory for a trading station, there has arisen a question about the defence of its residents, trade houses, and craftsmen shops against infringements of dashing neighbours. A low but a fairly spacious hill which was afterwards named "Karantinny" suited best of all for the arrangement of a strengthened part of the town. And on it in the XIV century the Italians built their fortress which consisted of 26 (according to a definite information) towers eleven metres high connected by walls two metres thick.

The tower of Krisko (Christ) has lasted out well

Some towers have partially lasted out till now. In order to see them you have to find yourselves in the old part of the town. For this you can take the town bus, but better, having armed yourselves with a map, to walk along the Feodosiya shady streets - on your way you will be able to see many interesting things and to plunge fully in the atmosphere of this ancient town, non-garish, but full of charm. The Lenina or Gorkogo streets lead to the fortress.

From all the medieval fortress constructions, except for the Konstantinovskaya which is in the centre, the towers of Kliment and Krisko (Christ), the view on which opens from the citadel gate, have lasted out well. If to move along the defensive walls, then soon below by the sea you will see the remains of the square Dokovaya tower. The rest of the objects - the Genoese bridge, towers of Foma and Dzhiovanni di Skaffa - are not so picturesque and after viewing the citadel will not produce a proper impression on you.

The temple of the God's Mother's Iverskaya icon is notable for its mellow atmosphere - Its walls radiate conciliation and peace. Stand for a while in front of the altar in order to fill that anxiety leaves your soul.

To the temple of the God's Mother's Iverskaya icon both tourists and Feodosiya's believers come

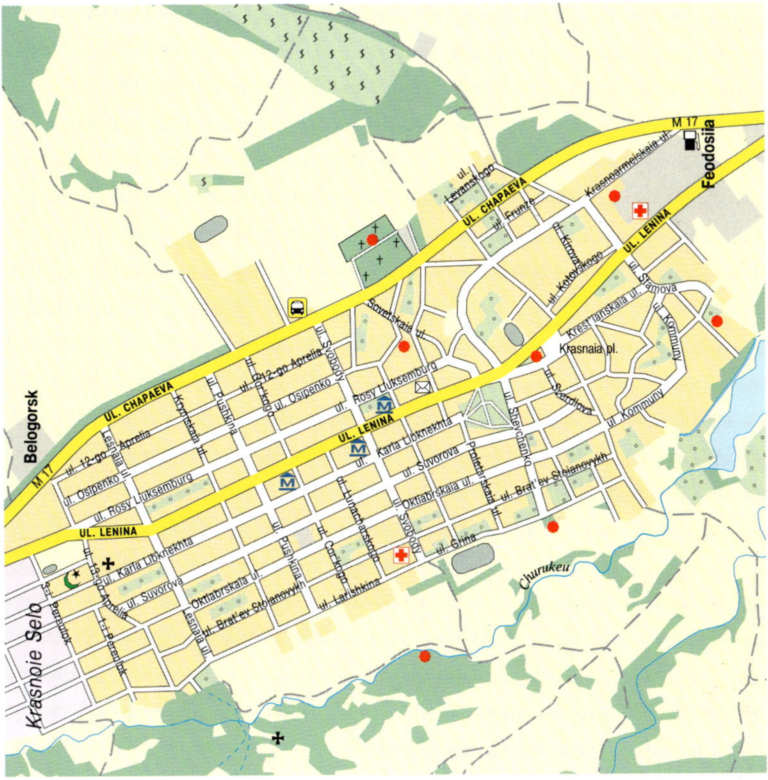

The Feodosiya holiday-makers must visit without fail the ancient Solkhat. Of course, here there is no sea and that special violence of nature characteristic of the sea-coast, but this town being provincial at present possesses an imperceptible charm - the charm of the great past. Antique pictures and ancient manuscripts smell so...

The first records about Solkhat date from 1266. Before this time Tavrs, ancient Greeks took their residence in these parts, but the town emerged only in the XIII century. To be exact, two towns as after the Golden Horde's forming the towns K'yrym where Moslems lived and Solkhat where Christians settled (Armenians, Genoeses, etc.) had emerged here. In the former one there was also the residence of the Golden Horde's khan's governor-general. Palaces, mosques, fountains decorated the town. Through the second one a caravan path went, here one could meet merchants from the whole world.

In the end of the XIV century both settlements were distracted by Tamerlan. Then Khadzhi-Girei had declared the peninsula an independent state and had transferred its capital to Bakhchisarai. Both Solkhat and K'yrym began to lose their positions, the trade stopped, the construction stood still. The two towns had united and received the name of Eski-Krym, i.e., Old Crimea. After the annexation by Russia they intended to make it the centre of Tavricheskaya province; Catherine II granted it a new name of Levkopol, that means a "quiet town". The Empress stayed here in May, 1787. But in several years Simferopol was appointed as the capital, and Eski-Krym remained the Old Crimea.

In the thirties of the XX century the town began revive - an antituberculous sanatorium and a polyclinics for health-resort visitors were opened here. The sanatorium "Old Crimea" exists till now.

The mosque and madrasah of khan Uzbek

WHAT IS WORTH TO SEE IN OLD CRIMEA

The ancient Solkhat is not a big town by the present standards. After the annexation of the Crimea by Russia a majority of the Tatar population left the town having emigrated to Turkey. During the years of the Second World war the Crimean Tatars were deported to the Middle Asia republics - that affected the small town's population size. Now, after returning of the Tatars to their own land, in Old Crimea more than 10,000 people live. Nevertheless, in such a small settlement many history and culture memorials have lasted out.

The museum of local lore, history, and economy

17 Svobody St.
9.00-17.00
tel. 21-244

The exact name of the museum is the literary-memorial-arts museum of "Town of Old Crimea", it is a branch of the Koktebel reserve of "Cimmeria of M.A. Voloshin".

Names of Aivazovsky and Voloshin, Bogayevsky, Grin, Tsvetayeva sisters, Petnikov, Okhotnikov, Drunina and Kapler, Amosov, and of other famous persons are connected with these places. In the museum exposition there are documents, photographs, personal things.

The bowler of Beibars

The A.Grin's museum

52 K.Libknekhta St.
9.00-16.00
tel. 21-444

In that small house the writer passed the last years of his life. "For a long time I felt no such a light world", - Grin wrote after his moving to Old Crimea. The house with two rooms and a tiny kitchen cost the Grins couple by far cheaper than a dwelling in Feodosiya. They were catastrophically short of money, his books were not published, his illness grew progressively worse...

Here his autobiography has been finished and a new novel "A thin-skinned person" has been begun.

Unfortunately, it has not been finished - the merciless cancer was on the offensive, and Aleksandr Stepanovich lost his strength quickly. In July, 1932 the writer died.

Not only the house, but, perhaps, the writer's literary legacy too have reached the present time owing to the selflessness of his wife, Nina Nikolayevna, to whom the famous "Scarlet sails" have been dedicated.

That woman's destiny was tragic. At the time of the occupation Nina Nikolayevna was left with her ill mother without livelihood. Saving herself from starvation, she had to start working at the printing-house attached to the town council. In 1944 her mother died, and N. Grin went to Odessa to her friends. But directly at the pier she was arrested and together with others sent to Germany for forced labour.

"She who runs over the waves" on the A.Grin's grave. Sculptor T.Gagarina

After her return home, in October, 1945, she was arrested again, the main charge being her work for the Germans.

Nina Grin spent ten years at Soviet camps. After her release she unsuccessfully petitioned for her rehabilitation, took care of the Grin's small house (which has miraculously lasted out owing to the fact that it had been bought in the writer's name) and of his creative heritage, living on a miserable pension. When Nina Nikolayevna has died the authorities did not permit to bury her at the Old Crimea's old cemetery beside her husband.

In a year the great romantic's talent admirers re-buried beside his grave the remains of Assol loved dearly by him.

The ethnographic museum of Crimean Tatars

29 Kalinina St.
tel. 22-196

The museum is a usual Tatar house with an exposition of articles of national way of life and decorative-applied arts. Here they have collected pots and pans, carpets, and also pictures of an Old Crimea artist, Nuri Yakubov.

In the courtyard of the museum the cafe "Muskus" ("Musk") where the Tatar cuisine dishes are made is situated. Tourists drop in the cafe with pleasure in order to fix the impression from being plunged in the household environment of the original Crimean nation.

THE HISTORIC-ARCHITECTURAL MONUMENTS

All the tourists visiting Old Crimea see the Uzbek's mosque and madrasah built in 1314. The Golden Horde khan, Sultan Mukhammed Uzbek during the first year of his rule introduced Islam as a state religion which contributed to the Horde's strengthening.

The restoration work is carried out at the mosque building at 5 Pobedy St. In the courtyard of the Moslem temple there are picturesque ruins of a madrasah - an ecclesiastical school.

The Uzbek's mosque is not the oldest in the town. At 39 Krasnoarmeiskaya St. one can see the Beibars's mosque constructed in the XIII century.

The second sultan of Egypt from the Mamelukes' dynasty has become a legend. It is supposed that the Crimea was his birthplace. The small polovtsian

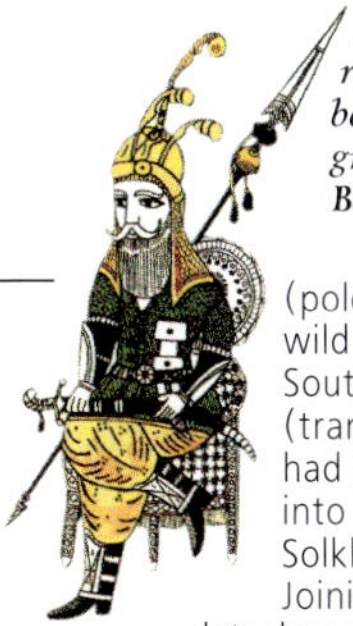

A former warrior-slave had become the great sultan Beibars

(polovtsians - a wild tribe at the South of Russia (translator's note) had been sold into slavery at the Solkhat market. Joining the detachment of Mamelukes ("slaves" in Arabic), he managed to rise from the ranks owing to his bravery and intellect. In 1250 the Mamelukes overthrew the dynasty of Ayubids ruling in Egypt. Having become the sultan, Beibars threw back from the state borders the crusaders and the Mongols. Not forgetting his native places, he allotted 2,000 dinars for building a mosque in Solkhat. The constructed building was notable for the splendour of its decoration. Of course, nothing remained of its former grandeur, except for its demolished walls. The rest has to be completed by your imagination.

The ruins of a caravanserai, musk and lead mosques have also lasted out in the small town. Here, by the maintain of Agarmysh, now broken by quarries, the I. Aivazovsky estate was from which a water-main has been laid to Feodosiya.

The name of the French adventuress, Zhanna d'Lamott-Gashe-Valua who had become the prototype of the famous heroine of A. Dyuma's novels (who was involved in stealing royal valuables) is bound up with Old Crimea. Having escaped from Bastilia, Zhanna had settled for a time at the Russian emperor's court, but soon she was recommended to choose an out-of-the-way place as the place of her residence. The disgraced countess had settled in Gurzuf, then she moved to Old Crimea where, according to a legend, she died. Before her death she had burnt down her papers which, by the way, representatives of Europe's ruling Houses were greatly interested in. Where the grave of the adventuress, on whose shoulder they had supposedly discovered a royal lily before her funeral, no one knows. M. Voloshin taking a walk from Koktebel to Old Crimea along the old pre-Revolutionary road has supposedly seen the gravestone, but there is no more information about it.

Zhanna d'Lamott-Gashe-Valua

We recommend the walking-lovers to repeat the way of Voloshin, Paustovsky, Drunina, and Kapler. The old road is exceptionally picturesque from it a view on fascinating landscapes opens.

A medieval Armenian cloister Surb-Khach ("Holy Cross") founded in 1338 is situated in the vicinity of the town. At its territory there are holy springs.

Surb-Khach - a specimen of the medieval Armenian architecture

Addresses and telephones:

Hotel "Karagol"
102 Lenina St. *tel. 36-335*

Tourist Centre "Primorye"
124 Lenina St. *tel. 36-275*

Boarding house "Goluboi zaliv" ("Blue bay")
120 Lenina St. *tel. 36-331*

Writers' House of creative work
110 Lenina St. *tel. 36-406*

In a town with such a reach history and a wonderful climate everyone will be able to spend his spare time to his taste. You like to dream taking a walk in shady lanes, don't you? You give preference to walking tours along cool museum halls, don't you? You don't like any entertainment, except for the beach ones, do you? You crave for driving the balls on the green cloth, don't you? In short, any whim for your money and even without it. From Feodosiya to Koktebel a bus and a minibus go, therefore you can perform your country trip independently. Plan to spend about 4 hours for the excursion - that will be enough for seeing, unhurriedly, the settlement itself and its sights, for ascending to M. Voloshin's grave, and for roaming about the famous pebbly beaches along the bay looking for Karadag semi-precious stones.

WHERE TO STOP

Many tourists choose this part of the Crimea as the place of their summer rest. The inhabitants will willingly let their dwellings, true, the prices here are fairly high - what to do, a popular health resort! In Koktebel the peninsula's largest tourist centre, "Primorye" ("Seaside") is situated. True, for an "unorganized" tourist to get there represents a problem, agreements on residence are concluded, in the first place, with groups, and if something remains... As a rule, there remain rooms without conveniences: only a wash-stand with cold water, the rest is, as the saying goes, on that storey. Such a room will cost you about UAH 50, with three meals a day.

Nevertheless, the tourist complex is situated in a beautiful place, has sports grounds and its own beach, which gives advantages over the private lodging. There are no municipal hotels in Koktebel. A private hotel "Karagol" is situated beside the Writers' House of creative work, in the park zone. During the high season to rent a double room de luxe with nourishment will cost you fairly much - at least UAH 500 a day. A usual double room costs about UAH 340. The cost includes the transfer from Feodosiya.

In the settlement there are several boarding houses and rest bases.

WHERE TO EAT

Cafes and small restaurants make uninterrupted lines along the embankment (to get there is easier of all from the Desantnikov street). One can choose an establishment to his taste and depending on how much he can afford. The chaikhana ((Uzber tee-house (translator's note)) "Aziz-Sevilya" where they serve viands of Uzbek cuisine attracts one's attention. A helping of quite good pilaff costs about UAH 5. The trestle-beds on which you have to sit crossing your legs and the drawings on the walls with views of Middle Asia towns shape an eastern colour of the interior.

We advise the lovers of sea gifts to visit the cafe "Osminog" ("Octopus"). The dishes of sea products - the special "Osminog", fish special dishes, the trout "Andreyevskaya" - will force you to get rid of earthly troubles and to plunge into the wonderful world of delicate culinary. True, the prices "sting". As, by the way, at any fish restaurant.

Also here, at the embankment, not far from the Poet's House, the famous cafe "Bybny" is situated which the Voloshin's guests under the leadership of their host liked to drop in.

Coffee-house-club

When the Greek Sinopli had opened his coffee-house at the sea shore, the Voloshin's house lodgers arranged here something like a club. The walls of the cafe were covered with primitive verses and caricatured drawings. In one of them A. Tolstoi had been depicted, the inscription told: "The passer-by, stop! I am Aleksei Tolstoi!". Under the picture of a pleasant young person in a tunic the inscription warned that "the Koktebel temptations are numerous and various!". The men of letters and artists had a jolly time scandalizing the respectable public.

Photo of the beginning of the XX century

The entertainment at the beach in Koktebel are not notable for special eccentricity - a hillock, going for a drive on a "banana" and outboard-motor boats. But may be the flights above the sea...

In the chaikhana "Aziz-Sevilya" hey will serve pilaff and a drinking bowl of green tea for you

The great mystifier

In the Voloshin's house practical jokes and mystification often took place. Once, in order to intrigue a Moscow publisher Maksimilian advised a poetess Ye. Dmitriyeva to sign her works by an exotic pen-name of Cherubina d'Gabriak, giving herself out

M. Voloshin

to be a women passionate, ecstatic, and unpredictable. And what was the result?! The practical joke has turned out very well: soon not only the publisher-lady-killer, but a half Moscow Bohemia craved to meet her. When the lies have been discovered, a scandal broke out. But N. Gumilyov who was then in love with Dmitriyeva suffered most of all. A challenge to a duel followed...

WHAT IS WORTH TO VISIT IN KOKTEBEL

The M. Voloshin's house-museum

The embankment
tel. 24-437
10.00-18.00

Having settled at these places, Maksimilian Aleksandrovich Voloshin decided to build a house at the sea shore by his own project. In 1903 the first version of the house was ready. But the owner was not very pleased with the construction. In 9 years Voloshin added a workshop, changed a little the internal lay-out, and the house has received that appearance which it has now. Maksim Gorky and Aleksei Tolstoi, Andrei Bely and Mikhail Bulgakov, Kornei Chukovsky and Osip Mandelshtam, Tsvetayeva sisters and Sofia Parnok, Nikolai Gumilyov and Vsevolod Rozhdestvensky were under its hospitable roof... The list can be prolonged and prolonged. Often from Feodosiya his intimate friend, Konstantin Bogayevsky has come to the writer, sometimes Aleksandr Grin came. Maksimilian Aleksandrovich also was an excellent walker, he liked long walks.

"Both Greece and Genoa have passed...". *Voloshin often sent his works to his acquaintances in the form of postcards*

Guests stayed with Voloshin free of charge. Here is an extract from the house owner's private letter with an invitation to come for the summer: "There are no servants. One has to bring water by oneself. This is not a resort at all. A free friendly cohabitation where everyone who is wanted becomes a full member. And the following is required: a joyful perception of life, love for people, and introduction of one's share of intellectual life". After the revolution which was welcomed by Voloshin, owing to A. Lunacharsky's intercession, they succeeded to preserve the poet's house. In March, 1924 a charter of immunity of

In the tsarevna's (a daughter of a tsar (king) (translator's note) Taiakh cabin (such was the name of a part of the workshop) literary readings often took place. Voloshin's mother resembled that enigmatic Egyptian whose bust Maks has brought from Berlin

some sort was issued: "Maksimilian Voloshin, with a full approval of the National Commissariat of Education of RSFSR, organized in Koktebel in the house which belongs to him a free of charge house of rest for writers, artists, scientists...". In such a way the Poet's House has arisen which gave Maks the possibility to remain at that complex time not only the owner of the house, but a man of letters in general. Before this, at the time of a constant replacement of powers, Voloshin proved to be a real humanitarian - he hid in his house the poet Mandelshtam, rescuing him in this way from an inevitable death because of the white terror, and an officer of the voluntary army - from the red one.

Voloshin died in 1932. His widow has succeeded to preserve the atmosphere of the house also after his death - men of letters and artists came as before "to Voloshin" for a long time after his death. By the way, Maria Stepanovna rescued the Voloshin's heritage during the years of occupation. She has refused to leave the house offering to blow it up together with her. Fortunately, the Germans have not dared to do it.

Maksimilian Aleksandrovich was buried on the peak of one of the hills of the mountain range Kuchuk-Yenishar in accordance with his will. The tree growing by the grave of the Voloshin couple (Maria Stepanovna was buried also there in 1976) can be seen from the windows of the workshop. But who was additionally buried a little lower (by the peak of the hill there is a table telling that here the poetess Iya Mikhailova was buried), we have not succeeded to ascertain with the help of the house-museum workers. Mystification continues...

The state farm - plant "Koktebel"

Long since the Otuzskaya valley was famous for its vineyards. Here the raw materials for famous fine wines and cognacs are cultivated. The head enterprise on cognac production is in the settlement Shchebetovka (the former Otuzy). The best cognac is "Kutuzov" which is kept to mature in oak tuns during 25 years! The name is symbolic, as during one of the Paris exhibitions this unique product ranked first. The "Napoleon" was once more defeated by "Kutuzov". In Koktebel the biggest Madeira site is situated (the Madeira is kept to mature in tuns not in basements, but in the sun). Tourists can visit the plant's own shop "Koktebel" situated by the plant entrance check-point and to buy the products at first hand. It is no secret for anybody that the farther from the manufacturer the wine was bought the farther it is from the original by its quality...

The Koktebel cognacs are in a constant demand

In the centre of the settlement, at Lenina street, not far from the settlement's Soviet, there is one more plant's own shop. A wine-tasting hall is situated also here.

The glider sports centre

Koktebel became the centre of the glider sports in the thirties. It has been founded by K. Artseulov - the I. Aivazovsky's grandson, a pilot and an artist. Here, on the mountain Uzun-Syrt, to the north-east of Koktebel the training base of the "small aviation" adherents is now too.

The preparation for a flight. On the Klementyev's mountain (Uzun-Syrt) there gather together those who like to fly not only by gliders, but also by hang-gliders

The first Crimean glider

The flying apparatus was built in 1925 under the Aleksandr Sharapov's leadership. A former military pilot who graduated from the Gatchinskaya flying school worked as a driver-instructor of the Simferopol professional technical school. The glider made by his project has been named "Alim - the Crimean robber". The legend about Alim - the defender of the poor tells about a popular national hero, the last Tatar Dzhigit (a skilful horseman (translator's note) who had been exiled to Siberia.

In the first years of the XX century a Moscow physician-neuropathologist, T. Vyazemsky founded here at his own expense a scientific station which was the first in the world. It is at its base that they have created a natural preserve where, in addition to a prepared volcano, a rich animal and vegetable world has remained intact. Practically a half the Black Sea ichthyofauna representatives live in the sea section of the preserve... The mountain-mass is a real wonder of nature. One can get here only with an excursion because here a state preserve has been organized. Those who wish to walk along the ecological path gather into groups and carry out a walk with a guide. Excursions to Karadag are organized by all town excursion bureau. If you don't want to make use of their services, you have to get to the dolphinarium located at the territory of the former biology station in Kurortny. The village is situated 4 km from the settlement Shchebetovka on the sea side.

The groups are usually formed near the library, tickets are also sold there. The cost of the three-hour excursion is UAH 9. Take trouble about your equipment - a light jacket for protection against spring and autumn winds (in summer - a shirt with long sleeves), a wide-brimmed hat, comfortable shoes (better - running shoes). Take water with you - there is nowhere above you could get it from.

In the course of the excursion you will see the famous mountain range Karagach with its Royal Couple, Throne, and Suite which has become the visiting card of the range, you will hear about the Karadag semi-precious stones, secluded bays, and fantastic rocks, and above all, you will see this wild, majestic, bewitching beauty!

Waiting for the walk along the Karadag paths, one can roam about the luxuriant park, to see the performance of dolphins and fur-seals (a ticket costs UAH 15).

It is convenient to carry out a sea trip from Feodosiya or Koktebel along the sea-coast, to steam past the Golden Gate, to look in numerous bays and grottoes of the majestic Karadag.

The Karadag monster and the little bird of love

In ancient times there lived in the Black Mountain entrails a giant-cannibal. He kept in fear all the surrounding villages. In order to cajole the monster, the residents of the Otuzskaya valley sacrificed him bulls, sheep, and goats. But the giant wanted more and more: he ordered them to give him in autumn, in the month of marriages, one of the brides, otherwise the monster threatened to ruin everybody living all though the neighbourhood. Many years the monster jeered at the villagers, but here a daredevil turned up who decided to kill the man-eater. He went before his own marriage on Karadag and, making himself comfortable on a big stone, began to sing a beautiful song about a small bird of love, that is to be caught with one's eyes - and then love will enter directly to one's heart. He sang and thought about his bride - the beauty Elbis.

Suddenly the giant's thunderous voice was heard: "To-morrow they must bring a bride to me, I want to see the small bird of love too!"

"Well, - the youth answered. - You will see it to-morrow."

On the next day the boy and the girl came together. Having taken her stand on the peak of a high rock, Elbis called the cannibal: "I have come and brought you the small bird of love. Go out and look at it!" Out of the precipice the giant's head appeared, on its forehead there flashed his only eye which he had opened widely in order to have a good look at the magic bird. And having drawn the bow, the courageous girl instantly shot a poisoned arrow into this staring eye. Howling with pain, the blinded cannibal went headlong into a fathomless pit. From the peals of thunder of his howl the boulders began to fall from the rocks. They had buried by themselves the thrown down giant. The whole night the mountain was trembling and spitting with fire until it broke down into separate rocks and cliffs. Everything had died down at daybreak, Karadag had acquired those fantastic contours which we admire till now...

Kerch is an Eastern Outlying District of the Crimea

The Kerch antiquities, excavations and findings are of a particular interest, which are not only the subject of studies for scholars-archeologists, but they also attract the tourists visiting the city of Kerch...

G. Moskvich

The Kerch emblem

The tourists interested in the archeology and military history come to this city, which is 40 km widespread along the eastern edge of the Kerch peninsula. In his guidebook published in 1910, G. Moskvich noted in part, that the Chokrak lake and Bulkhanakskiye Hills located nearby, the mud of which is notable for its curative properties, turn Kerch into a resort.

The swimming season opens starting from the last decade of May till the first decade of October; the average air temperature in summer is +24°C, in winter -1°C.

This most ancient city of the Crimea was founded by the Milesian Greeks more than 26 centuries ago. The first trade station - Pantikapeum - initiated the Hellenic colonization of the peninsula.

Soon other settlements sprang up nearby, such as Nimfei, Mirmekiy, Tiritaka (at present, archeological digs are carried out there). Having created the union, the city states created a powerful Bosporus Empire. In the course of nine centuries the Pantikapeum was its capital.

A view of the city from the Mithridates Mountain

When the kingdom started to fall into decay, the Tsar Perisad V decided to become the vassal of Pont (a Greek state in Asia Minor), but he was killed by the insurgent Scythians. The Pontus ruler Mithridates VI Eupatore stifled a rebellion and annexed the Bosporus to his possessions. In some decades, Pantikapeum got into the bondage of Rome. The city changed several times both its masters and its names: it was called the Byzantium fortress Bosporus; the Khazars called it Karsha or Charsha (which meant "market" when translated from the Turkic); it was included into the Kievan Rus under the name Korchev. The following masters - the Genoeses - named it Cherkio...

Gradually, Kerch was losing its former eminence. A. Pushkin, who visited the city in 1820, was disappointed having seen a small settlement, where only heaps of stones reminded of its former glory.

Kerch started to recover from the ruins only a century later. A fishermen's settlement turned into a large industrial center.

During the Great Patriotic War the city was practically destroyed. In memory of those heroic battles numerous monuments have been erected.

In the post-war years, all the efforts were exerted to recover the national economy, at the same time, not so much attention was paid to the resort construction. We hope that in the course of time the resort and tourist branches of Kerch region will occupy the proper place in the life of the city.

History in a few lines

The 6th century B. C. *- the city of Pantikapeum emerges on the place of modern Kerch.*
The 4th century *- Pantikapeum is ruined by the Huns.*
The 6th century *- The Byzantium fortress Bosporus was erected.*
The 7th century *- The Khazars' rule was established.*
The 10th century *- Kerch is included into the Kievan Rus.*
The 13th century *- The start of the Tatar domination.*
1318 *- Cherkio becomes a Genoese colony.*
1475-1774 *- The city gets under the Turkish rule.*
1774 *- Kerch and Eni-Kale are included into the Russian Empire.*
The middle of the 19th century is noted for the rapid development of industry.
1855 *- The city is ruined by the English.*
1920 *- The Soviet power was established.*
1939 *- The construction of the Kerch Iron-Ore Industrial Complex.*
November 1941 - April 1944 *- The period when Kerch was occupied by the Hitler forces.*
1973 *- Kerch was awarded the title of the Hero City.*
2002 *- Close to 170,000 people live in the city.*

It is possible to arrive to Kerch by sea, air, and railway.

A queue to the ticket office near the ferry berth

Addresses and telephones:

City Militia Department Tel.: 20-441

Traffic Police Duty-Officer Tel.: 21-238

Ambulance Station Tel.: 20-203

Drugstore (directory inquiries) Tel.: 0-59

Life-Boat Station Tel.: 24-725

City Information Tel.: 21-132

Custom House
9 Furmanova Street Tel.: 20-575

The Kerch Post Office

Post Office, Public Telephone Call-Boxes
1 Kirova Street Tel.: 20-500

Trunk-Line *23 Lenina Street*

Office for Advance Sale of Tickets
9 Gaidar Street Tel.: 21-126

"Pryvatbank"
9-a Marat Street Tel.: 21-000

Taxi Tel. 20-314

Railway Station

Pryvokzalna Square
Tel.: 20-029

The railway station is located on the square at the approach to the city. From this railway station trains are departing to Kiev, Moscow, Dneipropetrovsk, Dzhankoy, Kherson, and Simferopol. Provided you don't like to be jolted in the bus, you take the train in the evening and early in the morning you arrive to the capital of the Crimean Autonomous Republic.

Kerch Airport

6 Vokzalnoye Highway
Tel.: 23-044

The airport is located practically at the city approach. Unfortunately, it serves only the local lines.

Marine Passenger Terminal

12 Kirov Street,
Tel.: 19-339

One of the largest Crimean ports is located in Kerch, which includes the passenger, fishing, and cargo ports.

Ferry Port-Crimea

Tel.: 49-509

As is well known, Kerch is the port of two seas. The ferry is arranged between the ports "Crimea" and "Caucasus". The ferry will bring you and your car to the territory of Russia, hence you should pass the frontier and customs examinations. The ferry goes every 1.5 hours.

Bus-Station

30 Yeremenko Street
Tel.: 53-572, 57-589

The buses from Kerch arrive to the central bus station of Simferopol, as well as to the bus station of the "Zavodskoye" airport. From the comfortable Kerch bus station the bus routes go to Sevastopol, Yalta, and other cities of the Crimea. From this bus station the suburban traffic and practically all city routes have been arranged.

In the waiting room of the bus station

The Urban Transport

The buses, inter-city taxies, and taxies connect the city centre with its outskirts - the settlements of Arshintsevo, Bondarenkovo, Voikovo, Adzhimushkai, Sipyakhino, as well as with the "Crimea" port.

The Kerch infrastructure is not well developed in the resort city, but the tourists should not be afraid, they will be able to find a dwelling and a cozy restaurant, and a place where they will be able to have a rest and entertainment.

DWELLING

The "Kerch" hotel, which is the most respectable hotel in the city, is located in the centre of the city near the marine passenger terminal. A double room with conveniences is about 70 hryvnias per 24 hours, and more. There is a restaurant with the European cuisine in the hotel.

The "Lazurny" preventorium hotel is suitable for those going to stay in Kerch for a couple of days. Their neighbors - noisy young sportsmen, who arrived with the aim to participate in the competitions, would prevent you from staying in the hotel for a longer period of time. Prices for accommodation are moderate: a double room with all modern conveniences is 50 hryvnias. The car parking is located not far from the hotel; the price is two hryvnias per 24 hours. The newcomers can also be accommodated in the "Parus" (Sail) and "Moriak" (Seaman) hotels.

Cafe in the central boulevard

FOOD

Along the Lenin and Karl Marx Streets many inexpensive bars, cafes, and restaurants are located. In summer, the tables are set on the open-air terraces, where it is pleasant to sit in the evening, in particular, since these streets are pedestrian ones. Those preferring the vegetarian food can visit two food markets.

ENTERTAINMENT

The theatre-lovers can visit a wonderful city theatre. In the Park of Recreation and Entertainment the open-air theatre is functioning, and the youth center "Iskra" (Spark) is open for teenagers. The best discotheques are held in the "Tornado" club. The "Joker" casino is waiting for the clients who like the gaming.

Drama Theatre

BEACHES

There are not so many beaches within the precincts of the city: one is in the vicinity of the site of the "Mirmeky" ancient settlement excavations, another one is located along the Kamyshburunskaya Spit. The local citizens prefer the Azov coast and the beaches of the Bulkhanakskaya Bay. The beaches of the holiday homes and recreation departments located in the vicinity of the Eltihen settlement are also very popular with the holidaymakers.

Addresses and telephones:

CAFES:

"Assol"
47 Lenin Street Tel.: **21-020**
"Pogrebok" (Wineshop)
44 Lenin Street Tel.: **20-376**
"Griphon" Tel.: **22-078**
35 Teatralnaya Street

HOTELS:

"Kerch"
11 Kirov Street Tel.: **21-155**
"Lazurny" (Ske-Blue)
9-a Yeremenko Street
"Parus" (Sail)
9 Marat Street Tel.: **21-493**
"Moriak" (Seaman)
3 Gagarin Street Tel.: **57-257**

CLUBS AND CINEMA THEATRES:

"Druzhba" (Friendship) Tel.: **34-200**
39 Ordzhonikidze Street
"Ukraine" Tel.: **20-569**
11 Sovietskaya Street
"Tornado" Tel.: **33-570**
88 Ordzhonikidze Street
"Iskra" (Spark)
30 Voikov Street Tel.: **42-905**

PARKS

In the Park of Recreation and Entertainment there are boating station and an open-air theatre. In the public garden located in the Lenin Square there are side-shows for children; the holidaymakers will also like the shady Komsomolsky Park.

The boulevard is the most favorite place for walking

It is unusual for a city, which is some years younger than the eternal city of Rome, to have no museums. Of course, they are not so numerous than in the notable city of the same age...

The Historical and Archeological Museum

7 Sverdlov Street
Tel.: 20-475
from 9.00 a.m. till 5.00 p.m.

The museum founded in 1826, has the richest collection of the ceramics of the antique city, from the marble statues, which formerly decorated the houses and squares of the majestic city and objects of the Scythian culture, to the exhibits illustrating the recent times. Unfortunately, the funds of the museum are not so large: during the Crimean War of 1853-1856, the city and its museums were actually plundered by the English.

The exhibit of the Archeological Museum

In the Soviet period, the most valuable archeological findings of the Kerch peninsula have been sent to the collection of the State Hermitage (St. Petersburg). The museum belongs to the Crimean Historical and Cultural Preserve, which has the branch museums, such as the Adzhimushkaisky Quarry Museum, and the Eltihent Landing Operation Museum.

The picture gallery

The Picture Gallery

36 Teatralnaya Street
Tel.: 22-086 from 10.00 a.m. till 6.00 p.m.

In this gallery, a permanent exhibition is organized of the works by the artist N. But, T.Shevchenko Prize laureate, who dedicated the decades of his creative activities to the theme of the heroic defense of the city of Kerch from the German Nazi invaders, by partisans who had found refuge in the Adzhimushkaisky catacombs.

Here also an exposition of the "Masterpieces of the Antique Art" is displayed.

The Ethnographical Museum

7 Buvin Street
Tel.: 53-093
from 10.00 a.m. till 5.00 p.m., except for Monday and Tuesday

The museum exposition acquaints the visitors with culture of the peoples living in the most ancient city on the peninsula.

The Museum of Oceanography and Fish Industry

2 Sverdlov Street
Tel.: 21-065
from 10.00 a.m. till 5.00 p.m., except for Monday

A visit to this museum will bring much pleasure to children; here they will see the representatives of ichthyofauna of the seas and oceans, including the Black Sea fauna.

John's the Baptist Church

2 Dimitrov Lane
Tel.: 22-293

The archeologists did not arrive at the common conclusion concerning the time when this most ancient Kerch historical monument of the Christian age came into being. They suggest that the church was built between the 8th and 10th centuries. The building is unique due to the combination of different styles - basilica Byzantine style and the Russian cross-domed style. In honor of this cathedral, preserved since the times of the Tmutarakan Principality golden age, one of the city's names was St. John's Port.

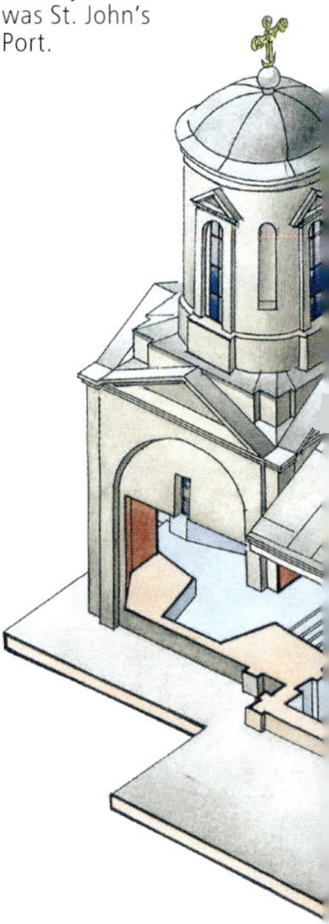

The bell tower of John's the Baptist Church

The dome of the cathedral is located on the high drum; its walls are noted for the original masonry consisting of alternate rows of the white stone and red bricks.

At the beginning of the 19th century, the church was expanded at the expense of the outhouse on the western part due to the fact that the interior space of the church was too small and could not include all wishing to be present at the divine service.

Inside the ancient church, a heavy vault is supported by four well-proportioned grey columns, topped with refined capitals of the Corinthian order. During the times of the Soviet power (before the church was closed), there were ancient icons of the Savior, Mother of God and John the Baptist, as well as items of the church plate. The wooden cup of the 6th century with hardly distinguishable representation of holy faces was particularly valuable. In the church library, ancient manuscripts of the "Gospel" (11th century) and the "Books of the Apostles" (12th century) have been preserved

At present, the John's the Baptist Church has been handed over to the believers and divine services are held there.

John's the Baptist Church

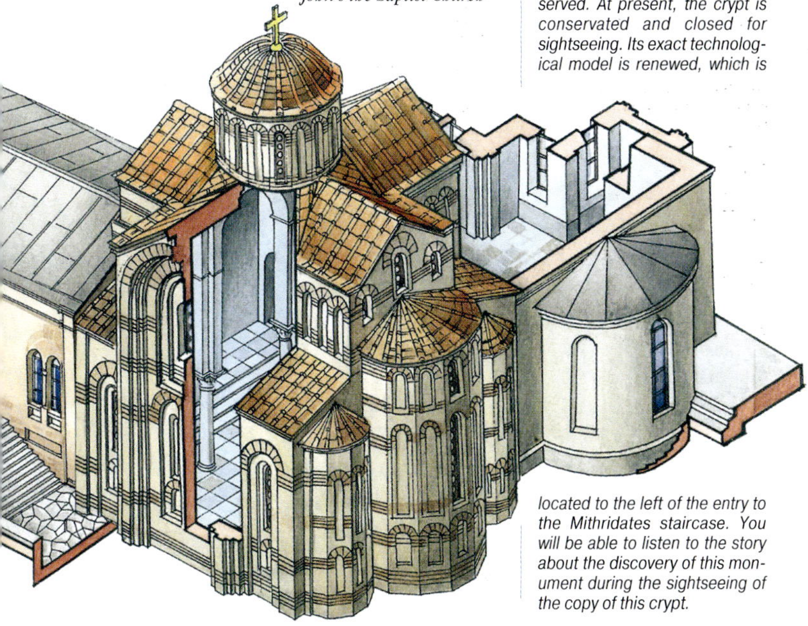

The Demetra's Crypt

In the middle of the 19th century, the archeologists discovered the most interesting monument of the antique funeral architecture in the territory of the city in the private possessions of the mistress Zaitseva. It was called the Demetra's Crypt.

The sarcophagus with the mortal remains of the noble Bosporus citizen was in the burial chamber, painted with wonderful frescos depicting the kidnapping of Persephona, daughter of the goddess of fertility Demetra byAides, God of the Underworld. Demetra is depicted on one of the frescos with her eyes full of grief and despair, and her lips impact. The mother's sorrow, which cannot be repressed by anything in the world, is revealed to the viewers. The artistic power of the image strikes to the innermost of one's heart...

Alas, the burial place was robbed by the landowners, only the paintings and small items of the funeral have been preserved. At present, the crypt is conservated and closed for sightseeing. Its exact technological model is renewed, which is located to the left of the entry to the Mithridates staircase. You will be able to listen to the story about the discovery of this monument during the sightseeing of the copy of this crypt.

Tsar Mithridates

The militant ruler of Pont waged war with Rome during all his life. The last years of his reign he had to flee to Pantikapeum. The Mithridate's armchairs were on the mountain; from that place the Tsar admired the outskirts. Here, according to the legend, he died having come to know that he had been betrayed by his native son Farnak, who organized a rebellion against his father. Mithridate attempted to take poison, but it had no effect on him, since the Pont's lord was getting accustomed to poison for a long time. Then Mithridate ordered the chief body-guard to kill him with the sword. It was not for a long time that Farnak, the successor to the throne, reigned. His troops were defeated by Julius Caesar, who had informed the Senate about his victory in the following way: "Came, saw and conquered"... Dinamia, the Mithridate's granddaughter, and daughter of Farnak, became the only woman ruler of the state in the history of the Crimea.

Mithridate VI Eupatore

The Kerch land is rich in historical monuments. Today it is possible to see only a small part of unique exhibits preserved after the plundering raids of the adventurers of every stripe...

THE ANTIQUE CITIES

The excavations are held throughout the territory of Kerch. The scientists-archeologists and students of the historical higher educational establishments sift the earth looking for the pieces of antiquities.

The ancient Pantikapeum on the slopes of the Mithridate Mountain is a historical center of the modern city. Once there was the acropolis with its vast squares and streets, white-stone palaces and cathedrals decorated with statues of gods. Only people having rich imagination can see the above pictures on the place of scattered stones. Thanks to the painstaking labor of archeologists, the remains of walls and foundations became visible from under the earth; many of the articles found there are the true works of art.

It is possible to get to the excavations from the St. Athanasius Church (19th century) located in 1 Pantikapeyska Street.

The research is carried out on the place of the Mirmekiy site of ancient settlement (6th century B. C. - 3rd century A. D.). The beach is located next to it. A wonderful view of the Kerch Bay with stone blocks in the strait is open from this beach. The buses Nos. 1, 18, 19 and 32 ("Kazakova" bus stop) go from the center of Kerch. It is possible to go to the excavations along the Moskovskaya Street.

The remains of the site of ancient hte settlement Porfmiy ("Port") are located on the hill mounting over the Krasnaya Street. The Meotiiskoye Highway leads to these excavations (it is necessary to go to the crossing "Port-Crimea"). On the hill in front of the crossing students-archeologists are working, who will tell about the antique settlement on the shore of the Bosporus Kimeriysky (the ancient name of the Kerch Strait is translated as the "Ox Crossing").

Other sites of ancient settlements, such as Nimfey, Tiritaka, Ilurat and others, are interesting only for experts.

BURIAL MOUNDS

The burial mounds are the monuments of the antique funeral culture. The most significant of them is the Tsars Burial Mound (4th century B. C.), which has been preserved till nowadays. The burial-vault of one of the Spartokid dynasty members, discovered in 1837, was built on the hill. The 17 meters height tomb consists of the burial chamber and a 36-meter corridor (dromos), erected from the finished stone blocks. The buriall chamber resembles a pyramid; the corridor is arranged in such a way that it seems to be located so close when looking inside the burial place,

The remains of Pantikapeum. The columns of pritanei - a public palace

The Tsar's Burial Mound

and the way back is much longer. The burial mound is located in the Adzhimushkai settlement, bus No. 4, departing from the bus station, will bring you there. The museum is open each day from 9.00 a.m. till 5.00 p.m., tel.: 54-713, the entrance fee is three hryvnias.

The Melek-Chesmen Burial Mound is next to the bus station. The corridor leads to the burial chamber. Unfortunately, the robbers visited this burial mound before the archeologists had discovered it. This burial mound was discovered in 1858, the items, which had remained, were brought to the Hermitage, and only the duplicates were left in this burial mound as exhibits of this small museum. The entrance fee is one hyrvnia.

In 1830, near Kerch the burial mound of a Scythian ruler was found (4th century B. C.); this burial mound is called Kul-Oba. The crypt was built according to the Greek pattern, but the funeral rite was Scythian, as scientists proved it. The ruler was buried in the wooden crypt, his wife or concubine was buried with him. In this burial place the items made of gold were found, as well as a vase made of electra (the alloy of gold and silver). The burial vault was not robbed by the treasure finders. All the valuables were sent to the Emperor's Hermitage.

The history of the Gold Burial Mound, which was simply blown up in the 20-ies of the 19th century, can be an example of vandalism. The excavations held later proved that it had been robbed still in the ancient times. Gradually, the stone blocks were taken away as stones for building. It is suggested that this burial mound was made in the Kimeriysky period and even in the earlier times... Yuz-Oba or one hundred of burial grounds are located in the vicinity of the TV center. The scientists hope that not all hills have been visited by the "amateur archeologists".

The Large Mithridates Staircase

STAIRCASES

The Large Mithridates Staircase is one of the main city point of interest. 432 steps lead from the Lenin Square to the peak of the Miithridates Mountain. (91.4 м). The staircase was built in the 19th century by the design of the Italian architect A. Digbi. The sight platforms were decorated with stone gryphons and vases. The staircase became a decoration for the city of Kerch. On the peak of the Mountain the Museum of the Antiquity was located, which was a copy of the Theseos Temple. But during a landing of the English troops and during the bombardment of the city from the ships, the museum and the staircase had been destroyed.

The staircase was reconstructed only 130 years later. They succeeded to find the remains of stone sculptures in the earth and the Kerch sculptor R. Serdyuk made their copies. At present, the upper circle of the reconstructed staircase is decorated with winged stone lions.

In addition to the Large Staircase, there is the smaller staircase in the city called Konstantynovskaya (1868), it leads to the picturesque ancient part of the city.

YENI-KALE

The Turkish fortress was built in 1703. The Turks had never used it as a fortification work - not a single shoot was made from this place. The task of this fortification was to control the narrowest part of the Kerch Strait.

In 1774, the stronghold came into possession of the Russian garrison. The fortress is not a museum, and it is possible to come there any time you like and see the remains that had not been ruined by the time. You can go to the ruins by bus No. 32.

Yeni-Kale

An Example of Staunchness and Heroism

Everyone who walks along the dark labyrinths of the Adzhimushkai quarries has the same thought: how could they stay in these stone graves during one hundred and seventy days - without sun light, food, and water and having a scanty ammunition supply - they not only lived there, but repulsed constant attempts of the enemy to suppress the resistance?! It seems that these people were made of stone... The Hitlerites were at a loss: where could the partisans hide

The motor boat of the Eltigentsky paratroopers

on this almost plain and woodless area? They did not know about the entry to the underground labyrinths of the quarries. But the traitor betrayed the underground activists. And then the entries to the labyrinths had been blocked and the poison gas was compressed into the galleries. Thousands of people died during the gas attacks, but Adzhimushkai did not surrender... When at the end of the October of 1942, the Nazis attempted to take Adzhimushkai by storm, it turned out that during the last days the stronghold had been defended by a handful of fighters...

The monument to the Adzhimushkai heroes at the entrance to the catacombs

Adzhimushkai Quarry Settlement of Adzhimushkai

36 Malchenko Street
Tel.: 54-001
from 10.00 a.m. till 5.00 p.m., except for Monday

The first liberation of Kerch from the Hitler troops took place in December of 1941 in one and a half months after a start of the German invasion. A half year later, Kerch was captured again. Part of the Red Army soldiers and citizens found refuge in the underground quarry and waged the partisan war. Many of them died in the catacombs.

You will be able to know in details about those heroic days after visiting the underground museum. It is possible to come there by bus No. 4. You should take into consideration the fact that it is rather cold in the catacombs, so you will need warm clothes provided you go there.

The Museum of the Eltigen Landing Operation History

The settlement of Geroyevskoye

The bridgehead captured by the Soviet paratroopers on November 1, 1943, during the Kerch-Feodosiya operation near the fisherman's settlement Eltigen went down in history of the Great Patriotic War under the name "Fiery Land".

The tiny sector of the shore was fully exposed to fire. In the course of almost forty days the paratroopers, who actually buried themselves in the earth, held their positions there due to their endurance, courage or miracle. Their task was to draw away considerable enemy forces. Sometimes, they had to repulse over ten enemy attacks during a day! The paratroopers were supported by the fire

Ttraditionally, the newly married come to the obelisk on the peak of the Mithridate Mountain

from the cutters, by the heavy artillery from the opposite shore of the strait, and by night bombardments of the enemy positions carried out by the fighter pilots of the 46th women air regiment. On December 7, 1943, the paratroopers, having broken through the enemy circle, reached the city of Kerch and went to the Mithridate Mountain. In the course of four days they combatted in the rear of the enemy, then the fearless soldiers who remained alive had been evacuated by the cutters. For forty days battle 61 persons were awarded the highest military awards - the Star of the Hero of the Soviet Union.

On the place of the landing operation, a museum was opened in May of 1985. The memorial complex resembling the sail was erected by the design of the architect A. Shakhov and sculptors S. Kovner and L. Tazba. It includes a hospital, operating room, the remains of the war trenches and a ditch, a common grave of the paratroopers, as well as the motor boat, lifted from the ground.

On the peak of the Mithridate Mountain the Obelisk of Glory has been established at which the Eternal Fire burns in order to keep the memory about the immortal feat of arms of the Hero-City defenders.

Bakhchisarai - the capital of the Crimean Khanate

It seemed that we roved to a Turkish or Persian city, with the only difference that we could quietly view everything, not afraid of humiliation displayed to Christians throughout the Orient...

Marquis de Segur

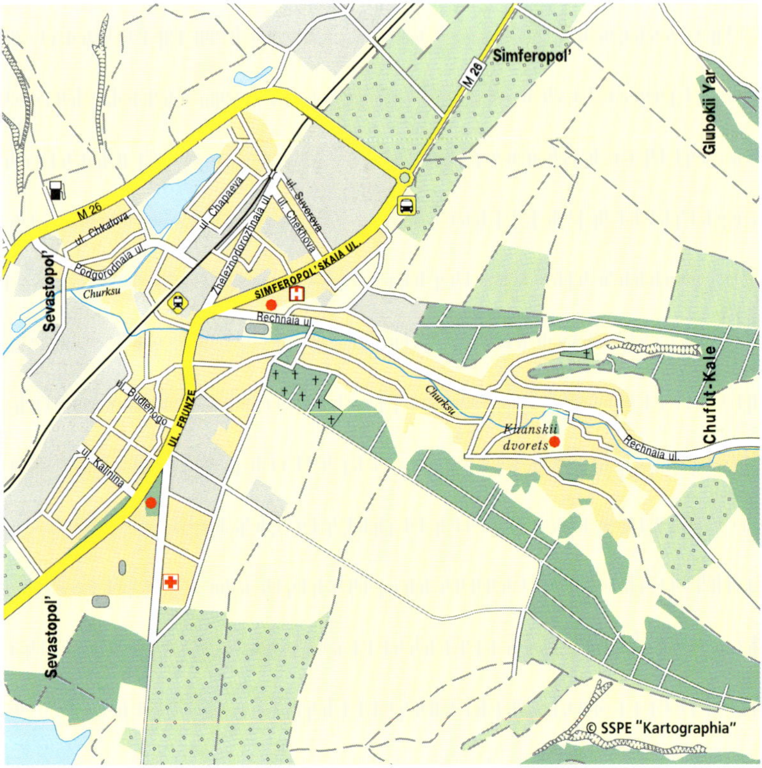

History in a few lines

The 2nd half of the 14th century - Eski-Yurt founded by nomad Tatars.

***1363** - battle of Syni Vody. Prince Vitovt of Lithuania defeats the army of the Tatar Khan, sovereign of the fortress of Qirq Yer. Later,*

Prince Vitovt of Lithuania

Bakhchisarai has been standing for half a millennium how. It lies in the picturesque valley of the river Churuk-Su pinched between rocks of fantastic beauty.

The area around Bakhchisarai is cut with narrow fertile valleys lying among steep spurs of the Inner and Outer ridges of the Crimean Mountains. The mixture of marine and steppe air masses in the ravine contributed to the formation of a pretty healthy climate. Permanent circulation of the air brings freshness, the shady banks of the river are cool in the heat of the summer. The average temperature in July (the hottest summer month) is +21.7°C, in February +0.8°C.

The Bakhchisarai valley houses beautiful orchards and vineyards. The plateaux are covered with forest. One should come here in spring, when everything around blossoms and smells sweet: around Bakhchisarai, they grow lavender, salvia, and roses - raw materials for the manufacture of the best volatile oils in the Crimea. By the way, the produce of the local "aroma factory" has attracted even the French perfumers - world-famous experts and connoisseurs of fine flavours. Your vacation in Bakhchisarai will be equally nice in the Indian Summer, when time comes to gather grapes.

Lithuanian princes helped Hadji Girai to take the Crimean throne.

1478 - *Hadji Girai I moves his residence to the Qirq Yer fortress.*

Beginning of the 16th century - *construction of the Ashlama Khan's palace.*

1532 - *construction of the Bakhchisarai palace is completed under the rule of Sahib Girai.*

The 17th - 18th centuries - *Bakhchisarai is the trade and industrial centre of the south-western Crimea.*

1736 - *during a campaign of the Russian army led by Minikh the city was plundered, the Palace burnt down.*

1787 - *Empress Catherine II visits Bakhchisarai.*

1820 - *A. Pushkin comes to the city.*

1887 - *outstanding Crimean Tatar enlightener I.Gasprinsky, a local native, returns to Bakhchisarai.*

1932 - *commissioning of the volatile oil factory.*

1974 - *commencement of production of wine in Bakhchisarai.*

2002 - *the city population makes some 28,000.*

The city lies rather far from the sea - 15-20 km, but if you wish to take a sea bath, a mini-van will promptly take you to the coastal settlements of Kacha, Uglovoye, or Peschanoye with their comfortable beaches.

Prior to the foundation of Bakhchisarai the capital of the Crimean Khanate several times changed it place. First, Khan Hadji Girai I, who announced the independence of the Crimean Khanate, moved his residence to Qirq Yer (later known as Chufut-Kale), then - to Salachik, where the Ashlama summer palace was built. At the beginning of the 16th century, the Khan's Palace was built - the main sight of today's Bakhchisarai. It served as the residence of the Girais who ruled the Crimea from 1443 till 1783. With time, a city grew around the palace. Its dwellers were engaged in trade, tanning, and armoury. Handworkers were united into 32 trades. Tradesmen settled in separate quarters, each with a separate mosque. The remains of some of them may be seen even now.

Trade in humans was an important item of revenues. "Merchandise" was seized in raids on Ukrainian, Lithuanian, Russian lands. Noble captives for whom a huge ransom could be obtained were led to the Khan.

After the demise of the throne by the last Khan Shahin Girai and annexation of the Crimea by Russia, Bakhchisarai gradually fell into decay.

Now, this is the centre of a prosperous agricultural area and a popular tourist sight.

Bakhchisarai sphinxes

Addresses and telephones:

City police department
3 Kooperativnaya St. tel. 42-616

Duty-officer of the traffic police tel. 26-957

Ambulance tel. 41-798

Drugstore (central)
15 Sovetskaya St. tel. 43-477

Mine-rescue service
31 Karla Marksa St. tel. 47-722

Central Post Office
7 Sovetskaya St. tel. 41-780

Long distance phone
Station Square tel. 42-678

Railway booking office tel. 25-086

Airline booking office
17/45 Tankistov St. tel. 32-585

Excursion office
106 Lenina St. tel. 39-826

Privatbank
92 Frunze St. tel. 44-862

Taxi tel. 43-879

Bakhchisarai is suitably located on the road from Simferopol to Sevastopol, so, one can quickly and easily get there.

Railway station
Station Square
Tel. 42-637

The Bakhchisarai railway station is situated in the centre of the city. Suburban trains going from Simferopol to Sevastopol and back stop there (see timetable on p. #). The trip from Simferopol takes 50 minutes, from Sevastopol - 1 hour 25 minutes.

Few passenger trains stop at Bakhchisarai, so, tourists prefer to come to Simferopol first and then to take a suburban train or a bus.

Bus station
Station Square
Tel. 42-825

Buses depart for Bakhchisarai from "Zapadnaya" ("Western") bus station in Simferopol. Buses from Simferopol to Sevastopol also go via Bakhchisarai. They depart from "Tsentralny" ("Central") bus station in the Crimean capital.

You can get to nearby villages by mini-vans.

City transport

Bus routes connect the city centre with its suburbs. Buses 1 and 2 go to the Khan's Palace, bus 2 - to Staroselye and the Dormition Monastery, buses 3 and 4 - to the central market and department store.

HOTELS

"Bakhchisarai"
3 Simferopolskaya St.
tel. 42-598

Typical hotel for persons on a business trip not far from the railway station. You may encounter problems with hot water. Accommodation cost: UAH 30 for a very modest double room. Rooms with conveniences cost almost twice as much.

Hotel of tourist centre "Prival"
43 Shmidta St.
tel. 47-846

Located 500 metres from the Khan's Palace. Comforts offered to any taste and purse: from double room without conveniences (UAH 15 a head) to luxury family cottages (UAH 500 per day and above). It is nice to stay there for several days and visit the sights of the city.

Private hotel
11 Vostochnaya St.
tel. 47-740

Private mansion on the territory of museum-estate of Ye.Nagayevskaya and A.Romm. Ideal for painters and photographers coming to Bakhchisarai to work. Single, double, and triple rooms with shower and lavatory are homely cosy and comfortable. Accommodation costs UAH 10 a head per day.

"Avtomobilist"
12 Krymskaya St.
tel. 26-872

The hotel's name speaks for itself: drivers and motor tourists caught by the night stay there. Undemanding but cheap.

As a rule, people staying in Bakhchisarai for a few days, are lovers of backpacking - folks not fastidious in the issues of "bread and circuses". Sightseers coming to see the palace of the Crimean Khans, the Dormition Monastery, or Chufut-Kale prefer to have a snack at nearby catering facilities.

MEALS

To view the Khan's Palace complex and not to taste Crimean chebureks would be an inexcusable mistake! Moreover that one does not have to go a long way: cafe **"Crimean Chebureks"** is situated right opposite the entrance to the palace museum. That national food is also offered on the square: the clamour of tradeswomen competing for buyers imparts the area true oriental colour.

"Queen of the Night" - one of the best Bakhchisarai wines

In Bakhchisarai, you will easily find eating houses where dishes of the national cuisine are served: restaurants **"Bakhchisarai"** and **"Elita"**, cafes **"Esma"** and **"Salachik"**. The latter is located near a parking by the path leading to the Dormition Monastery and Chufut-Kale cave city. One can refresh oneself after a long excursion on an open-air terrace of the cafe. Lunch will cost you UAH 10-12.

Many tourists are attracted by the cheap local fruits and splendid wines of the Bakhchisarai winery **"Fontan"**. The tasting room is located next to the Khan's Palace.

ENTERTAINMENT

As we already mentioned, Bakhchisarai is not a sea resort, and amusements are not in plenty there. Amateurs of dancing are invited to "Esma" disco bar whose interior is adorned with beautiful aquariums with exotic fishes.

Travellers staying at the tourist hotel "Prival" may marvelously spend a night in bars, gambling rooms, or cinema halls of that tourist community.

And the main entertainment of Bakhchisarai is an unhurried walk along the beautiful old streets that still preserve the unique atmosphere of an oriental town, tours along its suburbs and picturesque valleys.

Addresses and telephones:

"Bakhchisarai"
40 Frunze St. *tel.* **25-500**

"Elita"
110 Lenina St. *tel.* **32-634**

"Otdykh"
53 Lenina St. *tel.* **47-471**

"Crimean Chebureks"
104 Lenina St. *tel.* **42-561**

"Esma"
5 Simferopolskaya St. *tel.* **42-557**

Brisk trade in chebureks near the cafe "Crimean Chebureks"

"Lakomka"
72 Lenina St.

"Severnoye Siyaniye"
7 Simferopolskaya St.

Tasting room
106 Lenina St.

Three hundred years ago, there were many Turkish coffee houses in the city

The fact that modern civilisation has had little effect on Bakhchisarai in the end played a positive role: it preserved the atmosphere of a medieval Tatar city.

Yelena Nagayevskaya

Paintress Yelena Varnavovna Nagayevskaya bought an old Tatar house at 11, Vostochnaya Street in 1952 after the death of her husband - known Orientalist and artist Alexander Georgievich Romm. She spent there the warm seasons, leaving for Moscow in winter.
The talent of the paintress - a disciple of Konstantin Bogayevsky and Alexander Kuprin - was the most fully revealed in the landscapes of the Crimea and Bakhchisarai that became native for her. Thanks to the beautiful

Old Bakhchisarai (fragment). Ye.Nagayevskaya

water-colours by Yelena Nagayevskaya we may enjoy the sights of the old city, many of which no longer exist. She had a dream - to make pictures of all monuments of the Crimea, Caucasus, and Central Asia. In the Crimea her dream came true. Her paintings, personal belongings, graphic works by Alexander Romm, diaries, archival documents are kept with care in the house of the paintress. Visitors of the museum will hear an interesting story of those amazing people - Yelena Nagayevskaya and Alexander Romm.

Tomb of the early Girais

Bakhchisarai is a unique city that has three different faces. In the area of Staroselye (former Salachik) we can see original Tatar architecture: adobe houses with high fences, narrow curved streets; the architecture of the central part (former Eski-Yurt) is typical for rural area; the modern look of Bakhchisarai is to be seen in the new micro-districts with similar high-rise buildings.

One of the oldest architectural and historic monuments of the city - the mausoleum of Bei-Yude-Sultan - is situated at the beginning of Frunze St. The tomb was built by the son of the deceased. Unfortunately, the dyurbe is located on the territory of a private estate, for which reason it is difficult to get there.

Not far from the old mausoleum near the market there is a complex of structures of the Azis. Near the settlement of Eski-Yurt, there was a large cemetery with tombs, mausoleums, and other sanctuaries. Previously, the complex was called Kyrk-Azis (Forty Saints). Today, tourists may see some of the survived structures. Ahmad Bei Dyurbe (presumably of the 15th cent.) is small in size and has no decor.

Beside the dyurbe you will see the ruins of a chapel (tekiye) of dervishes - itinerant Muslim monks. It represented a mimber, or pulpit - a small octahedral tower on a platform with 12 stone stairs.

In the territory of the

Entrance to Zindjirli-madrasah

market there are two more monuments: the dyurbe of Mohammed Bei (resembling an octahedral yurt) and the mausoleum of Khan Mohammed Girai II distinguished for its refined architecture.

In Staroselye, tourists should see the mausoleum of the first Girai - Hadji Girai, built in 1501 by his son Khan Mengly Girai I also buried there. Next stands the building of Zindjirli-madrasah - a religious school built by Khan Mengly Girai in 1500. Above the entrance there hangs a chain that gave the name to the building ("zindjir" means "chain"): every comer had to bow his head before the wisdom of Allah.

Once the religious school stood next to the palace of Ashlam, now entirely perished. By the madrasah there is the grave of the writer, scientist, and enlightener Ismail Gasprinsky. You may learn about his life in the house-museum of I.Gasprinsky situated further down the main street leading to the Khan's Palace.

Staroselye is the former eastern outskirt of Bakhchisarai. Near the entrance to a narrow ravine of Kanly-Dere ("Bloody Ravine"), in 1950s archaeologists discovered a site of ancient people who lived in the area 35-50 thousand years ago.

In the 16th century there was a settlement named Salachik ("noose") in the narrow valley squeezed between rocks. The ravine was blocked with walls stretching from rock to rock, and when the gate was closed, it was impossible to enter the settlement.

Zoi Kosmodemyanskoi Street leads to one of the oldest buildings of the ancient city - Eski-dyurbe ("Old Tomb"). It is a small structure with a portal and a square courtyard, accessible only from the sepulchre, almost deprived of decorations but distinguished for its masterly masonry. There is a legend that buried there was the master of the valley who ruled that land yet before the arrival of the Girais.

The Golden Fountain, or Magzub, was intended for ritual purposes

Not far from a nameless mausoleum at 5 Rozy Luksemburg Street, there stands Tokhtaly-Dzhami ("Mosque of Boards") built in 1707 by the daughter of Al-Hadji Selim Girai. Due to the deficit of space its minaret was half-built into the wall of the structure.

The most famous sight of Bakhchisarai is the Khan's Palace. The complex of the historic-architectural preserve consists of a great many structures. The palace was several times rebuilt and changed its appearance. The oldest exhibit of the museum is the portal of Aleviz, or Demir-Kapu ("Iron Gate"). The structure presenting a true pearl of the complex was moved from the palace of Ashlam. The author of the portal - the Italian architect Aleviz Novy, or Fryazin - along with other Italian masters was invited by Prince John III of Moscow to decorate the Kremlin. The mission was held back by Crimean Khan Mengly Girai I. From June, 1503, till September, 1504 Aleviz was busy adorning the Khan's Palace. The Khan was highly satisfied with the work of the Italian architect and let him to the Moscow Prince with a testimonial letter where he highly praised the architect.

The poem of love

In a desolate corner of the palace park there stands a lonely tomb of Dilyara-Bikech ("beautiful princess") - the untimely deceased beloved wife of Khan Kirim Girai. Supposingly, one of the facets of the dyurbe erected in 1764 previously housed the "paradisal spring" of Selsebil designed by great Omer - the famous Fountain of Tears that inspired young A.Pushkin to write the poem "Bakhchisarai Fountain", the sad story of love and hatred. The fountain kind of personifies the palace's soul. Interestingly, when in the Soviet times the wave of total renaming reached Bakhchisarai (intended to be renamed Pushkingrad), the work by A.Pushkin served as an argument in favour of conservation of the historic name - what "Bakhchisarai Fountain" may there be without Bakhchisarai?! Maria Kustova, then director of the palace museum, went to Moscow to defend the historic truth...

Fountain of Tears that inspired A.Pushkin to write the immortal poem "Bakhchisarai Fountain"

From the gate of the palace museum visitors go over the bridge across the river Churuk-Su to a spacious shady courtyard decorated with beds of roses. Tourists like to make pictures there, near the stone bowl of the fountain, in the clothes of the Crimean Tatar nobility.

To the left of the entrance stands the Grand Palace Mosque - Khan-Dzhami. Its simple proportions and harmonic minarets attract the attention of travellers from a distance.

In 1787, the household who accompanied Empress Catherine II in her Crimean journey stopped in the Svitsky (Household) building; now, it houses the exposition of objects of applied art representing the way of life of Crimean Tatars.

After several reconstructions of the palace the Hall of the Court and Divan, the Small Palace Mosque and, partially, the Grand Palace Mosque retained their original look, along with the above-mentioned Portal of Aleviz. Unfortunately, during restoration Omer's paintings on the walls of the palace halls ware painted over. Recently, they have been partially restored, in particular, on the walls of the summer pavilion.

Seeing the beautiful buildings and splendid expositions of the museum complex, you won't even notice the flow of time in the atmosphere of medieval Orient.

BAKHCHISARAI STATE HISTORIC AND CULTURAL PRESERVE

1. *Catherine's mile of 1787*
2. *Main Gate*
3. *Svitsky building*
4. *Grand Palace Mosque*
5. *Khan cemetery with the Northern and Southern dyurbes*
6. *Sary-Guzel bath*
7. *Stables*
8. *Southern Gate Tower*
9. *Mausoleum of Dilyara-Bikech*
10. *Falcon tower*
11. *Harem*
12. *Main palace building*
13. *Aleviz' portal*
14. *Ambassadorial court*

Address:
133 Rechnaya St. tel. **32-753**
🕓 10.00-17.00, except Tuesdays

Entrance ticket - UAH 6 (for students - UAH 3), photography - UAH 5, camera shooting - UAH 15.

Presentation of the wonder-working icon

In the olden times there lived a fierce serpent who ate people and cattle, brought grief and ruin to the settlement. Many fled, and those who stayed - Greek Christians - devoutly prayed to the Holy Virgin and asked her for protection.
And a miracle happened: high on a rock people saw the image of Virgin Mary with a lit candle in front of it. Having cut stairs in the rock, the amazed people ascended to the icon and saw the dead serpent beside it... After that, the people often came to pray to the rock selected by the Mother of God.

Image of the wonder-working icon of the Mother of God

Another legend tells that the icon was found by a shepherd who told about it to his master - the Manhup toparch. The latter ordered to solemnly move the icon to his house but in the morning the icon reappeared in its old place. It so happened three times before the prince realised that the Mother of God did not wish Her holy face to appear anywhere else but on the rock where it was presented to people. A temple was arranged in the rock. Since the presentation of the icon took place on August 15 - during the Dormition Fast, the new temple was dedicated to the Dormition of the Mother of God.

Bowl of the holy spring

The Dormition Church was presumably founded in the 8th century, during the resettlement of iconodulists to the Crimea, in the period of implantation of Islam among the population of Tavrica, and became a bulwark of Christianity on the peninsula.

During the Turkish rule it housed the Metropolitan chair. The holy icon was respected not only by Christians; Muslims, too, turned to it for help. For a long time Tatar Khans offered candles to the Dormition Monastery that were set on fire in front of the relic of the Christian temple all the year round.

At that time, the cloister was poor, there were no precious appliances because of the fear of predatory Tatar raids. When the relations between the Orthodox and the Faithful aggravated up to the hilt, Metropolitan Ignatius asked the Russian Empress for a permission to resettle with the flock to the Russian lands. The Empress helped fellow-believers and allocated more than 200,000 roubles from the budget. On 66 carts guarded by soldiers of A.Suvorov, the Crimean Christians left for the Azov steppes. On the Easter day, April 23, 1778, 31,386 persons left the Crimean peninsula under the protection of the Icon of Dormition of the Holy Virgin. The Dormition Skete and next to all Christian convents fell into decay.

However, not all Christians left Tavrica. The believers who refused to leave the native land were greatly confused to learn that not a single priest stayed on the peninsula. Having heard that in June, 1781, the Greek priest Konstantinos Spirandis came to the Crimea, Christians asked Shahin Girai to keep the Greek to serve liturgy. Spirandis hesitated but in the end was the only guard of the Dormition rock for 60 years.

The Dormition Skete was reopened in August, 1850, thanks to the efforts of Archbishop Innocent. Initially, there were only

7 monks there. In 1921 the Monastery was closed on the order of the Soviet authorities. The Dormition Monastery has been active since 1993.

As for the wonder-working icon, before 1918 it was kept in a temple in Mariupol, but later its traces were lost...

The steep spurs of the Chufut-Kale plateau look forbidding, only from the east a curvy path leads there. Several survived buildings look from below like nests of strange birds that settled on the flat top.

The area of the site makes 46 hectares, in that, 10 hectares were occupied by urban settlements. During military campaigns dwellers of the surrounding valleys

gathered on the rest of the territory of the Burunchak Cape to escape the assault. Although next to all surface structures perished, the site presents a good picture of streets, city quarters, and fortifications.

The last dwellers left that presently dead city a bit more than a century ago. Surveys prove that as early as in the 6th century there were settlements of Alan cattle-breeders there. Some time later a fortified town was founded on the mountainous plateau. The household caves cut in the rock have perfectly survived, by contrast to the wooden surface dwellings. Out of 16 cave cities of the Crimea, Chufut-Kale lasted longer than others.

From the crossing of four valleys a tourist path goes past the Dormition Monastery to an ancient necropolis rank with cornel and wild hazel-wood. Historians are not sure who buried there their dead from the 4th till the 10th century - either the dwellers of the sky city or the villagers who lived in the gully of Maryam-Dere.

The castle-town was well protected but could not withstand the onslaught of Khan Nogai's army. During one of his raids on Tavrica in 1299 he took the fortress and slaughtered next to all its dwellers. Later the fortifications were restored.

The main events in the history of the cave city took place during the struggle for power between the Crimean and Golden Horde Khans. The local rulers sought independence from the establishment of the dying Golden Horde. Then, that strongly fortified town that became a Tatar stronghold was called Qirq Yer. It housed the headquarters of the contender for the throne of the independent Crimean Khanate Hadji-Dawlat Girai, founder of the glorious Girai dynasty.

At that time, a woman appears on the political scene. Dzhanike-Khanym was the daughter of Khan Tokhtamysh (who reduced to ashes Moscow in 1382). History preserved the memory of her as a wise ruler, the

Abraham Firkovich

The known Karaite historian was born in Lutsk in 1786. The traditional education he got covered the Hebrew language, the Bible, and religious literature. Those subjects decided the future of Abraham Firkovich: he devoted all his life to the study of the history and spiritual way of his people.

When the province Governor Mikhail Vorontsov asked gaham (spiritual leader) of the Karaite community Simkha Babovich to gather historic reports about his people, he turned for assistance to A.Firkovich. They went to

A.Firkovich and Karaites. Drawing of the 19th cent.

Palestine to collect old manuscripts. Trips to the Middle East, the Caucasus, Egypt followed. The unique collection of 15,000 books and manuscripts was transferred to the Imperial Library in Saint Petersburg.

Abraham Firkovich had an indisputable authority among the Karaite community. However, he also had to listen to the public opinion: when, being an old man, the scholar wanted to repeat the act of Abraham and marry a 16-year-old girl, he had to give up the idea under the pressure of the community.

Rut beaten by wheels over centuries

1. *Mausoleum of Dzhanike-Khanym, the daughter of Khan Tokhtamysh*
2. *Northern slope of the plateau*
3. *Kenasa Street*
4. *Middle Street*
5. *Burunchak Street*
6. *Complex of household caves. Played a defensive role during invasions. Presumably housed a cave monastery in the pre-Tatar period*
7. *Small (Southern) Gate - Kuchuk-Kapu*
8. *Ruins of the Khan palace, a mosque and the mint*
9. *Small and Grand Kenasas - Karaite houses of prayer*
10. *Southern slope of the plateau*
11. *Gate of the middle fortification wall - Orta-Kapu*
12. *Estate of Solomon Beim (Cha-Boriu)*
13. *Rich estate with household caves Chaush-Kobasy, or "Master's cave"*
14. *Ruins of a bath*
15. *Great (Eastern) Gate - Biyuk-Kapu*
16. *Double ditch. The road along the outer ditch leads to Ashlama-Dere valley*
17. *Road to a cemetery in Josaphat's Valley*
18. *Remains of the basement of a palace built in 1897 for the reception of the Imperial family*

successor of the Genghisids. She offered the rebellious Khan a shelter in her patrimonial castle. With the support from Dzhanike-Khanym Hadji Girai could resist the Crimean emirs. Unfortunately, soon after his patroness died, and the Khan had to seek protection of the Lithuanian princes. (It is know that the future Khan spent his early years at the court of Prince Vitovt.) With their help Hadji Girai became the ruler of the Crimean Khanate. Qirq Yer was the capital of that state for half a century.

Mausoleum of Dzhanike-Khanym

At that time, the ethnic composition of the city population was mixed: Tatars were warriors, Armenians - builders, Karaites - craftsmen and merchants. The Muslim mosque stood in the main square next to the mausoleum of Dzhanike-Khanym, Orthodox Armenians prayed in their quarter, Karaites - dissidents of the Judaic faith who rejected the Talmud and read the Old Testament in their temples - kenasas.

Tatars settled Karaites behind the eastern wall, and they built another fortification there, for which reason the site was also called the Double Fortress (Dzhufut-Kale). Some sources referred to the town as the "Fortress of Jewellery". The Turkish traveller of the 17th century Evliya Celebi wrote in his "Travel Book" that the walls and gates of the city were adorned with precious stones.

After Tatars left the fortress and moved to Bakhchisarai, Karaites stayed in the town. Qirq Yer was renamed Chufut-Kale (Judaic Fortress). In addition to numerous caves, the house of the scholar A.Firkovich survived.

19. *Dwelling estate of the 19th century that belonged to Karaite historian A.Firkovich*
20. *Entrance to a cave communicating with a secret well. Speleologists discovered there an underground gallery leading to a former water reservoir. In February, 2002, a treasure was found at clearing of a corridor probably leading to an underground vault. A clay pot contained some 4,000 silver coins of Genoese-Crimean mint and 30 Venetian gold ducats. The treasure is presently kept at the museum of local lore in Simferopol.*

Kenasas - prayer houses in Chufut-Kale (restored)

How far are the stars?

Maybe much closer than you believe, if you get to Nauchny - a township of the Crimean astronomers. To get there, turn to the Bakhchisarai Travel and Excursion Bureau. If the timetable of excursions does not suit you, call the observatory direct at (06554) 71-164. It is convenient to go to

Telescope in the settlement of Nauchny

Nauchny by a mini-van from Simferopol or, still better, by your own car, since the stars are especially well seen at night, for which reason excursions are held rather late.
The astrophysical observatory founded in Simeiz in 1908 was ruined during World War II. In 1946 it was decided to build a new observatory. So arose Nauchny.
In August, 1974, a small planet was discovered there named Vladvysotsky, after the famous actor and singer.

The outskirts of Bakhchisarai are among the most interesting sites of the Crimea for a true tourist. There are no grand palaces there, but that land conceals a great many secrets and mysteries...

Mini-waterfalls of Belbek

Chufut-Kale is not the only cave city in the Crimea. In the mountainous part of Tavrica, between Inkerman and Bakhchisarai, there are many cave cities and monasteries: Manhup, Eski-Kermen, Kachi-Kalyon, Bakla, and others.

Cave settlements appeared in the mountains of the peninsula in the 5th-6th centuries. Some survived better, others - worse, but what unites them is that surface structures made from wood, stone, and clay were razed by the time from the ground while cuts in the rocks - caves, cisterns, tarapans (reservoirs for pressing juice out of grapes) - withstood for centuries.

Of great interest for scholars and for people interested in the history of this land is the site of Manhup. High (250-300 m) above the forests of the surrounding valleys, beneath the sky there stood the fortress of Doros on Mt. Manhup - the centre of the future Christian Principality of Feodoro whose lands before the arrival of the Genoeses stretched along the south coast from Alushta to Balaklava. The Genoeses pressed Feodorites to the mountains of Tavrica, and the Turks who came there in the 15th century destroyed the great principality, whose population was highly mixed: Taurians, Scythians, Goths, Alans, Sarmates, Greeks, Armenians, Karaites flocked there under the pressure of invaders...

From the north, the body of the mountain is cut by deep gullies into four capes: Chamny-Burun (Piny Cape), Chufut-Chergan-Burun (Cape of the Call of the Hebrews), Helli-Burun (Hellenic Cape), and Teshkli-Burun (Holed Cape). The tops of the capes were protected with a strong vallum. The Manhup fortifications were raised with assistance from Byzantine architects and engineers.

One can get to the site along the gullies or by an old road around the Cape of Teshkli-Burun. From the mountaintop a great part of the Crimea - from Sevastopol to Chatyrdag - is perfectly seen.

No description will substitute a trip to those mysterious cities lying beneath the sky.

By the Manhup Lake

Sevastopol - the city of the sea glory

It seemed that after the Crimean War last century the human imagination cannot imagine more heroic defense of the fortress... but the current Sevastopol epics exceeds the previous one many times.

E.Tarle

History in a few lines

The 5th century B.C. - *the foundation of Chersonese.*
The 5th - 6th centuries - *Chersonese becomes a fore-post of the Byzantine Empire in the Northern Black Seaside.*
The 9th - 10th centuries - *Strengthening of the ties of Chersonese ("Korsun" in the Rus annals) with Kievan Rus.*
The 13th - 14th centuries - *the period of the Genoese dominance.*
1399 - *the city is demolished by the hordes of murza Yedigey.*
June, 1783 - *there were laid out the first stone buildings of the settlement named Akhtyar.*
February, 1784 - *the foundation of the fortress named Sevastopol.*
1804 - *Sevastopol becomes the main military port of Russia on the Black Sea.*
September 13, 1854 - August 25, 1855 - *the First heroic defense of Sevastopol.*
1875 - *building of the railway.*
1892 - *the foundation of Chersonese Museum.*
November, 1920 - *establishment of the Soviet power.*

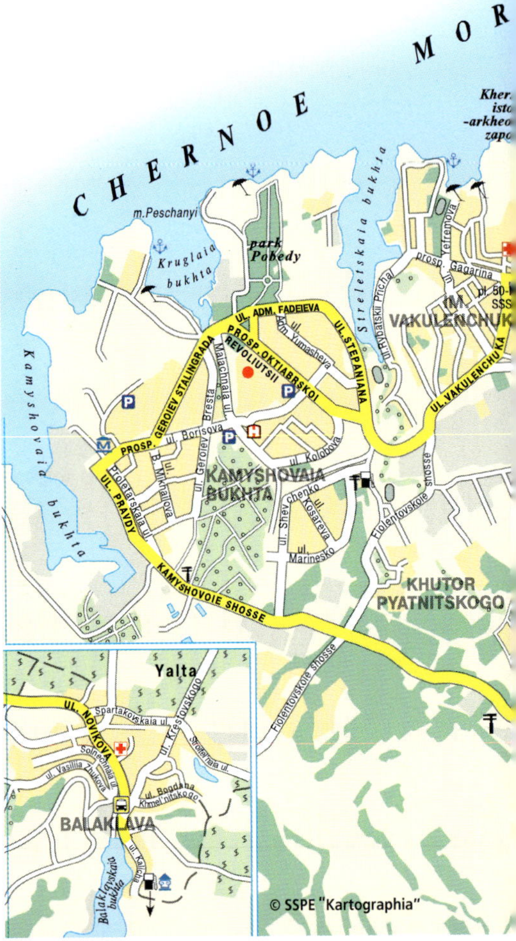

panorama Sevastopol

This city is both young and ancient. Sevastopol as it is was founded on the 14th of June 1783, i.e., a little more than 2 centuries ago, but Chersonese, an ancient city, the magnificent ruins of which are located in the territory of modern Sevastopol, is much older.

The city is located round Sevastopol (Akhtyar) Bay indented for more than 8 km deep into the land. Sevastopol runs along the coastline for about 40 km. Until recent times it was a closed region for tourists. After the entry to the city became free, the holiday-makers come here with pleasure. Greater Sevastopol is located on the borderline between the steppe and the mountainous Crimea. The territory of the region stretches from the Lukull Cape in the north to the Sarych Cape in the south.

The summer is usually dry in Sevastopol, the winter is warm, annual precipitation is low. Average temperature of February is +2,6°C, of July is +22,4°C. The bathing season lasts from June to September.

A car of General I.Petrov, Commandant of the Seaside Artillery defending Sevastopol

October 29, 1941 - July 3, 1942 *- the Second heroic defense of Sevastopol.*
1965 *- Sevastopol became the Hero-City.*
2002 *- there are about 350.000 inhabitants in the city.*

Gikiya - a daughter of Chersonese

Lamakh, the first arkhont (ruler) of Chersonese, was rich and powerful. He has got a huge house full of gold and precious dishes, fat herds, for whom they made a special gate in the city wall. But his daughter Gikiya, whose mind and talent were highly appraised by the wise men, was his main treasure.
Riches of Chersonese would not let Asunder, czar of the kingdom of Bosporus, a moment's peace. He schemed his son to get married Gikiya that would give his son an opportunity to become the ruler of the rich Polis after Lamakh's death.
The inhabitants of Chersonese agreed for that marriage but on the condition that after marriage the czar's son should not meet his father.
Soon Lamakh died, but Asunder's plans were not destined to implement - his son did not become an arkhont. Then the inhabitants of the kingdom of Bosporus decided to resort to cunning to seize the power. Small groups of warriors of the kingdom of Bosporus secretly penetrated into the city through the gate for the cattle and concealed themselves in Gikiya's house. By chance they were discovered by a female-servant. Gikiya understood everything: her beloved husband decided to seize the city during the upcoming holiday. She ordered to the reliable people to prepare brushwood and torches. During the holiday evening Gikiya lead her husband into the house, then went outside, locked the house, and ordered to get it fired. The enemies headed by the betrayer were killed, and the city was saved...

In Chersonese

The beaches are sandy, pebbled, with stony shore or gently sloping bottoms. They attract by their variety: one can find here well groomed, civilized places with the full choice of the beach entertainment or secluded corners for the lovers of evening meditations and underwater hunting.

The numerous bays (about thirty) attach a unique appearance to Sevastopol. They were the bays that determined the destiny of the city. When Lieutenant-General A.Suvorov came here for the first time, he immediately appraised the advantages of Akhtyar Bay. On his instruction the first ground fortifications were built here...

But everything started much earlier. In the middle of the first Millenium B.C. the ships of the Heracleotic Greeks (Heracleus was a Pontus

A bridge with dragons

colony in Asia Minor) moored to the shore of the modern Quarantine Bay. The ancestors of great Hercules were looking for a place for the future dominions. However, legendary Odyssey who, according to the opinions of some researchers, visited Balaklava Bay, can be considered a pioneer of this part of the coast. The meeting with the Tauri living here was not friendly. The aborigines of the Crimean peninsula acquired a stable reputation of cruel Barbarians. A Greek settlement set up on the St. Vladimir Cape was sheltered from their raids with the fortifications.

The Polis acquired the name of Chersonese in Taurida ("chersonese" means "peninsula" in Greek). The Greeks were engaged in winemaking, fishing, and trades. The Polis was steadily widening and soon it involved the whole Heracleotic peninsula and a part of the western coast with the cities of Cercinitidus and Kalos-Limen.

In the 3rd century the Scythians began to bother the Greeks, therefore the Polis had to be significantly fortified. Later the inhabitants of the Polis asked for help from

Mitridate IV Yeuvpatore, the czar of the kingdom of Pontus. They received help but lost their independence. Having united the kingdoms of Pontus and Bosporus, Mitridate was waging continuous wars with the Roman Empire. After the Mitridate dynasty suffered a defeat, Chersonese became tributary to Rome.

For several centuries the Polis was a cultural and trading center of the whole Southwest Crimea. Since the 5th century Chersonese was a forepost of the Byzantine Empire in the Crimea.

At this time Christianity began to spread here, though it was Andrei Pervozvanny himself who, according to a legend, set up the first Christian community as long ago as in the 1st century. St. Apostle built the first temple on the Phiolentus Cape. Later the Georgian Monastery emerged on its site. The Pope Clement, a successor of Apostle Peter was exiled to Chersonese in the end of the 1st century for the propagation of Christianity. There are evidences of the enlighteners Kirill and Mefody staying in the Sevastopol land.

In the end of the 6th century the Khazars showed up at the fortifications of Kherson (the way it was called in the Byzantine annals). In the 9th century the Slavs interfered into the development of the Crimean history. Economic rise of Cheers that started at this time was going on till the 8th century when the Tatars showed up in the peninsula. However, they were not the Tatars who brought death to the city but the Genoese who declined economy of Kherson. Later it was not difficult for the Tatar hordes to seize an impoverished city, demolish, and get it fired. It was the end of the existence of ancient Chersonese...

The first stone buildings of Sevastopol were laid out two months later after the well-known manifesto about the annexation of the Crimea by Russia. Catherine II decided to call a new port according to the fashion of that time for the Greek names. A

A city street

toponym is translated from Old Greek as " a city of glory; a sacred city deserving worship".

The development of Sevastopol was going on unevenly: rises in economy and construction changed for declines. A lot depended on the personality of the military Governor as well as on what resources were allotted by a regular emperor to the development of the fleet.

The world has heard about Sevastopol for the first time when the united troops of England, France, and Turkey landed to the north of the port and started an advance on the city. For 349 days the inhabitants of Sevastopol did not yield, holding in check the advance of the numerous enemy troops and demonstrating examples of courage, heroism, and inflexible will. This legendary time - from September 13, 1854 to August 27, 1855 came into the history as the First heroic defense of Sevastopol.

The second defense is connected with the Great Patriotic War. The advance of the Hitler's troops on Sevastopol started on October 30, 1941. For 250 days and nights the enemy was even unable to approach the city. Sevastopol was liberated from the invaders on May 9, 1944.

By the beginning of 1957 the city was practically restored from the zero level. It was a real labor exploit as far as after the liberation there were hardly ten buildings uninjured during the war. Historical and architectural monuments were restores from the ruins; new blocks of buildings and micro-districts were built. Therefore Sevastopol looks so young...

A submarine prior to going to the sea

Addresses and telephones:

City Police Department *Tel.* **54-6464**

Traffic Police Duty-Officer *Tel.* **45-1163**

Ambulance station *Tel.* **54-3802**

Drugstore *(information)*
25-a Ochakovtsev St. *Tel.* **54-2469**

Water-rescue station *Tel.* **54-3431**

Customs *Tel.* **54-3566**
5-aNakhimova Avenue

City Inquiry Office *Tel.* **52-4191**
15 Bolshaya Morskaya St.

Central Post Office *Tel.* **54-4881**
21 Bolshaya Morskaya St.

Railroad booking-office *Tel.* **36-7361**
3 Vokzalnaya St.

Air booking-office
13 Lenina St. *Tel.* **54-2829**

Privatbank
47 Lenina St. *Tel.* **45-6240**

Ukreximbank *Tel.* **55-5530**
15 Nakhimova Avenue

Order of taxicabs
Tel. **0-50, 0-52, 0-55, 0-57, 0-58, 0-60, 0-61**

Motor boats *(information)* *Tel.* **54-2465**

A train to Sevastopol.
An old photo

When going to Sevastopol the tourists can use various kinds of transport - railroad, coach service, or sea service.

Railroad terminal

3 Vokzalnaya Square
Tel. 54-3077, 36-6074

The railroad is the most convenient kind of transport communications. Sevastopol is connected by rail (through daily trains) with Kiev, Donetsk, Moscow, and Saint Petersburg. Local electric trains connect the city of sailors with Simferopol (trip time - 2 hours and a half), Yevpatoriya, Djankoy, and Melitopol.

Auto-terminal

2 Revyakina St.
Tel. 46-1632, 36-6011

The central auto-terminal is located next to the railway terminal. Coaches from Simferopol (from the coach station "Kurortnaya" and auto-terminal "Tsentralny" as well as from the airport "Simferopol") are coming here. Coach routes connect Sevastopol with other cities of the Crimea (Yalta, Feodosiya, etc.) as well as with the Ukrainian cities and with the cities of the near-by foreign countries. There are also several local bus stations in Sevastopol.

Marine passenger terminal

5 Nakhimova Square
Tel. 54-4082, 54-5201

Marine passenger terminal is located just behind the Grafskaya landing pier.

Motor boats and river trams are popular in the city. A ferry route is as follows: Artillery Bay - the "Northern side" (Zakharova Square)- interval 30-60 minutes. It is the fastest way to get with one's own car to the northern side of Akhtyar Bay when going to the settlements of Uchkuyevka, Lyubimovka, etc.

Motor boats connect the centre of the city with the "Northern side" (moorings Radiogorka, Zakharova Square, Holland Bay, Uchkuyevka Beach), Shipyard Side, and Inkerman.

City transport

Taking into account the fact that Sevastopol occupies a huge territory, studying bus and trolleybus routes becomes an important thing. In addition, there are about ten radio-taxi companies in the city.

There are more than ten hotels in Sevastopol located in the different districts of the city. They differ in categories and the level of prices.

"Gostevoy Dom" ("Guest House")
22 Chertsova St.
Tel. 55-3228

It is a private hotel complex with an aqua-centre and a parking place.

Cottages with all modern conveniences are located at the Quarantine Bay, not far from the reserve "Chersonese of Taurida". One can come here with one's water transportation means - the hotel organizes keeping, maintenance, and repair. One can hire yachts, motor boats, and underwater equipment. The cost of lodging is high, for example, to rent a cottage consisting of 6 double room in high season (August) will be approximately UAH 3,000 per night.

Inter-cruise Sailors' Holiday Home
22 Geroyev Stalingrada St.
Tel. 41-1219

This hotel can be recommended to those who like secluded vacation. Despite a severe name not only sailors but land tourists as well can find rooms here. There is a sauna, a decent cafe offering home cuisine dishes, a bar for the night party lovers. The hotel is located in the suburb of the city at the Kamishovaya (Rushy) Bay. There is a secluded wild beach in front of it. There is an "Omega" beach, one of the cleanest city beaches, within 10-15 minutes walk from here. There is a cheap market on the way to it. You can get to the centre of the city by trolleybuses # 10 and #18. The cost of lodging is low - from UAH 20 to 60.

"Ukraina" ★★★ ("Ukraine")
2 Gogolya St.
tel. 54-2127, 54-0398

The hotel is located in one of the mane and the most beautiful squares of the town. It is several minutes walk to the world-wide well-known Panorama, the Fleet Museum, the Aquarium, theatres, railway station, marine passenger terminal,

and the coach station.

100 comfortable rooms with an individual design and a wonderful view of the town wait for guests. For real connoisseurs of comfort luxury suites and rooms de luxe are prepared. The cafe and restaurant of the hotel are notable for their excellent cuisine, reasonable prices, and refined interior. Your beauty and health will be taken care of in the simulator room, massage room, hairdressers and barber services saloon available at the hotel.

Here they are always ready to assist you in your rest or taking decisions on business issues.

Hotels

"Krym" ("Crimea") Tel. **55-7154**
46-a the 6th Bastionnaya

"Vlana"
6 Podoltseva St. Tel. **46-0939**

"Yard"
9 Kesayeva St. Tel. **42-9857**

"Primorskaya" ("Seaside")
4 Partisanskaya St. Tel. **55-4001**

"Ukraine"
2 Gogolya St. Tel. **37-4333**

"Belbeck" Tel. **73-5205**
24 Fyodorovskaya St.

"Korabelnaya" ("Shipyard")
25 Pobedy Prospekt (Victory Avenue) Tel. **36-2810**

"Sputnik"
10 Voronina St. Tel. **54-0591**

Addresses and telephones:

RESTAURANTS:

"Grafskaya Pristan" ("Landing Pier")
3-a Nakhimova Avenue
10 a.m. - 6.00 a.m. Tel. 24-9615

"Italian Yard" Tel. 54-3921
4 Nakhimova Avenue *24 hours*

"Golden Dragon"
8 Nakhimova Avenue, Tel. 54-4136
24 hours9 a.m. - 11 p.m.

"Khreshchatik"
10 Bolshaya Morskaya St.
11 a.m. - 11 p.m. Tel. 54-2131

CAFES:

"Albatross"
21 Nakhimova Avenue
10 a.m. - 4.00 a.m. Tel. 54-4853

In the "Russian pelmeni" cafe-canteen they serve tastefully and cheap

"Magic Burger"
15 Bolshaya Morskaya St.
10 a.m. - 10 p.m. Tel. 54-3003

"Natalka"
72 Lenina St.
10 a.m. - 11 p.m. Tel. 54-2143

BARS:

"Nikita Club"
1-a Shestakova Descend
10 a.m. - 11 p.m. Tel. 24-9813

"Golden Rune"
2 Kornilova Seafront
24 hours Tel. 54-6504

"Merry Roger"
43 Bolshaya Morskaya St.
9 a.m. - 11 p.m. Tel. 55-4587

Wine tasting hall
38 Lenina St.
12 a.m. - 8 p.m. Tel. 54-3203

There are plenty of restaurants, cafes, and canteens in Sevastopol. A range of entities is wide enough - from a club restaurant to a decent canteen - one can look, taste, and choose.

The "Traktir of 1854" restaurant invites guests

"Traktir of 1854" ("Eating-house")

8 Bolshaya Morskaya St. (Big Sea) Tel. 54-4760
10 a.m. - mid-night

You will find an excellent Russian cuisine, stylish interior decorations of the Crimean War epoch, low prices, and girls wearing sailor's jackets. Quass and rolls are offered at the expense of the entity. An average price of lunch (without alcohol) is UAH 12-15. Those who like to have a sufficient meal will be pleasantly surprised - dished in the eating-house are rather big. There is a summer terrace for the smokers.

"Rybatsky Stan" ("Fishermen Camp")

300th Anniversary of the Russian Fleet Square
Tel. 55-7278
11 a.m. - 3.00 a.m.

An elite restaurant with the European cuisine offers a wide range of seafood dishes. Four halls with air-conditioning can fit 250 persons. There is a billiard-room. In the evening one can dance or see a show program. The level of prices is high, firm dishes - from UAH 30 to 110. A modest lunch - about UAH 100, an excellent one - about UAH 500. Time of servicing - from 15 to 40 minutes. Paintings, music, silver streams of the waterfall create a holiday mood. There are summer sites and a parking place.

Neptune at the fish restaurant

"Nostalgia"

1 Ushakova Square
Tel. 54-0686
10 a.m. - 2.00 a.m.

It is a fashionable entity with the European cuisine. One can seclude oneself in the pavilion. A family with little kids will like to have lunch on the lawn. The level of prices is rather modest: firm dishes (meat noblemen style, pike-perch stuffed with the trout liver) is UAH 15-18. Decent lunch (without alcohol) is UAH 50.

"Russian pelmeni"

5 Lenina St.
Tel. 54-5842
8 a.m. - 9 p.m.

A democratic cafe-canteen follows a motto "quickly, tastefully, and cheap". They cook excellent patties here. The cost of lunch or dinner is UAH 7-15.

Sevastopol is a big seaside city where everyone can arrange his leisure time according to his own taste.

BEACHES

The following beaches are located within the city limits: **"Khrustalny" ("Crystal"** - Artillery Bay), **"Solnechny" ("Sunny")** and **"Pesochny" ("Sandy"** - Sandy Bay, to go by trolleybus # 6). A pebbled beach at the **"Pobeda" ("Victory")** park is good for having a rest with kids - in the shadowy alleys one can wait until the full blaze of the sun is over. There are park-shows on the beach in the **"Omega"** Bay. In addition, there is a boating station here (to go by trolleybuses # 10, 14). In the wild beach of Chersonese the bottom is stony, but the water is wonderfully transparent.

But anyway the best beaches of Sevastopol are located in the settlement of **Uchkuyevka** (one can get there by a motor boat from the Artillery Bay). There is a pure sea and beautiful sand here; a green zone is located near-by.

We recommend lovers of wild beauty to bathe at the Phiolentus Cape (to go by

buses # 2, 19). But one should not go there with kids - bathing is dangerous there because of stones and rocks, and it is tiresome to go down to the beach.

CHILDREN'S LEISURE TIME

One can suggest to the kids to go to the Oceanarium, Museum-aquarium, and Dolphinarium, or to the Animals Theatre **"Country Dolphinia".**

Little kids will gladly spend time in the Children's

park in Ochakovtsev Street while riding ponies, driving electromobiles, and going rubber boating. Kids will also like a fairy-tale camp in Pobedy Avenue (to go by trolleybus # 9).

LEISURE TIME FOR ADULTS

There are walking, bus, and sea tours round the city. You will be told in detail about them at any table of the excursion office, which you can come across everywhere in the centre of Sevastopol.

City theatres are located in the centre of the city - the Drama Theatre named after B.Lavrenyov and the Drama Theatre named after A.Lunacharsky. In the latter one you can visit a theatre museum before the beginning of the performance.

Discotheques, billiards, etc. are available at the boarding houses, big hotels, and restaurants.

Addresses and telephones:

Oceanarium
9 Elronovskaya St. *Tel.* **24-0187**
8.30 a.m. - 12.50 p.m. and 1.35 p.m. - 5.30 p.m., except Saturdays and Sundays

Museum-aquarium
2 Nakhinova Avenue
10 a.m. - 7 p.m. *Tel.* **54-3892**

Animals theatre and dolphinarium
2 Kornilova Seafront *Tel.* **54-2385**
9 a.m. - 6 p.m., except Saturdays and Sundays

THEATRES:

The theatre named after B.Lavrenyov
Ushakova Square *Tel.* **54-3395**

The theatre named after A.Lunacharsky
6 Nakhinova Avenue Tel. 54-4330

CINEMAS:

"Druzhba" ("Friendship")
1 Shmidta St. *Tel.* **54-2657**

"Ukraine" *35 Lenina St.*

DISCOTHEQUES:

"Jam" *Tel.* **54-7099**
13-a Bolshaya Morskaya St.

"Green" *Tel.* **54-2727**
2 Klokacheva Seafront

BOWLING:

"Zolotoi Shar" *("Golden Ball")*
1 Admirala Fadeyeva St.
10 a.m. - 4.00 a.m.Tel. **24-6005**

Skittle-alley
Istorichesky Boulevard
2 p.m. - mid-night

On the stones of Chersonese

Panorama "Defense of Sevastopol in 1854-1855"

Istoricheskiy Boulevard
Tel. 57-9738
9.30 a.m. - 5.30 p.m., except Mondays

A panorama is a circlar painting 115 m long and 14 m high with the additional organic object plan. The work was performed under the guidance of F.Rubo, a professor of fine arts. The panorama depicts the assault of Malakhov Kurgan on 6 June 1855.

The building was specially designed for the location of the exposition. It was built by the 50th the anniversary of the First heroic defense of the city. In 1942 the pavilion was demolished, only several sections of the painting were managed to be saved. After the Great Patriotic War the work of art was in fact painted all over again by the art team under the guidance of V.Yakovlev and P.Sokolova-Skalya. The restored Panorama was opened for public in 1954. The building is decorated from outside by the busts of the defenders of the city mounted in the niches.

The entrance to the museum is only possible in the framework of an excursion, fee - UAH 6, using a photocamera - UAH 4.

Diorama "Assault of Sapun-gora on 7 May, 1944"

Sapun-gora
Tel. 54-4070
9.30 a.m. - 4.30 p.m., except Mondays

Artists P.Maltsev, G.Marchenko, and N.Prisekin depicted on a huge painting 25.5 m long and 5.5 m high one of the episodes of the battle for the liberation of Sevastopol from the Hitler's troops. An

Most of the Sevastopol museums - and there are more museums here than in any other city of the Crimea - is connected with its military history.

Diorama "Assault of Sapun-gora"

object plan of the immense diorama has 83 m^2.

On the open site not far from the building of the museum there are ship cannons, automobiles, shells, artillery installations of the Great Patriotic War times.

"Malakhov Kurgan"

Istomina St.
Tel. 36-6751
9.30 a.m. - 5.00 p.m., except Mondays

On the tallest hill of the Shipyard side there is a memorial complex of the Kornilov's bastion, a defensive tower, cannons of the First heroic defense of the city times, a monument to the Admiral V.Kornilov, mortally wounded on the defense line.

Museum of the Black See Fleet History

11 Lenina St.
Tel. 54-0392
10.00 a.m. - 5.00 p.m., except Mondays and Tuesdays

Seven halls of the museum tell about the glorious history of the Black See Fleet. In addition to the sample of the armament and models of the ships of war, one can see here the medical instruments that belonged to a well-known surgeon N.Pirogov, personal

Museum of the Black See Fleet History. Decoration fragment.

belongings of the military leaders headed the First heroic defense of the city - Admiral V.Istomin, Admiral V.Kornilov, and Admiral P.Nakhimov.

The building of the museum built in 1895 by an architect A.Kochetov and a sculptor B.Eduards is interesting as well. It is not big but decorated with stone carving, etc. There are cannons, anchors, and other elements of the ship armament and equipment.

Museum of Regional Studies

2 Suvorova St.
Tel. 54-5440
8.00 a.m. - 13.00 p.m.
2.00 p.m. - 5.00 p.m., except Saturdays and Sundays

The museum is located not far from the Vladimir's Cathedral standing high on the central hill of Sevastopol. The exposition tells about the rich history of this land - from ancient times to our days.

Sea Gallery

1-a Sovetskaya St.
Tel. 24-9036
10.00 a.m. - 5.00 p.m., except Saturdays

The tourists will find here everything connected with the marine theme: medals, uniforms, paintings, herald signs, souvenirs.

Art Museum named after M.Kroshitsky

9 Nakhimova Avenue
Tel. 54-4636
10.00 a.m. - 5.00 p.m., except Tuesdays

One of the most interesting buildings of Sevastopol was built in 1899. Its face is decorated with the decorative details of various epochs and styles - atlantes, mascarons and columns. The museum, created on the basis of the art gallery and palaces collections nationalized after the Great October Revolution, has one of the richest collections in Ukraine.

Museum-aquarium

2 Nakhimova Avenue
Tel. 54-3892
10.00 a.m. - 7.00 p.m.

The museum is set up by the Institute of Biology of the southern seas of the Ukrainian Academy of Sciences. Contrary to the traditional zoo aquariums there are not small exotic fishes but big inhabitants of the sea - sea-eels, skates, sturgeons, etc.

National reserve "Chersonese of Taurida"

1 Drevnyaya St.
Tel. 55-0278
9.00 a.m. - 7.00 p.m., (museum - till 5.00 p.m.)

The museum complex is located on the cape between Sandy Bay and Artillery Bay. One should go by trolleybus # 6 or # 10 to Dmitriya Ulyanova Street or Yeroshenko Street and further walk up to Drevnyay Street.

Vladimir's Cathedral is the most significant building.

The remains of the antique basilicas attract the attention of the visitors by the well-proportioned white marble columns. Well-preserved mosaic floors were discovered in one of the buildings, constructed, in the opinion of the researchers, in the 5th - 6th centuries. Count A.Uvarov studied the building in 1853. Probably the religious center of the medieval Chersonese was located in the Uvarov's basilica. Mosaics are exhibited under the shelters along one of the alleys of the reserve as well as in the museum located in two buildings of the former

Museum "Medieval Chersonese"

Chersonese "foggy" bell

A noticeable building dominates on the shore: a crossbeam with a huge bell is installed on the two massive supporting columns. It is a famous "foggy" bell cast from the trophy German cannon in 1776. During the Crimean war it was brought out with the other bells taken from the bell-towers of the city. In 1913 the bells turned out to be in the Notre-Damme Cathedral in Paris. On 6 December the same year "the prisoner" returned to Sevastopol.
It was installed on the bell-tower of the Chersonese

"Foggy" bell

Monastery (not preserved). One of the bells of the monastery rang during nasty weather warning of danger the ships floating by the shore.

In 1925, after the monastery was closed and the bells were dismantled, this copper giant was installed on the shore for the same mission. Now it one of the emblems of Chersonese.

monastery. A collection of ceramics, marble tombstones, family life tools is collected in the antique department of the museum. Coins, decorations, and other interesting findings are exhibited in the Middle Ages department.

A light summer pavilion is built on the supposed spot of christening Prince Vladimir who managed to include Kievan Rus into the number of the civilized Christian states. The monument to Prince Vladimir is located in the end of Drevnyay Street.

The antique theatre was supposed to be built in the middle of the 3rd century B.C. The fights of gladiators were arranged here in the epoch of the early Roman presence. Nowadays the Sevastopol actors and the participants of the theatre festivals perform on the stage of the theatre. The performances are also conducted near Zenon Tower and in the site at the Middle Ages museum.

The Chersonese reserve is of continuous interest for the tourists, coming here as a rule for the whole day, to walk among the unique monuments, to sit on the precipitous shore, to bathe in the caressing sea waves.

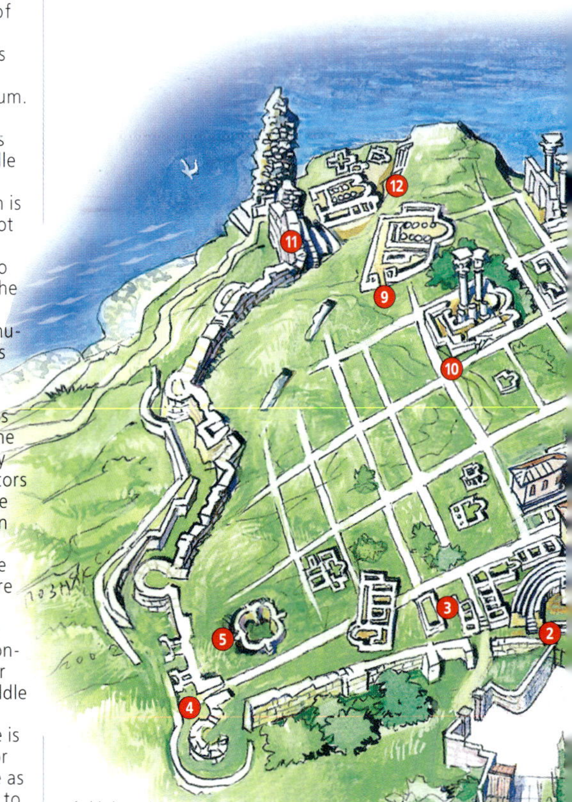

1. Main entrance
2. Antique theatre
3. A water reservoir
4. Western gate
5. Four-apse temple - memorial
6. Rich estate cellar premises ("a mint place")
7. Department of the Museum "Antique Chersonese"
8. Department of the Museum "Medieval Chersonese"
9. A basilica on the top of the hill
10. A basilica in a basilica
11. A fish-salting facility (5th -6th centuries)
12. A Western basilica
13. A basilica (6th - 10th centuries)
14. A rich inhabitant's estate (2nd -4th centuries)
15. "Foggy" bell
16. A Northern basilica (6th - 11th centuries)
17. Uvarov's basilica
18. St. Vladimir's Cathedral (1861-1892). Restored in 2001.
19. A christening site (6th century). Rotunda - a memorial sign in the commemoration of Prince Vladimir's christening (1997)
20. An embankment of an artillery battery (2nd half of the 19th century).
21. A seaside wall
22. Kruze's basilica (5th -6th centuries)
23. A harbor
24. Zenon's Tower
25. Roman barracks
26. An external wall (1st - 2nd centuries)
27. Internal gate in the peribolus between the internal and external walls
28. Near-wall burial vaults
29. Ancient city gate of Chersonese

Museum's address:

1 Drevnyaya St.

Tel. 55-0278, 24-1369

9.00 a.m. - 7.00 p.m., except Mondays

Magnificent churches dominate on some of the city hills. The history of each of the churches is unique in a way.

A burial-vault of admirals

Vladimir's cathedral was supposed to be built in the territory of Chersonese Monastery but Admiral M.Lazarev insisted that the temple was to be built within the

limits of the city. Nikolai II has chosen a site on the City hill and on 15 July 1854 laying out the foundations of the cathedral took place. The construction of the temple was interrupted during the Crimean war. Part of the money (18.000 roubles) was collected by means of selling cannonballs picked up on the battlefields.

In 1888 when the construction of the cathedral on the design of an Architect A.Avdeyev was completed, it was decided to set up a burial-vault of the outstanding admirals of the Black Sea Fleet - M.Lazarev, P.Nakhimov, V.Kornilov, V.Istomin. The cathedral became a kind of the monument to the defense of Sevastopol in 1854 - 1855.

In 1832 the cathedral was closed. The maintenance workshops and warehouses were located here. The remains of the buried officers (as the supporters of autocracy) were liquidated. This act of vandalism generates a feeling of shame and bitterness. I 1966 the decision was adopted to restore the building of the cathedral and to give it to the Museum of the heroic defense and liberation of Sevastopol. The tombstones were restored.

Since 1991 the cathedral was returned to the believers.

Petropavlovskaya Church

37 Lunacharskogo St.

The building itself is a very interesting example of the application of the elements of the Ancient Greek architecture when building an Orthodox Temple. A wooden Greek Church, earlier located on this site, was demolished during a storm. The temple erected in 1844 was restored twice. The columns of the Doric order surrender it along the perimeter. In Soviet times, just until the recent period, there was a House of Culture here - the building has extraordinary acoustic qualities. Now the church is returned to the believers.

Svyato-Nicolsky (St. Nicolas) Temple

Common cemetery in the northern side

The temple was built in 1870 by the design of an architect A.Avdeyev in the Common cemetery where the worriers perished during the defense of the city between 1854 - 1855 were buried. The cemetery consisted of the common graves (there were about 500 ones!) and monuments to the outstanding defenders of Sevastopol - General S.Khrulev, Prince M.Gorchakov, Counter-Admiral M.Kumani, etc.

More than 40.000 people were buried here. Now the new alleys are laid out in the Common cemetery where those who perished later are buried.

The church has a form of a pyramid, on the sides of which there is a list of the units of the Sevastopol garrison.

Pokrovsky Cathedral

36 Bolshaya Morskay St.

Pokrovsky Cathedral, the external side of which is covered with rich decorations, was built in 1905 by the design of an architect V.Feldman who participated in designing the building of the Sevastopol Panorama as well. For many decades the cathedral was closed for offering prayers. The church got its second life in 1992.

Pokrovsky Cathedral mosaics

All Saints Church

9-a Pozharova St.

All Saints Church built in 1822 was the only acting church in Sevastopol for a long time. It is located in the old cemetery in the Zagorodnaya (Countryside) gully.

The cathedral in commemoration of St. Prince Vladimir's christening

It turned out to be two Vladimir's cathedrals in Sevastopol. After the foundation of the first one was laid out on the City hill due to striving of Innokenty, archbishop of Chersonese and Taurida, a decision was adopted to built the temple in the territory of Chersonese Monastery. The cathedral was supposed to be erected to the celebration of the 900th anniversary of St. Vladimir's baptizing. An archeologist A.Uvarov has shown a site for the construction. He supposed that the God's Mother Christmas Temple, where Prince Vladimir was baptized, was located on this site.

The temple was erected by the design of an architect D.Grimm. Alexander II donated a part of the saint remains of Prince Vladimir. On 23 August 1861 the Emperor solemnly laid out the first stone of the future cathedral. The construction was completed in 1892 and 34 years later the temple was closed...

The cathedral was significantly demolished during the Great Patriotic War. In addition, they say that there were attempts to explode the building after the war. They started to hold praying in the half-demolished temple in 1992, and only 10 years later the restoration of the cathedral was completed.

Sevastopol is rightfully proud of his rich history keeping the memory of the well-known inhabitants of the city - politicians and worriers, enlighteners and artists...

A memorial bust of Gnat Shevchenko

Sirisk who lived in Chersonese in the 3rd century D.C. can be considered the first historian of this land. In the course of the excavations of the antique city the archeologists discovered a stone plate with an inscription: "The people appraises Sirisk... for the fact that he described the appearance of Virgo and studied friendly relations with the cities and czars truthfully and in accordance with the dignity of the state". Probably Sirisk described miraculous protection of the Chersonese goddess that saved the city from the attack of Barbarians.

Medieval Chersonese often turned out to be a place of exile of the political opponents of the ruling emperor. So, in the 3rd century in the course of the complicated intrigues the inhabitants of the city managed to enthrone to the Byzantine throne Vardan Philippic exiled from Armenia. He substituted Yustinian II who, by the way, was also exiled to Chersonese in certain time.

Alexander Suvorov and Grigory Potyomkin played a significant role in the history of Sevastopol. In fact, they are fathers of the city.

A literary glory of Leo Tolstoy starts here as well - being a lieutenant, the writer participated in the First defense of Sevastopol. He wrote the famous "Sevastopol stories" on the basis of his own experiences.

A surgeon Nikolai Pirogov who guided the activities of the nurses of the Krestovozdvizhenskaya community in the besieged city was also appraised at the same time. The professor was the first in the history of medicine who applied gypsum bandage. His numerous innovations saved lives of thousands of soldiers.

Michail Kazas, a talented Karaite artist lived a short life - only 29 years. During the four years only, prior to the beginning of the World War I, he painted several hundred canvases. Having become a victim of the Ref terror, Michail Kazas was shot in his native town. The biggest collection of his works is kept in the Simferopol Art Museum.

The name of Arkady Averchenko is also connected with Sevastopol. A satire writer was born and brought up in the city. Under his guidance in 1920 the theatre "A nest of the birds of passage" which was very popular at that time was set up. Soon the writer himself and his theatre were to immigrate to Turkey. In Constantinopol the castaway joined "A Black Rose" of Alexander Vertinsky. An excellent cabaret was set up which made great progress.

Sevastopol is a city of the military fleet. The vivid pages of the history are connected with the names of admirals, fleet leaders, and military leaders.

A sailor and a builder

The Admiral Michail Petrovich Lazarev was a courageous traveler. He made three trips round the world and together with F.Bellinsgauzen discovered Antarctica.

Being the captain of the ship of war "Azov", M.Lazarev did great during the Navarra battle (1827) with the Turkish and Egyptian Fleets. The ship of war "Azov" was the first one in the Russian Fleet awarded with the George Flag. A lieutenant P.Nakhimov, a cornet V.Kornilov, and a guardmarine V.Istomin participated in that battle... About 30 years later all the four of them were buried in the burial vault of the Vladimir's Cathedral in Sevastopol.

In 1832 M.Lazarev became the commander of the Black Sea Fleet and two years later became the Governor of the cities Sevastopol and Nikolayev. Since that time the epoch of city construction boomed: a building of the new Admiralty was erected in the Shipyard side, the Master Plan of the city was elaborated, etc.

In the square of ancient Chersonese

The city built out of the white Inkerman stones looks festive and decorated. Its sights are a subject of proud of each inhabitant of Sevastopol.

Catherine's mile
Northern side

An original road sign located at the turn to the beach "Uchkuyevka" was installed in 1786 prior to the arrival of Empress Catherine II to the Crimea. All the ten versts (3,500 feet, 1,06 km) on the way of czarina's train were marked with such columns.

The Volokhov's house
The corner of Pavlichenko and Suvorova Streets

The only preserved building of the 40-ies of the 19th century did not lose its strict symmetric faces despite the internal re-constructions. The owner of the building, a retired cornet D.Volokhov was a contractor of the construction of the first railway in the Crimea. The last apartment of Admiral V.Kornilov was located in this house.

A fountain at the former kenasa

"Wind Tower"
5 Frunze St.

An octahedral tower formed a part of the complex of buildings of the Marine library and served as a ventilating pipe. Bas-reliefs under the eaves symbolize the winds out of the Ancient Greek mythology.

The Sevastopol Central Post Office

The Palace of childhood and youth
4 Kornilova Seafront

The building of the former Institute of the physical methods of treatment, built in 1914 by the design of an architect V.Chistov, is notable for the splendor of its architectural forms and decorative ornamentation. A Corinthian portico of the main facade, an inner yard with a pool, sculptures along the both sides of the fronton lost after the restoration, depicting rushing carriers, attach a solemn and festive look to the building.

The building of the Central Post Office
21 Bolshaya Morskaya St.

The name of the designer of the building built in 1921 in the modern style is unknown. It is one of the several buildings remained uninjured in times of the Great Patriotic war.

It is impossible to tell about all the interesting buildings of Sevastopol - a famous small bridge with dragons, and a viaduct, and the building of the High Military and Engineering College (393 m long!), and many others.

Grafskaya Pristan (Landing Pier)

A wide white staircase guarded by stony lions is leading to the sea. An ancient frigate inviting the tourists to the excursion to the numerous bays of Sevastopol is peacefully strolling and pitching in the water...
Built in 1846, the landing pier is notable today as a king of an emblem of the city. It acquired its name due to the Count Mark Voynovich, Commandant of the Sevastopol Squadron. The landing pier had a formal name

as well, namely, the Catherine's landing pier, but the local people did not like it, and it disappeared.
When adopting a decision about the construction, Nikolai I first decided to reject the idea of building a colonnade, but Admiral M.Lazarev found the arguments that persuaded the sovereign to sign a project in the full scope. A funny event with a drunken cabman riding down the staircase directly into the sea in the twilight became one of the arguments in favor of building a colonnade. After the termination of the construction the columns were to hold back the reckless drivers of smart cabs.

As an example to the ancestors

The first monument in Sevastopol was erected in 1839, 10 years after a remarkable event - an exploit of the crew of the brig "Mercury", which under the command of captain-lieutenant A.Kazarsky won a victory in the battle with two Turkish ships of war. It took place during the Russian-Turkish war in 1828-1829. In the course of the reconnaissance in the Bosporus Strait an 18-cannon brig met a Turkish 110-cannon flagship and an accompanying ship with 74 cannons aboard. It was decided to fight to the bitter end and then explode their own ship together with the enemy's one. But masterly maneuverings of "Mercury" and inflexibility of its crew made the Turkish ships retreat. And although the brig had 22 shot-holes, the captain managed to bring a badly injured ship to the native harbor. Fearlessness of the crew and skillfulness of the captain deserved recognition and respect of the opponents as well as amazement and proud of the Black Sea Fleet sailors. Nikolai I ordered to make the following inscription on the monument in the commemoration of this event: "To Kazarsky. As an example to the ancestors".

On 9 May, when the inhabitants of Sevastopol celebrate a dual holiday that united the Victory Day and the day of the liberation of the city from the fascist German invaders, the festive columns of the military parade are marching along the streets of the city. The veterans of the former battles, crowned with glory and awards, followed by the military sailors of the Ukrainian and Russian Black Sea Fleets and by the students of the military colleges and schools open the parade. The celebration in honor of the veterans is not only restricted by the formal greetings on behalf of the city authorities. Each inhabitant of the City-Hero in the streets, in the cafes, and other public places will for sure express his gratitude and thankfulness to the participants of the combat actions. Of course, the number of those, who participated in the Second defense, becomes fewer and fewer. But, on the other hand, there are no people left at all who defended Sevastopol in times of the First defense, but the memory about them has been living for a century and a half! The city does not forget its heroes. The numerous monuments remind about them.

The monument to the Scuttled ships (1905, a sculptor A.Adamson) is the most famous among them. In the middle of the 19th century, Turkey, England and France, anxious by the increasing marine power of Russia, started combat actions against it without a declaration of war. The victory of the Russian fleet under the command of Admiral P.Nakhimov in the Sinop battle (in November, 1853 the Turkish Squadron was defeated at the northern coast of Asia Minor) made England and France act resolutely. It was a beginning of the Crimean war. To block the access of the enemy into the Sevastopol Bay, they locked the entrance by means of sinking the old sailing vessels. This decision of Admiral V.Kornilov's headquarters excluded the possibility of the enemy's attack on the Russian positions from the side of the sea. After the death of an admiral, when the sailors were leaving destroyed Sevastopol, they sank the rest of the Black Sea Fleet. The monument was erected in the commemoration of these events of the First defense.

The enemies were trying their best to capture Sevastopol - the military base of the Black Sea Fleet. Many glorious names were written into the history of the First defense. They are: legendary Admirals V.Istomin, V.Kornilov, and

Nakhimova square - the heart of Sevastopol

P.Nakhimov, perished in the Malakhov Kurgan; a sailor Gnat Shevchenko shielded by himself his commander N.Birulev; a courageous medical nurse Dasha Sevastopolskaya - a daughter of a common fisherman she was selflessly taking care of the wounded; a sailor Pyotr Koshka - an elusive reconnoiter, an angel-keeper of Admiral Kornilov - they were telling legends about him still under his life...

Sevastopol exceeding (in terms of both quantity of the troops and the quality of

A fort in the northern side

the armament) forces of the enemy due to not only military exploits of the sailors and infantry people. Properly built fortifications also had an important meaning. The fortifications were built under the guidance of an engineer E.Totleben. The monument to him is erected in Istorichesky (Historical) Boulevard.

Massive bombardments, which the city was inflicted to for a long time, destroyed Sevastopol. Fingers could count uninjured buildings. The defenders had to retreat to the northern side via a pontoon's bridge after the French managed to capture the Malakhov Kurgan...

In the course of the war all the participants were simply rendered lifeless, and in March 1856 in Paris a Peace Treaty was signed. The Black Sea was declared a neutral zone. Russia was forbidden to have a fleet in the Black Sea.

A half a century later they shot a movie "Defense of Sevastopol" in the style of military chronicles. In the end of the movie the veterans survived until 1911, both the Russian soldiers and their former opponents, were shown against the monument erected in the commemoration of the Crimean war. There is a Sevastopol Boulevard in Paris and a Crimean Memorial was erected in London, in Waterloo Square, in the commemoration of the events of 1853 - 1856.

Sevastopol was the first city to be bombed when the Great Patriotic war started and the enemy airplanes threw down the fist bombs on the sleeping city...

An interesting story is connected with the Sevastopol forts. In 1840 a French engineer de Gel visited the city together with his wife. Looking round the city, they were simply collecting information about its fortifications. The foreigners were not impressed very much with the docks and especially with the batteries. Having returned home, they described the defensive fortifications of the port as weak and unreliable and predicted that they would be destroyed in the framework of the first attack. Many people, who knew how strong robbery and stupidity were spread in Russia, believed it, including the employees of the military agencies. Soon they had to pay for it. The forts did not only survive attacks; coast batteries inflicted significant losses to the ships of the enemy.

Moreover the forts survived in June 1942 as well when their walls were inflicted to the storm of the German artillery shelling. These fortifications were the strong points of the defense in the northern side. Defense of Sevastopol became one of the most decisive moments in the course of the Great Patriotic war. Numerous memorials and common graves remind about those far away historic days.

"Dora" near Sevastopol

The biggest cannon of the World War II was called by this female name. In 1942 800 mm railway cannon with the weight of 1.350 metric tons and the length of the barrel about 50 m was delivered to Bakhchisarai in 100 railway cars.

One of the first shots, made at 5.25 a.m. on 5 June 1942, left the deepest shell-hole in the world with the diameter of 32 m. A shell covered a distance of 25 km for 44.8 seconds. About 50 armor-piercing shells were totally released; the weight of each shell under it was about 7 metric tons!

Between 1941 - 1942 the city was completely destroyed by the enemy artillery. There were concentrated from 37 up to 100 cannons on each kilometer of the frontline. No other city was inflicted to such a horrible shelling during the World War II.

Modern Inkerman (Belokamensk in the recent past) is the eastern suburb of Sevastopol. Many historical and architectural monuments preserved here.

Disgraced Pope

The legend says that the Pope Clement, one of the first Roman bishops, Apostle Peter's successor, was exiled for the propagation of Christianity to the wild places in the suburbs of Chersonese where there were stone quarries (Inkerman's stones were popular since ancient times). A cave that later became the St. Clement's Church was made in the rock by the exiled Pope himself. Clement did not stop his missionary activities in the stone quarries. He was killed for those activities on instruction of the authorities. Later he was canonized. A healing monastery spring is named after him. A chronicle of the 12th century says about the remains of an unknown saint, making different miracles. It is very probable that they were the remains of St. Clement. The author of the manuscript - an Orthodox priest Yakov, a member of the Russian embassy - tells about his attempt to extracts the remains and bring them away to Russia. A saint whom he saw during a dream forbade him to do it.

Cave cells

The ruins of the defensive towers on the top of the Monastery rock attract the attention of the tourists. The fortress Kalamita ("rushy" - in ancient Greek) built by the sovereigns of the Feodoro Principality was located here. The fortress performed the function of the guard fore-post in the narrow estuary of Akhtyar Bay protecting Avlita, a port of the Feodoro Principality inhabitants, located in the shore. The trading vessels were unloaded in the port, and further boats transferred the commodities - the estuary of the bay was too shallow for the vessels.

At that time Kalamita was a reason of hostility between the Genoese and the Feodoro Principality inhabitants because the port and the fortress compete with the Chembalo trading business. In 1433 the Genoese conquered and got fired Kalamita, but soon the fortress was restored, and the former enemies had to unite before the face of a new danger - the raids of the Turks.

In the period of the Osmanian Empire dominion the Turks strengthened the Kalamita fortress and the settlement acquired the name of Inkerman, i.e., "a cave fortress". It was called in such a way because of the fact that it was located on the top of the hill, in which the caves of the Christian Monastery were made. Modern researchers date setting up of the monastery to the 7th - 9th centuries. There were about 200 caves here, several churches, two of them have been preserved - named after St. Clement and St. Martin. The Byzantine Greeks who escaped into Taurida founded a monastery. Later exiles were sent there.

Ruins of Kalamita and the St. Trinity Church

At the foot of the rock there is the St. Trinity Church. In 1852 the Inkerman kinoviya (a small monastery) was set up here. It was active up to 1926. The Soviet authorities closed the monastery. Its activities only resumed in the 90-ies of the 20th century. The St. Clement's Monastery is located here nowadays. The headquarters of the Chapayev's infantry division was located in it during the last months of the Second defense of Sevastopol. A memorial plague and an obelisk on the common grave remind about it.

Those coming to Sevastopol via the railway can see cells and the other monastery facilities through the windows of the train. The monastery is closed for visitors.

Similar to the St. Clement's Monastery, St, George's Monastery is closed for visitors as well. But one can make a walk in the picturesque suburbs of the monastery.

The legend says that in 890 several Greeks were captured by a horrible storm on the rock eastwards the Phiolentus Cape. Feeling an inevitable death, the miserable people started to pray to George the Winner asking for protection. And a miracle occurred: the storm was immediately over, and the image of the St. George appeared on the rock. A year later the saved set up a small and secluded monastery on the remains of the basilica of the 6th century. They started to call the rock itself as the rock of the Saint Image. For many centuries the cave monastery remained a worshiped Christian relic in the southeastern coast of the Crimea.

A cross rock

In the 19th century the territory of the monastery was significantly enlarged. Two more temples were built - the St. George's Church (1815) and the Exaltation of the Cross Church (1850). The latter was located on the top of the cliff. The longest stony staircase in the Crimea led to the lower temple.

In 1891 in the commemoration of the 1.000th anniversary of setting up a monastery the lower cave temple was restored and, in addition, they installed a stony cross with the image of George the Winner killing a dragon on the rock of the Saint Image.

Grigory Moskvitch mentioned in the Crimean tourist guide in 1910 that in the monastery "there is a hotel with a sufficient number of rooms with a very modest furniture". The visitors could get a samovar here, eggs, milk, and butter. There were two monastery dachas at the shore to let. They were coming here to improve their health - they noticed that the air in this locality was of a healing nature. "Many hopeless nephritis patients, hard anemia patients, who suffered from chronic bronchitis, recovered themselves significantly here within two months".

Phiolentus Cape

There is no unanimous opinion as to the origin of its name. In ancient times the cape called Perpetium, i.e., "girlish". Probably, it was the very place where the temple of Virgo was located in pre-Christian times. The today's name of the cape is to some extent an echo of the old legend about the bloody sacrifices committed by Iphigenia in the Tauri sacred place - "Violent" in Latin means "cruel". Isn't it a reminder of the cruelty of the Tauri who threw the miserable foreigners, unfortunate enough to turn out themselves near the coast of the Tauris, down into the sea from the high rock.

A beach at the rock

Phiolentus Cape

How old is the picturesque settlement turned from the regional district centre into a part of the city district of Sevastopol after 1957? The historians suppose that there was a settlement on this site 30 centuries ago. Correspondingly Balaklava is one of the most ancient cities of the country...

A number of the researchers of creative activities of great Homeros are inclined to think that this locality was a bay described in the 10th song of "Odyssey". According to the poet, the cruel and bloodshed listrigons lived here.

The history of Balaklava starts from the 8th century B.C. In that time there was an early Tauris settlement here.

The Greeks called this locality "Le Sumbolon limne" that means "a Bay of symbols". The Genoese who conquered the Crimean coast in the middle of the 14th century erected a fortress of Chembalo over the bay including the upper and lower towns. The remains of the Genoese fortifications are viewed in a good way on the top of the cliff at the entrance of the harbor.

"Balaklava" Restaurant

Since 1475 the Turks became the masters of Chembalo. The town acquired a new name - Balaklava (a distorted own from the Turk's "balyk-yuve", i.e., "a fish-pond"). Three centuries later the Turks left the city in compliance with the terms of the Kuchuk-Kainardjiysky Treaty. A Greek battalion was located in the city.

In 1787 when Catherine II was approaching Sevastopol she was met by the detachment of "Amazons" formed from the Balaklava female-Greeks...

During the Crimean War a British battalion was located here. The British built the fist railrway in the peninsula (after the termination of the combat operation it was dismantled and brought away).

Later Balaklava turned into a small resort settlement. A writer Kuprin liked to come here. In addition to the ruins of Chembalo the tourists are attracted by the Twelve Apostles Church (41 Rubtsova St.), built in the 14th century.

After viewing the local sights one can attend a fish restaurant "Balaklava" located in 1 May Square or a cafe "Listrigons" located in Kalicha Street.

Suburbs of Greater Sevastopol

A borderline between Greater Yalta and Sevastopol region is in the picturesque places. The Aya ("saint, sacred" in Greek) Cape, Laspi, Batiliman or Sarych Cape (the most southern spot of the Crimea and of the whole Ukraine) - these beautiful corners of the Crimean coast attract the lovers of the beauty of nature. A wonderful panorama of these sites is open from the Baidarsky mountain-pass: transparent waters of Laspi

A view on the Aya Cape

Bay, relic groves of the Aya Cape sight. A rock with the remains of the Kokiya-Isar fortress (10th - 13th centuries) dominates over the cape. Balaklava is notable for the remarkable beaches located in small bays. The local people call Micro-yalo ("small shore") a Silver beach, Megalo-yalo ("big shore") - a Golden beach. It is easier to get there by sea. Balaklava boatmen will bring you to the secluded bays with their mysterious grottoes at symbolic price.

A view on the bay

Saki - a kingdom of curative mud

Here, on the bottom of the lake, the earth which heals illnesses lies...

Pliny Senior

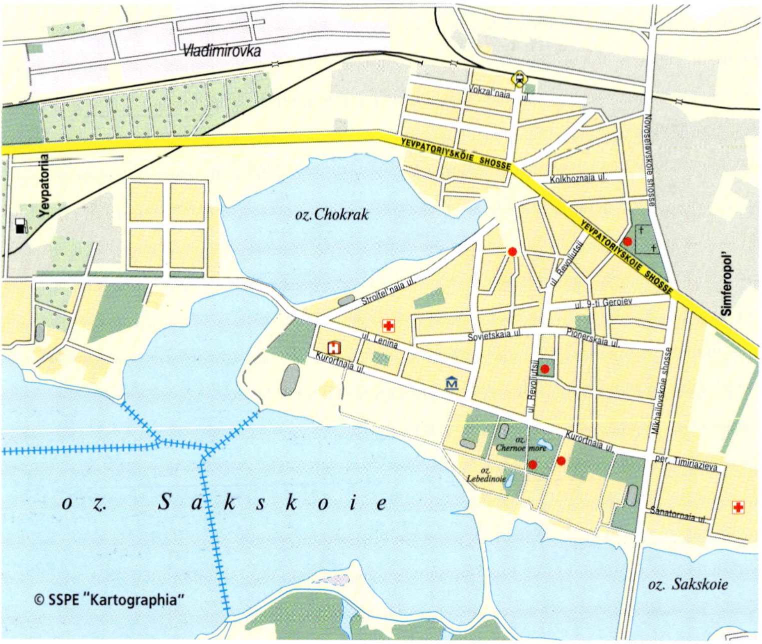

History in a few lines

1827 - *foundation of the first in the country mud-baths.*

February, 1855 - *the settlement was destroyed during the bombardment of the general S. Khrulyov's forces by the English-French artillery.*
1858 - *migrants from Poltava province, and later - Konstantinopol Greeks come here.*
1917 - *the building of the Saki bromine plant.*
1952 - *giving the status of a town to Saki.*
2002 - *more than 30,000 people reside here.*

One of the oldest balneological health resorts of the country is situated on the shore of the salt Sakskoye lake, near the Crimean western sea-coast washed by the waters of the Kalamitsky bay. Long since the famous tchoomaks' (Ukrainian ox-cart drivers') carts moved slowly for salt to Saki. The salt extracted here was transported on carts with yoked oxen. On this unhurried transport the tchoomaks had travelled more than 1,000 km.

The name Saki reminds of a nation who lived in ancient times in the territory of the Crimea - the Scythians were named Saks by the Persians. The settlement received its name from the Russian sovereign Catherine II only a couple of centuries ago when there was no trace of the Scythians already.

The unique medicative factors of the famous lake are successfully supplemented by the combination of the sea and steppe climates. The average temperature of June is +22°C, of February - about 0°C. The summer heat is softened by sea breezes, the cool nights are warmed by the steppes mild breath. The caressing sun shines here about 2500 hours a year.

The Saki mud wonder-working properties have been known from the old times, the ancient scientists Pliny Senior (the I century), Klavdy Prolomei (the II century), and others had mentioned them. In 1807 the mud of the Sakskoye lake was researched by the French chemist Desser, and since 1882 scientific medical observations concerning mudtherapy were carried out by the Yevpatoriya uyezd (district) physician N. Ozhe. A large-scale building of health resorts spread here at the end of the XIX century - the beginning of the XX century.

The prominent physicians N. Burdenko and S. Nalbandov who have given the most valuable scientific recommendations concerning the mudtherapy worked at Saki health-centres in the middle of the last century.

Many cafes have a ramp

The small health-resort town is at a distance of 20 km from Yevpatoriya and of 45 km from Simferopol.

TRANSPORT

The railway communication connects Saki in summer with Kiev, Kharkov, Dnepropetrovsk, Minsk, Moscow, St. Petersburg. Electric trains often leave Simferopol for here.

Coaches leave for Saki from Simferopol coach station every half-hour. The coach communication connects Saki with the airport "Tsentralny" (Central") situated in the capital of the Autonomy.

The town transport of the health resort is represented by several bus routes. The buses will take the holiday-makers to rest bases, sanatoriums, and boarding houses.

RESIDENCE

Those who have come to Saki without a voucher (and people come here in the main for treatment) can settle at the only town hotel "Chaika" ("Sea-gull") planned for 104 lodgers. At the hotel there are single, double, and three-lodgers rooms at a price from UAH 8 up to UAH 40 for a person a day, depending on the level of the lodging comfort. The hotel is situated next to the sanatoria where one can purchase a voucher-order for treatment. The voucher for treatment costs about UAH 900 for 24 days, the telephones for receiving information: 24-574, 23-444. In order that local physicians could prescribe you necessary procedures, you should collect medical certificates at the polyclinics at the place of your residence. By the way, a voucher for a sanatorium can be also bought there. The second version of choosing a lodging is the private sphere. The apartment-intermediary bureau will help you in your search for an inexpensive apartment.

NOURISHMENT

In Saki there are enough good inexpensive cafes and dining-rooms. An approximate cost of a dinner - UAH 10. Most of the establishments are located in the health-resort zone, there are restaurants and bars attached to sanatoriums.

People suffering from illnesses of the locomotor system often come to Saki, and the town powers try to give them everything necessary. In order that it should be convenient to enter premises on an invalid carriage the entrances to cafes, barber's and hairdresser's, shops have the form of a ramp.

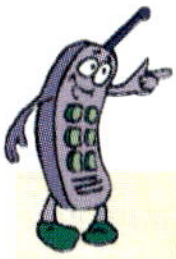

Addresses and telephones:

Municipal department of militia *tel. 23-655*

Officer on duty of the State Traffic Inspectorate *tel. 25-233*

Emergency aid station *tel. 23-703*

Water-rescue station *tel. 99-273*

Chemist's shops *tel. 27-578*
(information bureau)

Health-resort polyclinics
Kurortny park *tel. 27-345*

Head post-office
Revolyutsii square *tel. 24-222*

Bank "Privatbank"
2 Revolyutsii St. *tel. 26-131*

Coach station
5 Simferopolskaya St. *tel. 26-380*

Railway station *tel. 27-679*

Hotel "Chaika"
71 Kurortnaya St. *tel. 23-36*

A higher category room at the hotel "Chaika"

Apartment bureau
12 Lenina St. *tel. 24-290*

CAFES:

"Tabako"
4 Kurortnaya St. *tel. 21-394*
working hours: 11.00-01.00

"Monte-Carlo"
25 Lenina St. *tel. 24-239*
working hours: 11.00-24.00

"Zelyony mir" ("Green world") *tel. 21-796*
5 Kovalyova St. round-the-clock

The private residence of Cesarevitch (the heir to the throne in tsarist Russia)

Nikolai II and Cesarevitch Aleksei

The building in which the museum of local lore, history, and economy has settled was erected in 1913. The two-storey private residence in the park zone has been built for Cesarevitch Aleksei - the only son of emperor Nikolai II. The boy was notable for his poor health, suffered from hemophilia - this is a hereditary blood disease handed down by the woman's line, but only men fall ill with it. The court physicians hoped that the Saki miraculous mud will help to have cured the successor to the throne. But the First world war had begun, and the royal family had no longer come to the Crimea.

Saki is not a tourist centre, but one can perfectly well combine one's treatment with a cultural program.

THE MUSEUM OF LOCAL LORE, HISTORY, AND ECONOMY

29 Kurortnaya St.
10.00-17.00,
except for Saturday, Monday

In the museum halls they have developed an exposition which tells about the history of the health resort, a part of it is dedicated to the mudtherapy. On the first floor there is a show-room where local artists' works are represented.

The Cesarevitch's private residence

The museum workers organize temporary subject exhibitions, for instance, an exhibition of samovars, etc.

THE HEALTH-RESORT PARK

"For entertaining the patients there are a shady park, well maintained, in which a musical orchestra plays every day, trips to the sea, some games, as, for example, lawn-tennis, skittles, musical and literary parties at the clinic common hall, dances, etc.", informs the guide-book to the Crimea published at the beginning of the last century.

Actually, the Kurortny park, laid as far back as 1890-1892 by the health-resort keeper, P. Melnichenko, is a real pride of the small town. On a spacious area of more than 60 ha one can count more than 80 species of trees and shrubs, among them there are many exotic forms. The shady park lanes and lawns, small ponds and fountains attract us at a hot noon. Several sanatoriums, a lot of cultural compositions and monuments are situated in the park zone.

THE TOWN TEMPLES

The orthodox believers can attend service at the Svyato-Ilinskaya church situated at 38 Simferopolskaya St. In 2003 the temple marks its centenary by celebration.

A mosque was recently built at the entry to Saki from the side of Sevastopol.

The Svyato-Ilinskaya church

LAKES

Saki is a land of salt lakes. There are as many as three of them in the town's vicinity, not counting shallow estuaries. The Sakskoye lake - by far the most well-known of them - has turned the out-of-the-way settlement into a unique health

resort. The Saki mud-baths which were opened in 1827 were broadly known not only in the tsarist Russia, but also far out of its bounds.

A dam divides the lake in two. Its western part is the raw materials base of a chemical plant: here they produce hydrogen peroxide, ethyl bromide, and potassium permanganate. In the eastern part they extract silt for sanatoria of the Saki health resort and other Crimean health-centres. The lake area is about 15 km2, it depth does not exceed 1 m.

The lake Kizil-Yar separated from the Kalamitsky bay by a sand embankment is situated to the south of the Sakskoye lake. At the Crimean war beginning the forces of the French-English coalition landed at the territory between the lakes. That army besieged Sevastopol during many months. In February, 1855 the forces under the command of the general S. Khrulyov, who later undertook the storm of enemy's fortifications in Yevpatoriya which has ended unsuccessfully, were quartered here.

The new mosque

Sasyk-Sivash, the biggest salt lake of the Crimea which had been formed of a sea bay several thousand years ago is located to the north-east of the town. In spite of that venerable age, it is younger than other Crimean lakes. Along the sand embankment on which a branch-line has been laid the lake stretches from the Saki outskirts up to Yevpatoriya. Here the main salt extraction was carried out. The area of the watercourse is over 75 km2, the maximum depth is 1.2 m.

How had salt lakes arisen? Many centuries ago sea bays which penetrated deep into dry land had been separated from the sea by sand barriers. Because the estuaries were shallow the following processes proceeded in them under the action of natural factors: evaporation of water from the surface under the action of the sun rays increased the salt concentration in the lake, the atmospheric precipitation influenced the chemical nature of the estuary water. Gradually there formed the brine, that is, a concentrated salt solution.

The origin of the silt mud is organic. In summer in warm water the reproduction of microorganism takes place at a vast rate. They perish with the lapse of time, accumulate on the bottom, and decompose. The complex oily mixture arising as the result of this process has curative properties.

In addition to the silt and brine it is worth to mention the mineral springs. Wells, the deepest in the country, have been drilled in Saki - the water is extracted from the depth of about 970 m. The slightly alkaline water "Krymskaya mineralnaya" ("Crimean mineral") (the "Yesentuki-4" type) is used for treatment of digestive organs.

Saki in persons

At the territory of the Saki oldest mud-baths, bearing now the name of N. Burdenko, professor N. Golovkinsky, a well-known Crimean hydrogeologist, organized in 1897 a water observatory for controlling the local lakes. A tower which is called the "Golovkinsky tower" has lasted out up to the present time.

Nikolai Gogol who was treated at the local health-centre lived in Saki some time. At the building of the block No. 5 the Ukrainian poetess Lesya Ukrainka lived in summer of 1890. In the park of the sanatorium "Saki" there are monuments to well-known men of letters.

One of the Saki health-centres bears the name of a talented physician, academician Nikolai Burdenko. Owing to his research hope and health have been returned to many patients. A monument to the scientist has been erected by the entrance to the main building of the sanatorium.

The Saki district has a reputation for its balneological factors: curative mud, estuaries brine, splendid sea beaches. It is considered that by its characteristics the bottom silt of the Sakskoye lake surpasses the famous mud of the Dead Sea. Only the Moinakskoye lake in Yevpatoriya possesses similar properties. The mudtherapy gives a tremendously strong result, but one should be engaged in self-treatment in no circumstances - the effect might be exactly opposite.

The salubrious influence of silt deposits had been noticed as long ago as by ancient Egyptians who applied the following procedure: sections of skin, and more often the whole body was coated with pre-heated mud, and the person was exposed to the influence of the sun till full drying of the mud mask. After this the patient had been washed in the lake and some time was in the salt water taking a brine bath.

But such a procedure was not fit categorically for people with violation of the cardiovascular system. Therefore later there has been a switch to the principles of the so called "medallions". The mud mass in the form of oval flat cakes was put on wooden platforms protected reliably from the wind. The patient was coated with mud pre-heated up to 48-50°C, except for his neck and head, and left to lie for 15-30 minutes. Then he was washed under a warm shower. Also, they tried to dilute the mud with heated water, but this procedure as before created large loading on the heart and vessels. It was necessary to look for sparing technique and new methods of treatment, and the Saki mud-baths doctors set to it in the end of the XIX century.

Gradually several sanatoria specializing in treatment of the locomotor system, nervous system, respiration organs, gynecologic diseases, of male and female infertility, etc. have been erected on the lake-side.

We want warn the holiday-makers once more against the temptation to set to self-treatment, the more so, that the necessary consultation can be received in the town's health-resort polyclinics.

Healing with mud

In the anthology "Picturesque Russia" (volume 5) which was published in 1898 a curious legend was cited.
A tchoomak passed by his cart heavily loaded with saltbags through the estuary. And what a nuisance: the oxen has stopped exactly in the middle of the swamp not wanting to go farther. However hard the infuriated coachman whipped the pigheads, the cart did not move from the place. The felling had gone far forward, and the poor wretch had to come down from the cart in order to force the animals to move ahead. But the cart had stuck fast in the mud. The whole night the tchoomak stamped in the mud trying to help the oxen to pull out the cargo. Only before daybreak things have taken a turn for the better. The muzhik, collapsed and exhausted, had sat down on the cart, and the tired oxen pushed off along the dusty road... And already at home the tchoomak had found out that his effort was not left without a reward: the chronic pain in his legs had disappeared without leaving a trace after the night he had passed away in the wonder-working swamp.

Dinosaurs by the Saki health-centre

Even usual bathing in the estuary demand fulfilment of definite rules:

1. one should bath at the air temperature no less than +29°C;
2. one should not bath more often than once a day, the best time for water procedures - from 14:00 till 16:00;
3. the first bathing is to last no more than 5 minutes;
4. one should not bath at once after taking food;
5. after bathing one should take a fresh-water shower, it is dangerous to dry or bask in the sun.

Yevpatoriya - the charm of the "wild" West

... I feel sorry very much for those who have not been to Yevpatoriya...

V. Mayakovsky

History in a few lines

■ The town by the sea in the flat part of the Crimea is renowned for excellent sand beaches, warm caressing sea, and moderate prices of lodging and products. Families with small children like to come here for their rest.

The VI - V centuries B.C. *- the foundation of Kerkinitida by Greeks-settlers.*

The IV century B.C. *- the polis becomes dependent of Khesones.*

The II century B.C. *- the beginning of the Scythian plundering raids.*

The I century B.C. *- the Mitridat's VI forces come to the aid of the Greeks.*

The XV century *- the foundation by Turks of the fortress Gezlev.*

1736 *- the town was seized and burnt by the Russian forces.*

A combination of dry steppe air and salt iodic fumes creates a healthy microclimate in the Yevpatoria region. The shallow Kalamitsky bay gets warmed quickly, the bathing season in Yevpatoria begins early, at the end of May, and continues till the end of September. The average temperature of July is +23°C, of February - 1°?. The sun shines here for 2,384 hours a year.

The first Greek vessels came in the spacious bay of the future Yevpatoria in the VI - the beginning of the V century B.C. The ancient settlement Kerkinitida was formed over 2,500 years ago. Gradually its possessions were expanded, the khora (an agricultural district) had included the settlements by the Moinakskoye lake and in the area of the present children's camp "Luchisty". The Kerkinitida residents were occupied with fishing, farming, stock-breeding. The polis had become a large trade centre of the peninsula north-western part. By its western extremity, on the cape Tarkhankut, the port Kalos-Limen (the "excellent harbour" if translated from Greek) had emerged soon. At present on the spot of the ancient port the settlement Chernomorskoye is situated.

A century later Kerkinitida and all the small settlements along the Crimea western seacoast up to the Kalos-Limen became dependent of more powerful Khersones. With the appearance of nomads-Scythians in the Tavrida steppes (from the II century B.C. till the III-IV centuries) the polis more than once became the military spoils of the Scythian tsars. The Pont's tsar Mitridat VI Yevpator had not once rescued the Greek towns, defended them from plundering raids, but still Kerkinitida had gradually fallen into decay under the nomads blows... In the memory of those times the town which emerged by far later on the spot of the perished Kerkinitida was given the name of Yevpatoria by Empress Katherine II.

After the seizure of the Crimea by Turks on the spot of the Greek polis the fortress Gezlev had grown. At present not a trace remains of the powerful stronghold walls - with the lapse of time they were pulled down for construction of houses. There had formed a sad image of the Turkish town - as well as in Kafa , a centre of slave-trade was here. Gezlev was occupied by Russian forces several times during the Russian-Turkish wars. The town was substantially destroyed in 1736 by the general Minikh's army, it managed to rise from the ruins only at the end of the XIX century.

In 1886 on the shore of the Moinakskoye lake mud-baths were built. The "Primorskaya

An old narrow street of the town

sanatoriya" has become the Yevpatoria first private health-centre. In the early XX century buildings of country-cottages and boarding houses spread widely.

At present Yevpatoria is, in the first place, a children's health resort. The Black Sea natural peculiarities in that region are not the least of the factors. The depth here is small, the sand shore is sloping, there are no stones, rocks, and holes, sudden tides do not occur - the parents may with a clear conscience send their child to the Yevpatoria children's camp.

1905 - *the opening of the first private health-centre of Yevpatoria.*
1913 - *the mud-baths were connected with the centre of the town by a tram communication.*
1915 - *the building of the railway.*
1965 - *Yevpatoria receives the status of a children's health resort.*
2002 - *more than 110,000 people reside in the town.*

Addresses and telephones

Municipal department of militia *tel.* 21-587

Officer on duty of the State Traffic Inspectorate *tel.* 60-557

Emergency aid station *tel.* 33-164

Water-rescue station *tel.* 30-577

Town information bureau *tel.* 30-224

Railway station
Privokzalnaya St. *tel.* 51-411

Coach station
124, Internatsionalnaya St. *tel.* 33-224

Port arrival and departure building
Moryakov Sq. *tel.* 32-495

Head post-office
3/5, Bratyev Buslayevykh St.

Trunk-call office
33, Frunze St. *tel.* 60-002

Bank "Privatbank"
41/28-a, Nekrasova St. *tel.* 33-295

Bank "Kreditbank"
100, Demysheva St. *tel.* 28-490

TRANSPORT

Yevpatoria is located aside of the Crimea main highways. The railway and a motor-car route connect the town with the Autonomous Republic's capital. The distance to Simferopol is 66 km.

In winter the long-distance trains go to Yevpatoria only from Kiev and Moscow. From June the town is additionally connected by through service with Kharkov, Dnepropetrovsk, Minsk, and other towns.

If one has not succeeded to take a ticket to Yevpatoria, one can reach the station Ostryakovo by any train bound for Simferopol, than to take the electric train bound for Yevpatoria. The electric trains depart every 1.5-2 hours.

The Yevpatoria coach station is located next to the railway station. Over ten trips a day to Yevpatoria are carried out from the coach station "Kurortnaya".

The town transport of Yevpatoria consists of buses and trams. The "narrow-gauge railway" which remained intact from the early XX century is something worth seeing in the town. The tram slowly crawls on the rails laid as far back as before the First world war. Very likely, this is rather an exotic than an operational type of transport.

Those who wish to carry out a trip to Istanbul are to apply to the information bureau of the marine passenger terminal. Motor ships depart to the capital of Turkey twice a week.

The tram-"narrow-gauge railway"

RESIDENCE

Most of the Yevpatoria hotels are concentrated not far from the coastline, in the health resort zone.

The tourist hotel "Yevpatoria" is the remotest from the sea, but on the other hand it has its own beach, and real tourists are not afraid of walking tours.

The hotel "Ukraina" ("Ukraine") is intended for 300 tenants; the chamber hotel "Apogei" ("Culmination") has only 24 rooms, of them - 5 rooms de luxe, 11 - semi-de luxe ones, the rest ones - rooms of the I category (only the rooms de luxe are equipped with air-conditioners).

The hotel - boarding house "Volna" is situated on the Moinakskoye lake shore

"Volna" ("Wave") situated practically out of town works as a boarding house: nourishment, improving from a health point of view, it is next to the Moinakskoye lake, the sea-coast is behind - this is a real recreation centre.

An alternative to the stay at hotels is the residence at the private sector. Apply to the apartment-intermediary bureau or directly to the Yevpatorians - they meet new-comers at the town's station.

The popularity of Yevpatoria as an inexpensive health resort grows swiftly. The health resort infrastructure including the public catering system and the network of establishments for passing the leisure-time develops accordingly.

NOURISHMENT

Moderate prices with a wide assortment of offered dishes are a pleasant peculiarity of the Yevpatoria cafes.

We offer to those who are fond of the national cuisine tasting to visit the cafe "Karaman" where they serve Karaite dishes: yantyks ((pies resembling chebureks (kind of meat pasty eaten in the Crimea and the Caucasus), but fried without oil)), khamur-dolma (soup with "small ears"), koi-kavurma (roast mutton), etc. The cafe is situated in a shady small courtyard next to kenasas.

The Greek restaurant "Kasper" is cosy establishment with medium level of prises (the cost of a dinner is UAH 30-40).

Those who wish to dine out quickly and inexpensively and also those who prefer the dietetic cuisine will leave satisfied having visited the cafe "Molochnoye" ("Milky"). Here they make a baked omelette, tasty pies, dishes of curds, etc. The cost of a dinner is UAH 5-7.

The cafe "Belfigor" attracts by a large selection of vegetarian dishes. The cost of a dinner is UAH 10-15.

The fast food restaurant "Kolizei" is located in the town's centre and is open round-the-clock.

In the town there are many cafes and small restaurants the menu of which is intended from small visitors, for instance, "Lakomka" ("Gourmand"), "Snezhinka" ("Snowflake"), "Alyonka", and others.

LEISURE-TIME OF CHILDREN AND ADULTS

Good sand beaches stretch in the west from the marine passenger terminal to the settlement Zaozyorny and from the Plyazhny lane at the east sea-coast along the embankment by the lake Sasyk-Sivash.

Cinemas, two children's theatres, a dolphinarium, an attraction park - here children also will have a jolly good time.

Attraction park

To adults, in addition to bars, discotheques, billiards halls, etc. we offer to visit the entertaining centre "Solnyshko" ("Caressing sun"). At the territory of the vast out-of-town complex there is a unique dancing hall for 1,500 visitors.

The "Caressing sun" at the highway between Yevpatoria and Saki

Addresses and telephones

"Alyonka"
43, Tokareva St. *tel.* **61-586**
10.00-23.00

"Karaman"
68, Karaimskaya St.
12.00-22.00 *tel.* **33-035**

"Kolizei" *17, Gogolya St.*
00.00-24.00

"Kasper"
105, Demysheva St.
11.00-24.00 *tel.* **27-828**

"Belfigor" *tel.* **60-441**
160, Demysheva St.
10.00 - till the last client

"Molochnoye"
55, Revolyutsii St.
8.00-21.00 *tel.* **36-131**

Cinema-concert hall "Otdykh"
Frunze park

A.S. Pushkin theatre
Teatralnaya Sq. *tel.* **32-490**

Puppet-show "Poteshki"
4, Muzeiny lane *tel.* **61-671**

Children's centre "Zolotoi klyuchik" ("Golden key")
5, Barteneva St. *tel.* **62-524**

Cinema "Raketa" ("Rocket")
1, Lenina St. *tel.* **31-078**

Dolphinarium *tel.* **58-900**

Tennis-courts *tel.* **33-047**
25-a, Polupanova St.

Water club
Gorky embankment

Entertaining complex "Solnyshko"
the 51-st km of the highway Yevpatoria-Simferopol

The Yevpatoria temples had been erected at the expense of numerous communities (Armenian, Moslem, Karaite, etc.) professing various religions, therefore the cult architecture of the town is so diversified.

The Karaites' spiritual centre

By tradition the Karaite meeting-house interior is very modest. It is characterized by the simplicity of the decoration, a wooden carved altar and benches for those who are praying - to decorate the walls of a temple by drawings, pictures, icons is not usual. Antique chandeliers are the sole decoration of the kenasa premises.
In addition to the kenasas, the complex of the Karaite spiritual centre includes a religious school, an ethnographic museum where there are materials on history, culture, religion, and literature of the Crimean Karaites, and also articles of their way of life, clothes, etc. Also here there are a library and a cafe where they make dishes of the national cuisine.
The small marble courtyard with vines looks solemnly and smartly - everything here breathes freshness, peace, and pacification.

Kenasa
68, Karaimskaya St.

The Yevpatoria Karaite community, the most numerous in the Crimea, was formed at the close of the XVIII century when the Karaites had left the cave town Chufut-Kale near Bakhchisarai. Having settled down in Yevpatoria, the Karais (the self-name of the Karaites) built meeting-houses - kenasas by the project of brothers Babovich. The Cathedral kenasa is designed for festive divine services, the Small one - for everyday services. In addition to their cult meaning, the kenasas are of enormous historical-cultural value as a masterpiece of national architecture. The complex can be examined on an excursion, the admission to its territory is a paid one (UAH 2) - the kenasa is both a temple and a museum.

An enormous vine grows immediately behind the gate put into shape of an ancient portico, to the left of the wall. They assert that it is about 200. At photographs imprinting the Emperor Nicholas' II visit of the Karaite object of worship this vine thickness is already considerable. Near the ancient vine in the wall there is a small fountain for lavabo erected at the expense of the community ecclesiastical Head's daughter means. In the courtyard of the complex there are a lapidary, memorial plaques on which the names of the Karaite nation sons who lost their lives in battles for their fatherland have been inscribed.

The meeting-house in Demysheva St.

The Greek church
1, Bratyev Buslayevykh St.

The temple in honour of the holy prophet Illya built in 1891-1892 is situated by the embankment, near to the yacht-club wharf. The church is an acting one now, it is protected by the state as an architectural monument.

The Armenian church
44, Internatsionalnaya St.

A beautiful cult building being an architectural monument was built in 1885 by the town's Armenian community.

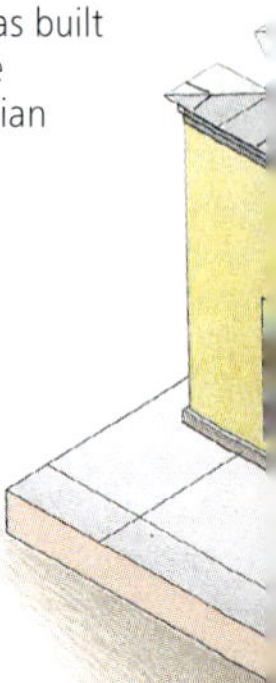

The interior of the mosque

The Saint Nicholas - wonder-worker cathedral

the corner of Revolyutsii and Tuchina streets

The Orthodox temple was sanctified in 1898 in the memory of the town's liberation in the course of the Crimean war. Together with the Pyatnichnaya (Friday) mosque situated beside, it forms the inimitable face of Yevpatoria. The acting church accommodate up to 2,000 parishioners.

The mosque Dzhuma-Dzhami

36, Revolyutsii St.

The Cathedral Moslem temple was built in 1552 by the project of the famous Turkish architect Khodzha Sinan (the creator of the mosques Shakh-Zade and Suleimaniye in Istanbul, Selimiye in Edirne. Sinan is the author of projects of about 300 prominent constructions).

The Pyatnichnaya mosque ("Dzhuma" in Turkish is Friday. On that day, according to legends, the prophet Mukhammad was born) had been built to order of the Crimean khan Devlet-Girei I. According to his intention, the firman, the right to the Crimean khanate received from the Turkish sultan, should be announced only here. The document signed by the khan had to be kept in the mosque.

The silhouette of the building reminds one of the Istanbul's Ai-Sofia in a decreased form. From both sides of the many-dome mosque two 30-meter minarets, surrounded by small balconies - sherfe, take the air. From there the muezzin calls the faithful for a prayer.

The axonometry of the Tatar mosque Dzhuma-Dzhami

Unfortunately, many a page of this ancient town's history has been lost, but that which lasted out is, without doubt, interesting and captivating.

Dervishes - wandering monks

A "dervish" means a "beggar" if translated from Persian. So the devout people striving for salvation of their sole are called according to the Moslem religion. Dervishes' communities, according to legends, were already founded in the I century of Khidzhra (the beginning of the Moslem chronology). The dervish way of life made its start from India. This trend totals about 70 orders, the monks' clothes differ by their colour and cut. The order of the so called "revolving dervishes" arouses a special interest. In the evening the monks gathered together at the mosque for a prayer and, having stood in a circle, began to yell the word "guve" ("He, that is, the God, moves everything"). The dervishes were held sacred, it was considered that their prayers heal. Therefore people brought invalids and feeble to the mosque, laid them on the floor, covered them with robes, and the monks standing around began to offer prayers and at the same time to spin. Their movements grew quicker and quicker, their yells - louder and louder, running into frenzy. Then their spinning gradually slowed down.

The dervishes' tekie

The house of the town mayor, S. Duvan

Tekiye of dervishes

the corner of Internatsionalnaya and Karayeva streets

The complex of the XVI-XVIII centuries constructions is a unique monument of the Crimean-Tatar architecture. The tekiye (Moslem cloister) in Yevpatoria is the only lasted out one in the Crimea. The cloister square building is surrounded by a not high outhouse with cut off angles in which the cells are located. The mosque by the entrance to the tekiye was built later. A minaret joins it from the east. The constructions are surrounded by a blind fence on the top of which they had poured in broken glass protecting against uninvited visitors.

Now restoration work is carried out here. The Tea house (the XIX century) joining the courtyard from the west will be included in the cloister complex. Its name gives rise to a light perplexity, as it is well known that on the ground floor a coffee-house was formerly, and on the first floor - hotel rooms.

The remains of Kerkinitida

The museum of local lore, history, and economy

11/2, Duvanovskaya St.
☎ 62-727 ⌚ 10.00-18.00, except for Wednesday

The museum collections total about 80,000 exhibits: ancient ceramics and articles of the town way of life of the XIX - the early XX centuries, ancient coins and documents of the Crimean war times, old photographs and personal belonging of well-known Yevpatoria citizens. In the department of nature the Crimean steppe rich fauna is produced.

The site of ancient settlement "Chaika" ("Seagull")

Settlement Zaozyorny
23, Druzby avenue

A site of a Greek-Scythian ancient settlement has been revealed by the Yevpatoria north outskirts, near the children's camp "Luchisty".

The remains of ancient Kerkinitida

The fragments of the once a glorious ancient settlement

fortress wall can be examined in Duvanovskaya St., at the Military sanatorium park.

The Turkish bath-house

20, Krasnoarmeiskaya St.

The baths built in the XVI century functioned till the 90-ties of the XX century. Already after the construction was declared an architectural monument, it has been simply destroyed. They have taken away everything that was at least of any value: copper cocks, marble slabs of coating. The half-collapsed walls, heaps of rubbish, dirt and desolation produce an oppressive impression. And, you know, people came here not only to wash themselves. By tradition the baths were a sort of clubs, especially for Moslem women. The baths seemed to children to be mysterious and enigmatic - through the lighting holes in the ceiling stars were seen...

There were similar baths in Feodosia and Belogorsk, but, alas, there are no baths there already...

The town theatre

Teatralnaya Sq.

☎ *32-490*

The theatre bearing the name of A. Pushkin now was built in 1910 on donations of the town citizens. The building in modern style was erected by the project of architects P. Seferov and A. Genrikh. To the opening of the first theatre season there came actors of the Mariinsky theatre, the Muscovites had put on the Yevpatoria stage the M. Glinka's opera "Life for tsar".

The town theatre

The Pushkin reading-hall

23, Bratyev Buslayevykh St.

The building of the former Aleksandr II Public library also built by the project of A. Seferov is situated not far from the theatre. A library, only renamed in honour of another Aleksandr, is here too.

The old town narrow streets with Tatar and Karaite houses lasted out here and there, the Karaimskaya, Tatarskaya, should be classified as the town sights. In the streets Revolyutsii, Karayeva, Duvanovskaya there are private residences in modern style built in the early XX century.

A memorable badge in honour of Russian warriors who lost their lives during the unsuccessful storm in the course of the Crimean war has been erected in Vtoroi Gvardeiskoi Armii avenue.

In Revolyutsii street there is a monument in honour of warriors-paratroopers. In 1942, after bloody battles, a handful of paratroopers were annihilated by fascists. The reinforcement detachments could not come to the shore because of a heavy gale...

A badge in the memory of the Crimean Tatars deported from Yevpatoria mounted near the mosque Dzhuma-Dzhami reminds of one more sad page of that time.

Yevpatoria in persons

The name of the architect Pavel Yakovlevich Seferov is inseparably linked with Yevpatoria, quite a number of buildings were built by his projects. The house of the town mayor, S. Duvan who has done a lot for the town's prosperity, the country-cottage of Terentyeva, and others are among them, in addition to the theatre and the library.
The house of S. Babovich, the Karaite community spiritual head, which is not far from the kenasa, has also lasted out. In 1825 Adam Mitskevich stayed here. Wearers of a crown who came to the town from time to time also made use of Babovich family hospitality.
In the early XIX century Lesya Ukrainka lived in Yevpatoria, later - the writer Nikolai Ostrovsky who created the Pavka Korchagin's image.
There remained intact the house where at the beginning of the XX century Lenin's brother - physician Dmitry Ulyanov lived and took an active part in formation of the Crimea as a sanatoria and health resorts region.
The Yevpatorians honour the memory of the Hero of the Soviet Union Nikolai Tokarev. The monument to the fearless general, the pilot who has lost his life during the battle for liberation of the town in 1944 is erected at Teatralnaya square.

The monument to N. Tokarev

The Saint Yelisaveta and Zakhary church

In the 30-ties of the XIX century Mikhail Vorontsov moved a part of his peasants to his estate in the north-west of the Crimea. In order to fix the migrants at the new place the count had ordered to build a church in Ak-Mechet. The stone temple in pseudo-Gothic style with a beautiful fence and a high tower was erected in 1838 by the project of the architect G. Torichelli. The church was sanctified in honour of the Saint Yelisaveta - the countess Yelisaveta Ksaveryevna Vorontsova (nee Branitskaya) was a woman educated, clever, charming, enjoyed love and respect of her encirclement. A. Pushkin was in love with countess Vorontsova and dedicated to her the poem "A burnt letter". The high tower acted as a reference-point for the vessels coming in the Ak-Mechet bay and had been included in marine international sailing directions, that is why it has not been destroyed during the Soviet power years. They have decided to "dress" the belfry in a concrete housing, mounted the sheathing and poured concrete for the whole height. The reference-point for vessels has remained, but it has somewhat changed its appearance. A sports school has been accommodated in the church premises. After the Soviet Union's collapse the temple was returned to believers. There were attempts at taking off the concrete "clothes", but nothing has come of it - concrete has stuck too strongly to the belfry walls. The small "windows" near the top of the parallelepiped on which they again mounted a cross are the signs of these attempts. The fact that its bells are suspended on a metal horizontal bar mounted next to the entrance reminds one of the church "sports" past.

In concrete "clothes": the belfry of the church in honour of Saints Yelisaveta and Zakhary

This small settlement spread on the shore of the Uzkaya Bukhta (Narrow bay) has a rich history. The Crimean "wild west" sea-coast was occupied from ancient times. Nations replaced each other during millenniums - from Cro-Magnons to ancient Greeks and Scythians, from Crimean Tatars to Russian peasants resettled in the 30-ties of the XIX century.

Signs of the Stone Age people on the Tarkhankutsky peninsula have been revealed in the vicinity of villages Olenyovka, Mezhvodnoye, Dalyokoye. During excavations they have found out silicic knives, fragment of ceramics, etc. related to the IV-III millenniums B.C. Besides, the region is renowned for barrows erected during the period from the Bronze Age to the Scythian times.

In the XII century B.C. in the north-western Crimea there appeared Cimmerians. It is supposed that it was a Cimmerian settlement that has been discovered near the village Vladimirovka. A lot of Scythian settlements have been discovered at the territory from the lake Donuzlav to the settlement Chernomorskoye.

A warrior-polovets (Chernomorskoye historic-cultural museum)

In the VIII century B.C. colonization of the Crimean peninsula began. Greek polises emerged on the sea-coast. The port Kalos-Limen was on the northern outskirts of the Great Khersones possessions, it was mentioned in the Khersonessians' well-known oath: "I...shall betray neither Khersones, nor Kerkinitida, nor Kalos-Limen, nor other fortifications and lands belonging to Khersonessians..." A plaque with the oath text was found out during excavations of Khersones in 1891 and is dated the III century B.C.

Kalos-Limen was a port town and the centre of an agricultur-

An excursion near the remains of the Kalos-Limen stronghold constructions

Tarkhankut. The rock Cherepashka (small tortoise)

al district. In the district they grew wheat and grapes being the main article of export. The settlement was protected by a stronghold wall of thickness up to one and a half metres. The town passed repeatedly into ownership of Scythians who lived beside. In so doing the barbarians tried to use the Greek buildings, even completed them in their own way, true, Scythians were considerably inferior to Greeks in the building skill.
Centuries went, towns and nations became non-existent, the climate changed: coniferous forests on Tarkhankut disappeared, nomads arranged pastures on ruins of abandoned settlements.
During the period of the Crimean khanate on the Kalos-Limen spot there was a Tatar village the inhabitants of which were occupied with stock-breeding.
After Russia annexed the Crimea a part of the Tarkhankut lands have passed into possession of a Katherine's II court dignitary, Major-General Vasily Stepanovich Popov. He had founded a large estate, built a house (it has remained intact in the village of Olenyovka, now it is one of the sanatorium buildings), laid a big orchard. In order to populate the tenantless lands (many Tatar families after 1783 left the Crimea migrating to Turkey) the retired soldiers were offered to remain in Tavrida, migrants were brought from Ukraine and Russia. To be engaged in recruitment was a paying business, especially it concerned women: for every young she-settler the State paid the recruiting agent a large sum.
In manors at Tarkhankut they began to breed sheep. This branch had reached a considerable flourishing when in 1824 one of M. Vorontsov's numerable Crimean possessions formed here. Fells of Tarkhankut lambs were valued highly - the manors affairs went up in the world sharply. The village Ak-Mechet also was expanded and built. Owing to M. Vorontsov effort new houses, a church had appeared in it, good roads led to the settlement. The estate owner strove for transformation into a town of the settlement neglected before.

After the Crimean Tatars' deportation in 1944 the settlement Ak-Mechet had been renamed into Chernomorskoye.
The Republican historical-archaeological preserve "Kalos-Limen" is the main of the settlement's sights. Excursions are organized by the Yevpatoria excursion bureau.

Tarkhankut lighthouse

The Tarkhankut rocky shores are very beautiful, but not safe for navigators. Many a ship has been wrecked here. In order to prevent possible wrecks a lighthouse was built in 1816 on a cape protruding far into the sea. The majestic white-stone tower was erected at a distance of 30 m from the shore, its height is about 40 m.
A spiral staircase leads to an observation landing from where there opens a picturesque view of the sea-coast and sea distance. The lighthouse light could be

seen, according to data of 1862, from a distance of 23 km. In the presence of fog there began to work a pneumatic siren the sound of which could be heard from a distance of 11 km from the shore. A double stroke of a bell every three minutes also could be a sound signal.
The lighthouse serves the sailors up to the present. The entrance to the territory is allowed only with an excursion. At an extra charge one may go up to the observation landing.

Camp and extreme Tourism

He who breathes the Crimea breathes
The joy of life, the poetry of longevity.
So hasten to leave for the Crimea...

Ye. Markov

The Crimea was called a "museum of nature", a "magic land", a "copy of the ancient paradise". A wonderful spot of the Earth washed by the Black Sea and the Sea of Azov attracts travellers charmed by the beauty of its mountains, valleys, palaces, and parks.

Some people prefer to walk along the marvellous peninsula admiring the variety of landscapes. Others - infatuated with riding bikes - are sure that the "sun on the spokes, the blue over one's head" ((from a Russian song (translator's note)) are the integral attributes of a full-bodied rest. The third ones consider that "better than mountains only another mountains can be" ((from a Russian song (translator's note)), and the fourth ones strive for unravelling the secrets of the sea depth...

Departing for a trip, you are to remember several simple rules in order that your rest should not be overshadowed by an unpleasant incident.

THE FIRST RULE: SAFETY

The inhabitants of Crimean forests are non-aggressive. The largest predator in the peninsula is the wild boar. A sudden meeting with it may be of serious danger: if the animal will be made angry, one will have to save oneself on the nearest tree.

In local forests there are no venomous snakes, but on the other hand, there are harmful insects. Serious troubles are produced by stings of a Lathrodectus tredecimguttatus, tarantula, scorpion. One should bandage the spot of the sting as soon as possible having previously wetted the bandage with a strong manganese solution (be sure to have on you a first-aid set). Until a doctor comes provide the victim with peace, warmth, and plentiful drinks. The clothes for walking tours to the mountains and the forest are to be convenient, light, dense, not leaving, if possible, open areas of skin. Do not ignore head-dresses - in such a way you will make yourself secure against an assault of ticks. Spending the night in a tent, check carefully whether unwanted visitors have penetrated into the tent, fasten the entrance.

In the sea waters you will not feel pleasure from a meeting with a large jellyfish. A venomous fish scorpena and a ray represent a more serious danger.

Some Crimean plants can cause poisoning, burns, allergic reactions. So, for instance, bright fruit of berry yew-tree can be the cause of a tragedy - all the parts of the plant are very poisonous. The leaves and spectacular flowers of fraxinella cause the heaviest burns. Oleander, box-tree, lily of the valley are also poisonous. Do not pick and, all the more, do not put in your mouth wild plants - both you will be more easy in your mind and nature will be more safe and sound.

Wild piglets on Chatyrdag

THE SECOND RULE: NATURE PRESERVATION

In the Crimea the first territory protected by state appeared in 1923 when the Crimean State Preserve was founded. Forest and yaila landscapes of the mountainous Crimea are liable to protection. The task of the preserve consists in preservation of rare species of animals and plants. Its branch - Lebyazhi ostrova (Swan islands) - serves as the place of thousands of swans and sea-gulls nesting. This is a real kingdom of birds.

In all at the territory of the Crimea there are 6 preserves: Crimean, Yalta, Martyan

Cape, Karadag, Kazantip, and Opuk preserves. In addition to the preserves 75 nature monuments, 35 game reserves, 9 protected natural boundaries, 30 monuments of gardens-park arts have been organized.

The stay in protected territories is strictly regulated. One can visit them only in the presence of a corresponding permission or on condition that one is a member of an organized excursion. For an authorized staying on the peninsula protected lands a penalty is inflicted on the onfringer.

THE THIRD RULE: PRUDENCE

We recommend to leave for mountains only with a guide. Never start for a walking tour without a large-scale map or scheme of the region, a compass, and means of communication (portable radio transmitter, telephone).

Your footwear is to be comfortable, with a non-slippery sole, no heels, plimsolls, and sandals whatever. Be especially careful on complex sections of your way - rocky juts, screes, steep slopes. Avoid going to the mountains in rainy weather. Prefer beaten tracks. If you have no experience and equipment you should better not subjugate peaks, not descent to caves, etc.

Intending to carry out a walking tour to the mountains, you are bound to inform the Control-rescuing service on its terms and route.

SIMFEROPOL
24 Z. Zhiltsovoi St., tel. **25-3158**

BAKHCHISARAI
31 Karla Marksa St., tel. **47-722**

ALUSHTA
8-a Lenina St., tel. **35-010**

FEODOSIYA
32-a Fedko St., tel. **71-573**

YALTA
10 Pirogova St., tel. **32-8715**

SUDAK
28-a Primorskaya St., tel. **94-380**

SEVASTOPOL
20 Suvorova St., tel. **52-5318**

In the case of an unforeseen situation requiring the interference of rescuers one should pass a call to the nearest team of the Control-rescuing service using any available means.

An excursion on Karadag

L E G E N D

1	Autocamping-sites	6	Organizers of jeep-safari
2	Spontaneous parking places	7	Yacht-clubs
3	Tourist centres	8	Sea journeys
4	Equipped tourist stopping places	9	Cruise tourism centres
5	Spontaneous tourist stopping places	10	Underwater tourism centres

LEGEND

11 Walking tourism centres
12 Speleotourism centres
13 Horse tourism centres
14 Rockdromes
15 Winter tourism centres
16 Bicycle tourism centres
17 Aeronautic tourism centres
18 Nudist beaches
19 Regions for sail-boarding

A stereotype connecting the Crimea exclusively with the summer holidays has firmly taken root in many people' minds. And quite wrongfully, because this spot of the Earth is beautiful at any time of the year. If to digress from the idea that the Crimea is the summer sun and excellent beaches caressed by the Black Sea waves, then one can make for oneself many little wonderful discoveries in the marvellous peninsula.

The singing feather-grass

AUTUMN

September and October in the Crimea are much brighter than August when the summer heat burns grass and covers leaves with dust. Autumn guests will be made happy by the abundance of tasty grapes, by quiet sunny days, and by a condition of some special pacification when both the earth and the people rest after the invasion of tourists' numerous hordes... In the environs of Old Crimea feather-grass sings tenderly, firm capers on the Sudak and Koktebel hills, touched with grey, flourish in white and pink, woods and parks demonstrate their bright autumn costumes. Autumn is an excellent time for long, unhurried walks.

WINTER

Snow in the Crimean mountains lies down as a firm cover ordinarily only from January, but on the other hand, the ski season continues as long as till April. There are not many places for skiing - you know, the mountains are not high and are covered with woods and shrubs. There are ski bases near Angarsky pass and on Ai-Petri. One may come here with one's own skis, but one can also take advantage of rent services. There are routes both for beginners and more complex ones. One can get

The snows on Ai-Petri

A snow-tractor

The autumn Crimea

The lake Barakol

easily to the Angarsky pass, but the ascent on Ai-Petri is connected with difficulties: the rope-way is not working when a strong wind blows, and one not always succeeds to find a person wishing to take you along the snow-covered serpentine road. But the one who has overcome all the obstacles will be rewarded: in addition to excellent skiing (to the elevator the skiers are towed by means of snow-tractors, this entertainment is called skijoring), the contemplation of incredible Ai-Petri sunsets and sunrises will afford him real pleasure.

SPRING

At the South Coast it begins early, and in the Crimea mountainous part - a little later. The April blossoming in the gardens and parks of the Greater Yalta produces an indelible impression on the sole of every visitor of this Goddess Flora's fairy-tale kingdom. But still the picture of a blossoming yaila really is a staggering discovery. And what about the Bakhchisarai's foothills covered with poppies or the spacious plateau of Uzun-Syrt decorated by luxuriant candles of asfodeliya and crimson stars of peony narrow-leafed?! From here before your dumb-founded gaze there opens the view on the toy-lake Barakol which had fallen into a hollow like a blue mirror, and farther - on the dark mountain range of Karadag projecting into the sea... A mysterious "dead town" is situated on the back of an ancient volcano, where in spring luxurious clearings of pink peonies suddenly appear, and above them along the overturned sky blue there fly light feathers of white clouds

The Big Canyon decked by yellow, red, blue, green patches represents a majestic sight. The air is transparent, clean, and fresh like the light and delicate Crimean wine.

In the Kerch steppe

Don't miss the spring holiday which is organized for you by nature.

In conclusion we may repeat the Yevgeny Markov's call: "Hasten to leave for the Crimea". You must not deprive yourself of this fairy-tale beauty!

The beach "Solnyshko". Preparation for swimming

This region of the Crimea is of interest to lovers of an inexpensive rest preferring an active way of life, especially for lovers of cycle racing and underwater swimming.

Many tourists bound for the north-western part of the peninsula get to Krasnoperekopsk by train, and from there along the sea-coast ride bicycles in the direction of Tarkhankut. In the village of Vorontsovka it is necessary to turn to the road leading to Razdolnoye. The highway here is rather a desert one, without intensive traffic, therefore the journey will be pleasant and safe. In Razdolnoye one may turn to the sea and ride to Portovoye. Here on the shore a spontaneous parking place is situated, and next to it, at the preserve Lebyazhi ostrova (Swan islands), thousands of birds build their nests.

Farther the way goes to Bakalskaya spit: a narrow strip of sand projecting far into the sea, with a traditional spontaneous parking space, is an excellent place for a halt. If one does not want to sleep in a tent, one can stay overnight in the village of Steregushcheye. Also here one can buy cheap food products. The bathing season at Bakalskaya spit begins in early May and continues till the middle of October.

You can also stop in Mezhvodnoye, Chernomorskoye, Olenyovka. In the last settlement the selection of dwelling is diversified: there are cottages, rest homes, boarding houses, the residents of the village let rooms.

The Dzhangul landslide sea-coast and the rocks of the Big and Small Atleshes are the cult places of Tarkhankutsky peninsula. You will have to get there along country roads. For bicyclists this is not a problem, but many cars are far from passing there. A jeep is ideal for local roads. It is not worth to go out for a trip by a town car with a low carriage and a rear drive.

Tourists from many cities of CIS set up encampments on Dzhangul. Unfortunately, here practically there is no fresh water (you have to take it with you), but then you are provided with a good fishing, a captivating underwater hunting, and with diving (submersion with an aqualung).

An encampment near Olenyovka

Atlesh rocks are an extremely exotic place. Coastal country roads lead there from the Tarkhankut lighthouse. Shores of limestone indented in a whimsical way set off the emerald sea deep. The water on Tarkhankut is very clean, therefore underwater submersion gives real pleasure.

The Bolshoi Atlesh (Big Atlesh), with an enormous arch, caves, grottoes, and steps cut out in stone, towers above the sea. Beside a metal staircase is erected for the descent to water. The pass to the staircase is blocked, those who wish to descend along it are to pay from 1 (for excursionists) to 3 Hr (for individual tourists). A little farther one can descend to the sea free of charge, but with a lesser comfort. Here, by the cape, the tents of cycle tourists and lowers of underwater submersion stand. They take with them fresh water and fire-wood. On the Big Atlesh they fish by an ancient method lowering into the sea the so called karaviys - special fixtures invented as far back as by ancient Greeks.

The Maly Atlesh (Small Atlesh) is renowned for its tunnels. In the cape thickness the waves had knocked out a passage of length about 100 m. In that places a multitude of adventure films were shot, among them "The pirates of the XX century", "A man-amphibian", and others.

To the north of Atleshes the village Marino is situated where at the tourist parking place a not so Spartan way of life is accepted, although these places are not so beautiful.

Farther the road leads to a narrow and long lake Donuzlav. Unfortunately, across the spit separating it from the sea a canal had been dug, and one has to go round the lake through Novoivanovka. Then one can return to the sea and to stop in Popovka where during the season the tourists arrange a spontaneous camp. In villages along the sea-coast up to Yevpatoriya (Shtormovoye, Vitino, Zaozyornoye) one will find a place both for one's tent and for one's car.

In the Yevpatoriya environs you can make yourselves comfortable on a sand spit between the lake Sasyk and Kalamitsky bay. On the 51-st km there are a youth centre "Solnyshko" ("Caressing sun") with an autocamping-site for 100 visitors, a guarded parking place, a hotel, a disco equipped according to the latest achievements of technology, a cafe, bars, a restaurant, a children's playground, a diving-centre, etc. A well-equipped beach with a fresh-water shower-bath and bio-lavatories waits for lowers of a civilized rest. To install a tent costs UAH 5 a day (as well as a car). For those who have settled in the hotel a place at a guarded parking lot is given free of charge. Last season the daily cost of staying in the hotel amounted to UAH 40 per person. Here admirers of water kinds of sports come - lowers of yachts, sail-boards, diving. At the spit tents are set up by unorganized tourists - adversaries of an organized way of life when at rest.

In the Crimean steppe. *Windmills turn the wind into electric energy*

Cape Tarkhankut

Kazantip stones

The north-eastern region of Crimean peninsula is somehow similar to its north-western part - the same not high density of population, endless plains, and scanty vegetation. Kerch peninsula is of interest to cycle tourists, and to the Sea of Azov coast admirers of sailing sports like to come.

The road leading to the eastern outlying districts of the Crimea is not notable for picturesque vicinities, but on the other hand, the even a hundred kilometres highway connecting Feodosiya and Kerch was chosen by bicyclists, motorists, and rockers.

One can stop in the settlement of Primorsky situated along the sea-coast strip. There are here an excellent sand beach, inexpensive food products, and lodging. Farther the way goes through desert parts where small settlements are found every now and then. If to turn to the right after Lugovoye, not reaching the village of Vulkanovka, you will see the largest Crimean mud volcano Dzhau-Tepe. From Vulkanovka through Marfovka and Maryevka the road brings you to the village of Zavetnoye renowned for cheap and tasty fish. Here you also can stay overnight. To the west of Zavetnoye the Opuksky preserve including Koyashskoye lake and mountain Opuk (123 m) is situated. Beside the shore in the sea there have stiffened the fantastic Rocks-Ships.

Having turned to the boarding house near the sands of Tobechikskoye lake, fill up your supply of fresh well-water. Farther go along Kerchensky strait till the town-hero itself. It is better to stay overnight in a tent not in the town, but a little northward to the Bulganakskaya bay with an interesting relief of the landslide sea-coast on the shore of which the villages of Yurkino and Osoviny are located.

A whole field of small mud volcanoes near the village of Bondarenkovo erupting not magma but blue-green clay represents a striking sight. It is not recommended to approach closely to the small hills with small mud lakes - you can come down deeply in the mud slush.

By Chokrakskoye lake known for its medicinal mud the village Kurortnoye is located. Here, in the Azov sea-coast, boarding houses and rest homes are situated, in addition, the rent from the inhabitant costs not much. Take into consideration that in this region of Kerchensky peninsula the condition of road is disgusting.

In order to get to Kazantip one may, of course, take advantage of country roads, but only not in a rainy weather. It is better to drive out to the route M-17, to turn to Lenino, and to reach Semyonovka where near the shore the tourists traditionally set up their tents.

The camp of funboardists near Kazantip

In Kazantip, the other side of Aktashskoye lake, the unfinished building of a nuclear plant is situated. Here in 1995 the first festival "Kazantip" was conducted. During the next years the most cult and youth squeeze of the Crimea moved

At the excavations of ancient Pantikapeus

along the peninsula (the village of Kurortnoye near Karadag, the village of Popovka near Yevpatoriya, etc.), but everybody waits for its return to Kazantip. Now the exotic place by the entry to the settlement of Shchyolkino is chosen by funboardists - lovers of a sail-board with a neutral floatage. Next to the rest base "Riga" on the sand shore of the beach a spontaneous encampment functions. The cape itself is declared now a state preserve.

At the sea-coast of Arabatsky bay there is enough place for lovers of desert shores, secluded beaches, and a good fishing. Many prefer a "wild" rest at the sand strip of Arabatskaya spit.

Kurortnoye.
The cape in the Azov coastal waters

The charm of this place in the Crimea located between Alushta and Feodosiya consists in an unhurried replacement of natural landscapes, characteristic Cimmerian scenery.

The region can be conditionally divided into two parts: the mountainous and the coastal ones. The mountainous south-east Crimea does very well for lovers of active rest. The roads, in contradistinction to the south-coast ones, are not overloaded by transport, which will make happy the numerous bicyclists. In addition to a highway one (one can say, an outing one), here mountainous cycling tourism is also widespread. The admirers of this kind of extreme rest have chosen the region of mountain Demerdzhi above Alushta. Here also one of horse tourism centres is situated.

Admirers of walking tourism

The desert, wild landscapes of vast Karabi-yaila attract the adherents of speleotourism and walking routes. But take into consideration that this region of the peninsula is not adapted for light promenades. One must never start alone a walking tour along Karabi - too much difficulties lie in wait for a careless traveller. In order to avoid possible troubles the group has to be directed by an experienced guide or instructor, and the route is to be approved without fail by the Control-rescuing service. A visit to the caves on Karabi demands a professional preparation, among them there are no specially equipped ones, such as, for instance, the Mramornaya and Emine-Bair-Khosar on the plateau Chatyrdag. The Dolgorukovskaya yaila is also of interest for speleotourists.

ORGANIZING ROCK-CLIMBING TOURS:

Tourist firm "Turist"
town of Simferopol
tel. **25-0351, 57-5478**

Private businessman V.Yu. Kulinich
town of Yalta
tel. **35-0735, 35-0784**

Conkord-club
town of Sevastopol
tel. **53-0352**

In the south-eastern Crimea there are several rockdromes: these are mountain Sakharnaya Golovka (Sugar head) in Sudak near the Genoese fortress, and mountain Sokol (Falcon) by the settlement Novy Svet, and the rock Syuyuryu-Kaya near Koktebel, and Parsuk-Kaya near Solnechnaya Dolina (Sunny Valley). Rock-climbers have the opportunity to perfect themselves in the skill of subjugating peaks and rock walls in Nikitskaya crevice where a rockdrome is equipped with due regard for the world standards. For the beginners we can recommend Petrovskiye rocks in Simferopol. In the

Crimea there are several firms engaged in organization of rock-climbing tours.

The south-eastern sea-coast is a real paradise for lovers of "wild" rest. Along the highway connecting Alushta and Sudak a multitude of encampments are situated, starting with Semidvorye where tent by the shore are put in the main by "pedestrians" and bicyclists. On local steep slopes a car cannot be parked. But on the other hand, from Solnechnogorskoye to Morskoye several well-equipped tourist parking places have been organized. For example, last season in the village of Rybachye the cost of placing a tent and a car amounted to UAH 16 a day. At the camp territory there is drinkable water, lavatories, removing of rubbish has been organized. Spontaneous parking lots arise in summer by the cape Alchak behind Sudak, in the village of Pribrezhnoye, and behind the nudist beach situated by Koktebel bay. These parking places are free of charge, accordingly, there are no here even common conveniences - one will have to organize everything on one's own. But one can stop at the camping-site "Bon", true, not for one night, but for at least 5 days. Last summer one place in a small wooden house cost UAH 22 a day.

In the Koktebel sky

To Koktebel there come admirers of air kinds of sports. On the mountain Uzun-Syrt, which best of all does for flights with gliders and hang-gliders, the "ikars" centre is situated. And here, on the mountain, the most inveterate extremists set up their tents, in spite of the constantly blowing winds.

The Feodosiya region locks the south-eastern sea-coast. Between the eastern outskirts of the town and the settlement of Primorsky along the Zolotoi plyazh (Golden beach) tourists are waited for both by stationary camping-sites and by encampments spontaneously arising.

Delights of "wild" way of life

A camp in the village of Morskoye

This region is, perhaps, the most attractive for tourists, everyone will choose for himself a kind of rest to his taste. Because of the diversity of landscapes three tourist districts may be singled out: the South Coast of the Crimea (SCC), the western sea-coast, and the mountainous Crimea.

The Big Canyon charms

The South Coast, as a rule, is visited by lovers of the traditional, comfortable, and, correspondingly, not cheap rest. Various sanatoria, boarding houses, tourist centres, motels, and camping-sites are located here. For autotourists guarded parking lots are equipped practically in every one of them. One can also rent a private dwelling with a garage. To organize a free lodging for the night in the SCC is practically impossible, therefore for those who have got accustomed to save it is better not to come here.

The South Coast is a popular place for holding all sorts of congresses, conferences, seminars, and similar arrangements - from serious political summits to merry festivals and simply squeezes.

In the Western sea-coast boarding houses and rest homes are situated. In Nikolayevka, Beregovoye, Peschanoye, Andreyevka, Kacha, Lyubimovka one can rent a comparatively inexpensive lodging. Here there are splendid sand-pebbly beaches, convenient for holidays with children. Equipped parking spaces and camping-sites invite the adherents of motor tourism.

In the Sevastopol environs competitions of sailing sports lovers are traditionally carried out. In the town there are quite a lot of yacht-clubs, diving centres, and firms specializing on the sea kinds of tourism.

The Gerakleisky peninsula sea-coast was chosen by lovers of underwater submersion not loosing hopes to find priceless treasures concealed in the mysterious sea depth.

The mountainous Crimea is a place of active kinds of rest admirers' pilgrimage; bicyclists, speleotourists, and rock-climbers will find for themselves interesting routes. In winter desperate extremists - mountain-skiers and snowboardists assemble on Ai-Petri.

Local forests and watercourses are attractive for lovers of hunting with a camera and off fishing. Admirers of ecological tourism will visit with pleasure the Crimean natural preserve; the fighters for nature preservation will be glad to know about a so big quantity of protected territories.

Parking spaces are equipped near all the sights, one can spend the night at tourist centres in Bakhchisarai, Sokolinoye, on Ai-Petri. One can also set up an independent camp at grounds specially designed for this.

The mountainous Crimea is widely known by its "cave towns", cloisters, stopping places of primordial people, and other monuments of past centuries keeping their secret till now. Here the famous canyons - Chernorechensky (the longest in the peninsula) and Bolshoi Kanyon (Big canyon) (the deepest in the Crimea).

Owing to the fantastic variety of most beautiful natural landscapes - ringing waterfalls, mysterious canyons, mountain peaks, picturesque valleys - thousands and thousands of tourists come here year after year discovering for themselves new and new wonders which the Crimean land is full with.

The caves of Eski-Kermen

Information from A to Z

The one who possesses information possesses the world...

VISAS

For one's entry to Ukraine one is to register a visa at the Ukraine's diplomatic representation or consulate abroad. One should take trouble about it in advance - one cannot receive a visa at the airport or the custom-house. One can prolong the visa validity already at the territory of our country.

If you are in the territory of Ukraine, additional documents for entry to the Autonomous Republic of Crimea are not required.

TERMS OF ISSUING A VISA AND ITS COST

The standard term of issuing a visa is 10 working days. In case of necessity a visa can be issued during 2-3 days, but is will cost twice as much. Consular payments amount to USD40 - 150 and depend on the terms of documents presentation and the type of the visa (a tourist, guest one, etc.).

SOME CUSTOMS RULES

Information about articles and currency value transported through the Ukraine's customs is to be introduced in the declaration. You are to point out data about what and what for you are transporting and also other information on demand of the customs guard.

It is permitted to export articles, not being a goods consignment, to the sum not exceeding the equivalent of EURO100,000. For exporting works of art, cultural and historical values one is bound to receive a permission of Ministry of Culture. In case of an insignificant cultural value of the souvenirs purchased by you it is enough to have a bill of the shop, the arts salon where the purchase has been made.

TIME

The time in Ukraine is ahead by 2 hours of the Greenwich mean time. From the end of March up to October there acts the summer time.

ELECTRICAL DEVICES

The mains voltage - 200 volt, frequency - 50 Hz. An adapter may be needed for electrical devices of the USA and Japan manufacture. Sockets of European standard are not uncommon for a long time already, but sockets with more narrow jacks are found fairly often (in such a case a special adapter will prove useful).

One person is permitted to bring to Ukraine:

- vodka products - 1 litre;
- vine - 2 litres;
- tobacco products - 200 cigarettes (or 200 grams of these products);
- beer - 2 litres;
- food products to the sum not exceeding the equivalent of EURO50.

You will need a special permission in order to bring in or export:

- arms of military patterns; special means of self-defence charged with substances of tear action, etc. - a permission of Ministry of Internal Affairs of Ukraine;
- animals - a veterinary certificate;
- medicinal agents (no more than 5 packages of the same name or no more than the quantity necessary for one patient for one course of treatment according to a physician's prescription) - a permission of Ministry of Public Health, etc.

It is unknown when and where the wonderful tradition of bringing memorable trinkets from a trip has been born, but since then genuine tourists consider it to be their duty to purchase souvenirs reminding them of every new place of the Earth. The Crimean souvenirs assortment is broad and diversified. The choice depends on personal tastes and also on which part of the peninsula you pass your leave in. In addition to the traditional articles of juniper (beads, supports, etc.), dried crabs, exotic shells and coral twigs (by the way, not being relevant at all to the Crimean sea fauna), there is its own spirit in the souvenir set of every region.

Sevastopol

Chersonese ceramics are sold at the territory of the museum-preserve - by the entrance and at the hall of holograms. Visit also the town's opening day of an exhibition near the Grafskaya square where Sevastopol artists and photographers exhibit their works.

Yalta

Along the embankment there is a fair amount of booths and hawker's trays where one can find articles of stone, cockle-shells, wood. In memory of your stay in beautiful Yalta buy several wonderful water-colours, and at the Nikitsky botanical gardens purchase a box of bamboo.

Alushta

Here herb tea of Alushta valley and environing foothills and also volatile oils are sold. By the beginning of many foot routes they arrange "mobile samovars" - here one can taste medicinal species and choose the ones one liked.

Feodosiya

Here one can purchase articles of the famous Karadag semi-precious stones. Small many-coloured stones will decorate the home aquarium, one can also beautifully spread out them in flower-pots, for instance, around cactuses.

In the centre of the town the Feodosiya present-day painters of sea-scapes exhibit their pictures.

Kerch

large selection of clay vessels painted in imitation of ancient ceramics are represented in the Demetra's crypt (more exactly, in its technological model) by the Mitridatskaya stairs.

Bakhchisarai

Volatile oils, of course, rank first among Bakhchisarai souvenirs. In addition to a set of oils, purchase a ceramic lamp for aroma-therapy. The usage of it is very simple. The lamp itself is made in a form of a

luminaire, in the lower opening of which a light candle is put. The upper small cup is filled in with water with a several drops of the oil. As it evaporates the water is added. Buy also a book about medicative aromatic oils.

"If a person wants to know the other nation's soul, he has to do it by means of the language and also by means of his stomach".

(Popular wisdom)

What are the national cuisine peculiarities determined by? These are both the cultural traditions of every nation, and interconnection of different ethnic groups residing in the vicinity of each other, and the generosity of their native land presenting us with its excellent fruit, and, of course, the hosts' hospitality.

The Crimean land joyfully receives its guests bringing forward to them its best, including delicious food. Dishes made by traditional Karaite and Crimean Tatar recipes can be a real adornment of the table.

Koi kavurmasy
(stewed mutton in Karaite style)

To put mutton cut into large pieces in a frying-pan with fat, to salt, to pepper, to add sliced onions, and to stew on a small fire until the meat juice has evaporated. After that to fry the meat all over, stirring it slowly all the time, then to add parsley, dill, mint, boiled water, and to stew on a small fire until it is ready in full.

Mutton - 1 kg, fat - 2-3 spoonfuls, 2-3 onions, greens (parsley, dill, mint leaves) - 50 g, salt, pepper to your taste.

Imam-baildy
(vegetables in Tatar style)

Not only Crimean Tatars like to make this dish, the recipe is highly distributed with eastern nations. The word for word translation of the name is "the imam (a Moslem clergyman) has gone crazy". There exists a legend about a Moslem clergyman who, having once tasted this wonderful dish, had literally lost his head for delight.

To cut washed aubergines into circles, to salt them, and to leave them for half an hour, in order that a bitter taste should be absent. Then to wring out them, to wash, and to fry them all over with sunflower oil. To fry separately Bulgarian pepper, onions, segments of tomatoes, to stew the fried vegetables, having salted them and added sugar. To cover with the received sauce the aubergines put into a stew-pan, to sprinkle them from above with garlic cut finely, with greens of parsley and dill, to cover the pan, and to let it get cold. To put it into a refrigerator for 2-3 hours.

Aubergines - 4-6 pc., Bulgarian pepper - 4 pc., tomatoes - 4 pc., sunflower oil - 4 tablespoons, garlic - 3-4 tooths, sugar - 1 tablespoon, greens of parsley and dill, salt, pepper to your taste.

Yantyks (Karaite pies)

The pastry for the yantyks is prepared quickly by the leaven-free method. To grind the yeast with softened butter until a uniform mass is received. To shake up an egg with sugar, to dilute with milk or water, to add salt, to intermix the whole mass. To knead the pastry until it is ready (it is to come easily off hands and walls of the crockery). To leave for a short while covered with a napkin.

For preparation of the filling to grind meat together with onions by a meat-chopper with a grill with large openings, to add 2-3 tablespoons of water, salt, pepper.

To cut the swelled pastry into 10-12 parts, to roll out every of them into a circle of diameter about 10 cm. To put the filling on the flat cakes (1 tablespoon). To nip the pies in a form of tooths from the edges to the midst, to leave a small opening in the centre. To smear the top with an egg, to put on an oiled baking tray. To bake in an oven at the temperature of 210-230°C. To serve hot, before serving to put in the opening a piece of butter.

For 10 pies: *flour - 3 glasses, eggs - 2 pc., milk (water) - 1 glass, butter (margarine) - 100 g, yeast - 25 g, sugar - 1 tablespoon, salt - one-third of a teaspoon, mutton flesh - 0.5 kg, an onion, salt, pepper, greens of parsley to the taste..*

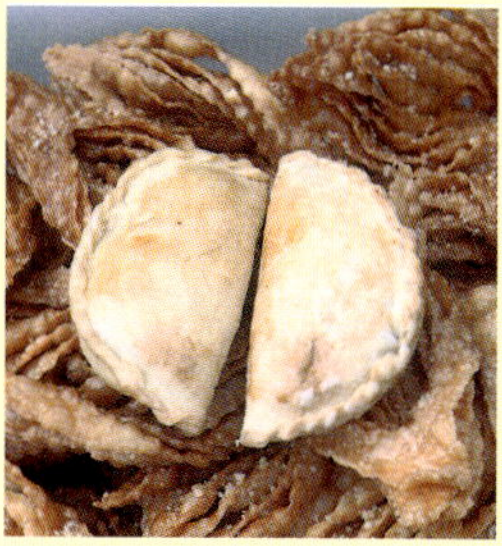

Pakhlava (a Tatar recipe)

To knead pastry, having taken only 150 g of butter. Having separated it into parts, to roll up balls, to put them in a stew-pan and to cover with a warm damp napkin for exfoliation.

To get the parts of the pastry one by one, to roll out into thin circles. To smear every one of them with butter and to fold into an envelope. To fold in such a way again and again, as long as possible, then to cover with a napkin and to put them in the refrigerator for half an hour. To repeat twice the operation of rolling out and folding the pastry.

To prepare the filling: to cook the syrup of sugar, water, citric acid. To add nuts, crumbs, and to intermix well. If liquid is lacking, to add some water or melted honey.

To roll out the pastry from the refrigerator to a thickness of 0.5 cm, to cut into squares with a side of 6-7 cm, to put the filling into the centre of every one. To nip the opposite edges, to put the small triangulars on a baking tray smeared with fat. To smear with butter the top of every pie, to put in a hot oven, in 8 minutes to decrease the fire, to bake until they are ready.

To cover the ready pakhlava with melted honey, to serve on a dish.

For the pastry: *flour - 3 glasses, butter (margarine) - 300 g, a glass of a mixture of 2 tablespoons of vinegar, salt, and water.*

For the filling: *ground nuts - 1.5 glasses, crumbled up dried crusts or biscuit - 1 glass, honey - 6-7 tablespoons, sugar - 1 glass, water - three fourth of a glass, citric acid - 0.5 teaspoons.*

...Drank and admired. Left comparatively sober - only because of lack of time. The most part of wine consists of the sun. Long live people who know how to make wine and by means of it - to bring the sun strength in souls of people.

M. Gorky

The Crimean wine-making is already several thousands years old, you know, vine is one of the most ancient cultures of the peninsula. For example, the sort of Muscat grows on this blessed land for two with a half millenniums. The vine delivered by ancient Greeks has brought fame and international recognition to many Crimean wines.

What the success depends on? Of course, on the fruitful interaction of the generous sun and painstaking human labour. As far back as several decades ago by the technology for receiving the Tokay "Ai-Daniel" it was necessary to twist every ripe bunch with special tongs in order that berries should become dry, more sweet. Then they were ground by hand for receiving juice. The wine from a tun was poured also by hand, not resorting to the help of automatic machines. As the result, a real masterpiece was born...

It is not known who was the first to invent the process of making wine of the grape juice, the history of wine arising is lost in the depth of mythology. It was already known to Egyptians as long ago as three-four millenniums. It was considered that they were taught wine-making by Osiris

himself - the God of dying and reviving nature. Greeks were given their first lessons concerning the life-giving drink preparation by the God Dionis, Romans - by the god Bakhus, and the Bible on this issue refers to Noi...

The Crimean wine-making founded as long ago as by the Greeks-colonists repeatedly experienced both a flourishing and a decline. In due course of centuries the ancient Greeks began to be pressed by nomads: primarily by Scythians, then by Huns, Khazars, Polovtsians, and others. By the way, the Greek wine suited the Scythians' taste. True, they drank it in Barbarian style, not diluting it with water, as it was accepted by the Greeks. From this the expression "to drink in Scythian style", that is, to get fully drunk, has been born. Afterwards the proverb was changed into "to drink like a pig", although poor pigs have here absolutely nothing to do with it. By the XI century the wine-makers' craft had practically gone out in order to revive with coming of Genoeses to the Tavrichesky shores. The next blow was delivered by Turks - as is generally known, Moslems were not allowed to drink wine. A new recovery in the business of production of drinks of grapes berries took place in the early XIX century. G. Potyomkin, M. Vorontsov, P. Gubonin, Kh. Steven, and L. Golitsyn played in it a great part. Wine-making economies were organized, plants and cellars were built, new grades of wine were born. At a fairly short time the Crimean wine-making reached the world heights.

Every Crimean region is renowned to-day for its original wines.

Above the Sevastopol highway, behind the village of Kamenka the famous Kizil-Tash (Red stone) is. A reddish rock of height 430 m was torn off once from the main ridge and slowly crawls to the sea. A small fortress was before on its upper site, here a patrol of feodorits watching the Genoeses' actions was.

In 1946 from the grapes growing by the Red stone the famous Massandra wine-maker A. Yegorov made the unique wine - "Muskat bely Krasnogo kamnya" ("Red stone white Muscat"). And already about sixty years it is the pride of the "Massandra".

YALTA

Numerous enterprises of the association "Massandra" and also the research institute "Magarach" are situated in the environs of Yalta. The "Massandra" produces the best sweet liqueur wines: Muscat "Yuzhnoberezhny bely" ("White South Coast Muscat") and "Yuzhnoberezhny rozovy" ("Pink South Coast Muscat"), "Livadiya" (white and red), "Magarach", pino-gri "Ai-Daniel", "Tokay Yuzhnoberezhny" ("South Coast Tokay"), and many others.

ALUSHTA

Several enterprises of the firm "Massandra" are situated in the environs of Greater Alushta. Here they grow grapes grades for production of Muscat, ports, sherry, Madeira, etc. It is accepted to consider the table red wine "Alushta" the best one among the table wines. It is made of grapes of Cabernet, Saperavi, Morastel grades. The red port "Malorechensky" also is worth of attention. Among the sweet red wines the aleatiko "Ayu-Dag" was marked by a multitude of gold medals.

SUDAK

The Sudak valley wine plants are renowned for various wines: these are both the sweet "Surozh", and white port with the same name, and the Crimean Madeira. It is considered that Madeira possesses the property to postpone the coming of old age, the English call it the "ladies' cognac".

The plant "Solnechnaya Dolina" ("Sunny Valley") specializes in unique wines "Chyorny Doctor" ("Black Doctor"), "Chyorny Polkovnik" ("Black Colonel"), "Solnechnaya Dolina" ("Sunny Valley"). The last was awarded 8 gold and silver medals at international competitions.

At the plant of champagne wines "Novy Svet" ("New Light"), by tradition established as long ago as by prince Golitsyn, they produce this excellent sparkling wine. The Champagne bryut contains up to 0.3% of sugar, the dry one - up to 3%, semi-dry one - 3.7%.

KOKTEBEL

Madeira, white Muscat, aligote, white port - here is an incomplete list of the Koktebel plant production. But most of all it is well-known due to its cognacs.

BAKHCHISARAI

In addition to the famous "Bakhchisaraisky fontan" ("Bakhchisarai fountain") and "Tsaritsa nochi" ("Night Tsarina"), they produce here table wines, and also balsams prepared from Bakhchisarai foothills and valleys medicinal herbs.

SEVASTOPOL

Several wine plants of the region (the Inkerman, Kachinsk, Sevastopol ones) specialize in the main in fine wines of type aligote, rkatsiteli, sauvignon. The "Cabernet Kachinskoye" may be considered one of the best red wines.

Balaklava agricultural firm "Zolotaya balka" ("Gold gully") produces sparkling wines notable for their excellent quality, as, for instance, the "Sevastopolskoye igristoye" ("Sevastopol sparkling wine").

How to combine wines with food

Wine must never suppress the taste of a dish, that is why good red fine wine is never served to white meat. But the dish also must not suppress the wine, for example, game does not combine with white of light red wine.

To select a drink to dessert dishes is especially difficult. Sweet wine very seldom goes with cakes. The simplest decision in this case is champagne. But ripe red wine, even a little strong, can perfectly combine with a cake or chocolate mousse.

The better the wine grade, the simpler and nobler the dish is to be: light white wines - fish; strong white wines - fish, white sauce; pink ones - white meat; light red ones - red meat; strong red ones - game.

The most squeeze place in Yalta
night club
Tornado
CHIC MUSIC, DANCE, AND LASER SHOW
TILL MORNING
ABSOLUTELY ACCEPTABLE PRICES
11 Lenina St. (entrance from the embankment), Yalta, tel. (0654) 32-2036

CAFÉ LE NOUVEAU GOURMAND
гурман
2002
A worthy place for worthy people
Restaurant "GURMAN"
гурман
11 Lenina St. (entrance from the embankment),
Yalta, tel.(0654) 32-0306

BRISTOL
HOTEL
Our address:
10 Ruzvelta St., town of Yalta,
98600, Autonomous Republic
of Crimea, Ukraine
e-mail:office@hotel-bristol.com.ua
www.hotel-bristol.com.ua

DEN TOURISTISCHEN SERVER DER KRIM
WWW.TOUR.CRIMEA.COM
BEHANDLUNG, ERHOLUNG, ABENTEUER
BEHANDLUNG UND AUSHEILUNG
KINDERPROGRAMME
JUGENDTOURS
ACTIVE ERHOLUNG
DIE RESERVIERUNG DER HOTELS, FLUGZEUG UND ZUG KARTEN DURCH DAS INTERNET
DIE ORGANISATION UND DIE DURCHFUHRUNG DER KONFERENZ
DEN KOMFORTABELEN TRANSPORT
+380 652 551222

Hotel Yalta

"Yalta" in Yalta - rest and business all the year round

The best hotel complex of the Crimea - "Yalta-Inturist" has received numerous tourists from various countries of the world over 25 years.

Situated at a distance of 1.5 km from the centre of Yalta, the hotel, like a snow-white ocean-going liner, swims amongst the emerald greenery of a XIX century landscape subtropical park into the sea spaciousness.

1,142 comfortable and cosy rooms can receive at the same time 2,272 guests. All the rooms are supplied with telephones, radios, and TV sets; hot and cold water is supplied round-the-clock; 75% of the rooms are conditioned and have an autonomous heating system.

Luxurious restaurants, refined bars and cafes are intended for 3,886 visitors who can choose complex or individual menus, a "Swedish table", or to order food to their rooms.

The "Yalta-Inturist" offers all kinds of rest, a complex of tourist and hotel services, and a large selection of tours and excursions along the Crimea.

For tourists' active rest there is a centre of sports and improvement of health which includes open swimming pools with pre-heated sea water, a room with simulators, tennis-courts, a bicycle club, a scuba-diver school, table tennis, billiards, a comfortable three-tier beach connected by high-speed lifts with the hotel complex, cutters, yachts, stations of hiring beach and water-sports appliances, including water bicycles, hydro-cycles, etc.

The "Yalta-Inturist" is the largest cultural and business centre of the Crimea. In concert halls and on concert grounds folklore and variety shows, festivals, cinema-tele- forums, ballroom dances, and variety songs competitions take place. Discotheques, variety shows with a constantly changing program, and a magnificent dolphin-show attract numerous visitors.

Businessmen meet at the hotel complex at seminars, symposiums, and conferences, commerce-and-industry and tourist fairs. On the basis of the "Yalta-Inturist" there take place meetings on high level, party congresses, and public-political forums.

---

50 Drazhinskogo St., town of Yalta, Autonomous Republic of Crimea, Ukraine, 98600
Contact telephones: (0654) 270 270, 270 260; fax: 353093
a-mail: info@hotel-yalta.com

Name	Address	Telephone
GREATER ALUSHTA		
Tridtsat let oktyabrya (30 years of October)	17 Glazkritskogo St.	30-544, 33-438
Alushta	8 Glazkritskogo St.	31-511,30-293
Alushta	16 Oktyabrskaya St., Alushta	30-514 30-477
Albatros (Albatross)	2-a Lenina St., Alushta	33-258,30-528
Veteran	4 Oktyabrskaya St., Alushta	31-091,30-446
Gorizont (Horizon)	7 Komsomolskaya St.	31-568, 31-198
Demerdzhi	4 Perekopskaya St., Alushta	30-310,33-269
Dubna	20 Naberezhnaya St.	31-588
Zhemchuzhina (Pearl)	14-a Sudakskaya St., Alushta	39-454
Zolotoi kolos (Gold ear)	9 Krasnoarmeiskaya St., Alushta	30-740, 30-569
Karasan	settlement Utyos	64-238, 64-269
Kiev	20 Komsomolskaya St.	33-713, 30-714, 31-274
Kiparis (Cypress)	9 Krasnoarmeiskaya St., Alushta	30-418
Krym (Crimea)	urban village Partenit	45-524, 45-711
More (Sea)	25 Naberezhnaya St.	31-131
Morskoi bereg (Sea shore)	24 Naberezhnaya St.	30-405, 30-796, 32-105
Rabochy ugolok (Working place)	6 Naberezhnaya St.	33-456, 30-374,33-359
Santa-Barbara	settlement Maly Utyos	64-387, 64-415
Severnaya Dvina (North Dvina)	4 Pyatnadtsatogo aprelya St., Alushta	31-246, 30-584
Slava (Fame)	1-a Krasnodarskaya St., Alushta	30-344, 30-298
Slavutich	20 Krasnodarskaya St., Alushta	34-482,33-488
Tavrida	22 Lenina St., Alushta	30-451,30-630, 64-348
Ukoopspilka	3 Chatyrdagskaya St.	30-581,
Utyos (Cliff)	settlement Utyos	64-217,64-331
Chaika (Sea-gull)	11 Krasnoarmeiskaya St., Alushta	30-586, 35-217
GURZUF		
Ai-Danil	urban village Gurzuf 3	33-5302, 36-3320
Gurzuf	10 Leningradskaya St.	36-3488, 36-3203
Gurzuf	10 Leningradskaya St.	36-3622
Pushkino	3 Naberezhnaya St.	36-3390, 36-3086

Name	Address	Telephone
YALTA		
Vremena goda (Seasons)	23 Rudanskogo St.	34-3045 32-6012
Dolossy	settlement Massandra-1	32-5057
Donbass	settlement Massandra	27-2074, 27-2000
Zaporozhe	29 Lomonosova St.	32-0010
Zarya	7 Kommunarov St.	31-6554,32-0334
Kuybysheva	11 Shcherbakova St.	31-7172,32-5830
Sechenova	11 Pushkinskaya St.	35-0512, 31-6313
Kiev	1 Morskaya St.	32-7576, 32-7536
Kirova	39 Kirova St.	32-7612, 32-6932,32-2106
Lastochka (Swallow)	12-a Naidyonova St.	34-2094, 34-1110
Livadiya	6 Baturina St., settlement Livadiya	31-5403, 31-5504
Malakhit (Malachite)	15 Shcherbakova St.	31-6370, 31-6381
Yalta	32 Sverdlova St.	32-7512
Niva	44 Kiyevskaya St.	32-4392, 32-3547
Nizhnyaya Oreanda	settlement Oreanda	32-2212, 31-2548
Orlinoye gnezdo (Eagle's nest)	5/8 Kommunarov St.	32-7867, 32-3061
Pribrezhny	settlement Otradnoye	33-6971, 33-5922
Rossiya (Russia)	12 Kommunarov St.	31-0471, 32-1837
Sevastopol	2-a Kirova St.	32-5992
Uzbekistan	1 Bakhchisaraiskoye shosse	31-2423, 31-4903
Fitotsentr (Phytocentre)	urban village Nikita	33-5543, 33-5617
Chernomorsky	25 Dneprovskaya St., settlement Otradnoye	33-5691, 33-5319
Chernomorye	12 Vinogradnaya St., settlement Livadiya	31-5558, 31-8489
Yalta	12/43 Sevastopolskaya St.	31-7284, 32-3860
Energetik (Power engineering specialist)	23 Pushkinskaya St	32-9304, 32-4690

Name	Address	Telephone
MISKHOR		
Ai-Petri	15 Alupkinskoye shosse, settlement Koreiz-1	72-2432, 72-1830
Belorussiya (Byelorussia)	2 Miskhorsky spusk, settlement Koreiz	72-21 81,72-2350
Burevestnik (Stormy petrel)	2 Koreizskoye shosse	72-3003, 72-1280
Gorny	Livadiya	24-8153,24-8149
Dnepr (Dnieper)	13 Alupkinskoye shosse, urban village Gaspra	24-7197, 24-7365
Dyulber	7 Alupkinskoye shosse, settlement Koreiz	24-1672,24-2308
Zhemchuzhina (Pearl)	5 Alupkinskoye shosse, urban village Gaspra	24-7376, 24-8267
Zolotoi plyazh (Golden beach)	settlement Livadiya-2	31-2495, 24-8584
R. Lyuksemburg	8 Sevastopolskoye shosse, urban village Gaspra	24-2427, 24-2307
Kurpaty	4 Alupkinskoye shosse, urban village Gaspra	31-5534, 24-8307
Marat	60 Alupkinskoye shosse, urban village Gaspra-1	24-2269, 24-2212
Miskhor	10 Alupkinskoye shosse, settlement Koreiz	24-2565,24-3826
Sosnovaya roshcha (Pine grove)	5 urban village Gaspra	24-2486, 24-2247
Ukraina (Ukraine)	urban village Gaspra-3	24-7413,24-7397
Yasnaya polyana	urban village Gaspra	24-2568,24-2403
ALUPKA		
Alupka	5 Litinskaya St.	75-1152
Alupkinsky klinichesky (Alupka clinical)	Ametkhana Sultana St.	72-2139, 72-2241
Zlatoust	28 Dvortsovoye shosse	72-3849, 72-3865
Bobrova	35 Lenina St.	72-6942, 72-6232
Mo Alupka	31 Ametkhana Sultana St.	72-2139, 72-2074
Predgorny	11 Svobody St.	72-2207
Solnechny (Sunny)	19 Frunze St.	72-2862,72-3266
Starinny osobnyak (Antique private residence)	58/62 Kulakova St., Sevastopol, "Gelika"	54-0544
Boarding school	1 Koshevogo St.	72-1201
Yuzhnoberezhny	29 Lenina St.	72-5304, 72-6481
SEVASTOPOL		
Baidary	34 Tenistaya St.	53-4260,53-4259
Kamadeya	2 Kalicha St.	63-4573

Name	Address	Telephone
SIMEIZ. FOROS		
Goluboi zaliv (Blue bay)	79 Sovetskaya St., urban village Simeiz	24-0150
Zori Ukrainy	Simeiz-2	72-7473
Baranova	5 Baranova St., urban village Simeiz	72-6973,72-6105
Semashko	urban village Simeiz	24-0326,24-0248
Krasny mayak (Red light-house)	35 Sovetskaya St., urban village Simeiz	24-0267, 24-0328
Moskva (Moscow)	Sovetskaya St., urban village Simeiz	24-0243, 24-0100
Pioner (Pioneer)	2 Paustovskogo St., urban village Simeiz	24-0325, 24-0100
Simeiz	3 Sovetskaya St., urban village Simeiz	24-0144,24-0392
Foros	settlement Foros	79-1351,79-2497
Yuzhny	settlement Foros-1	79-1000
PESCHANOYE		
Shevchenko	1 Bolshaya Morskaya St., settlement Beregovoye, Bakhchisarai district	96-125, 96-192
Orliny zalyot (Eagle's flying)	Lenina St., village Sokolinoye, Bakhchisarai district	64-492, 43-958
Prival (Halt)	43 Shmidta St., Bakhchisarai	47-846, 44-550
U lukomorya	settlement Peschanoye	92-544, 43-963
Yyut (Cosiness)	settlement Peschanoye	40-480,92-574
Chernomorets	settlement Peschanoye	43-502, 92-492
Chernyye vody (Black waters)	2 Yaltinskaya St., settlement Aromatnoye	42-740, 64-471
NIKOLAYEVKA		
Izumrud (Emerald)	settlement Nikolayevka	35-8635
Luchezarny (Radiant)	settlement Nikolayevka	35-8928
Energetik (Power engi-neering specialist)	settlement Nikolayevka	29-8650, 29-8573
YEVPATORIYA		
Sorok let oktyabrya (40 years of October)	48 Kiyevskaya St.	31-490, 33-484
Almazny (Diamond)	29 Lenina Ave.	36-424, 36-451
Brigantina (Brigantine)	31 Shestdesyat let SSSR St., settlement Zaozyornoye	22-193, 62-069
Burevestnik (Stormy petrel)	7/13 Morozova St.	32-041, 60-323
Druzhba (Friendship)	7 Mayakovskogo St.	61-645, 36-257

Name	Address	Telephone
Yevpatoriya	19 Moskovskaya St.	62-739, 62-720
Yevpatoriya-Mir (World)	19 Moskovskaya St.	31-339, 61-784
Zhemchuzhina (Pearl)	Shestdesyat let SSSR St., settlement Zaozyornoye	21-307, 21-831
Zvyozdochka (Small star)	25 Lenina Ave.	36-158,62-695
Zdravnitsa (Health-centre)	21 Gorkogo St.	61-429, 62-075
Izumrudny (Emerald)	49 Pushkina St.	33-565, 32-000
Krupskaya	97 Shestdesyat let SSSR St.	31-459,31-047
R. Lyuksemburg	35 Kirova St.	32-262, 36-189
Iskra (Spark)	91 Kirova St.	30-384
Lenina	6 Duvanovskaya St.	31-472, 31-369
Luchezarny (Radiant)	49 Pushkina St.	62-610
Mayak (Lighthouse)	39 Shestdesyat let SSSR St., settlement Zaozyornoye	21-437
Mediki Chernobylya (Doctors of Chenobyl)	4/25 Chekalova St., settlement Zaozyornoye	21-886, 21-436
Yevpatoriya	21 Duvanovskaya St.	31-400
Moinaki	30 Polupanova St.	62-506,60-730
Nagovitsyna	33 Moskovskaya St.	30-558,30-347
Oktyabr (October)	86 Kirova St.	30-418,30-410
Orei-Krym (Orei-Crimea)	17 Frunze St.	32-449,36-680
Orlyonok (Small eagle)	3 Mayakovskogo St.	30-259, 36-155
Voyenny sanatory (Military sanatorium)	7 Mayakovskogo St.	31-498, 31-059
Planeta (Planet)	29/73 Kositskogo St.	28-384,60-320
Pobeda (Victory)	4 Frunze St.	61-142,36-170
Priboi (Surf)	9/15 Moskovskaya St.	31-570, 36-225
Primorye (Seaside)	2/27 I. Franko St.	62-603,32-012
Prometei	13 Shestdesyat let SSSR St.	21-372,31-263
Rodina (Fatherland)	30 Franko St.	32-410
Rodnichok (Small spring)	68 Lenina St.	30-116,62-473
Sakko i Vantsetti	48 Kiyevskaya St.	31-589,32-572
Severny (North)	Shestdesyat let SSSR St., settlement Zaozyornoye	41-049
Solnechny (Sunny)	17 Mayakovskogo St.	32-235,61-548
Tavrida	64 Kirova St.	30-514,31-478
Tavriya	108 Kirova St.	31-029,36-727
Udarnik (Shock-worker)	7/3 Ushinskogo St.	36-241, 31-466
Solnechny (Sunny)	29 Shestdesyat let SSSR St.	21-158
Chaika (Sea-gull)	37 Shestdesyat let SSSR St.	41-972
Yubileiny (Jubilee)	1/3 Morozova St.	30-194, 30-118

Name	Address	Telephone
SAKI		
Burdenko	4 Kurortnaya St.	26-502,24-574
Golubaya Volna (Blue wave)	2 Morskaya St.	27-240, 99-298
MO Saki	2 Kurortnaya St.	91-404
Poltava	8 Morskaya St.	24-372, 25-254
Sakropol (Lenina)	4 Kurortnaya St.	24-574,27-494

Name	Address	Telephone
FEODOSIYA		
Aivazovsky	4 Lenina Ave.	30-113, 45-383
Ai-Petri	4 Lenina Ave.	71-871, 71-074
Volna (Wave)	37 Lenina St.	31-377
Voskhod (Sunrise)	27 Lenina St.	30-165,31-658
Vympel (Pennant)	6 Chernomorsky tupik	73-198
Zolotoi plyazh (Golden beach)	7 Kerchenskoye shosse tretyego kava-leriyskogo korpusa	30-401,73-175, 73-107
Mo Feodosiya	5 Generala Gorbacheva St.	33-065
Rodina Mira (Fatherland of peace)	45 Fedko St.	73-000, 45-572
Voyenny sanatory (Military sanatorium)	5 Generala Gorbacheva St.	33-000, 30-626, 30-962

Name	Address	Telephone
KOKTEBEL. KURORTNOYE		
Goluboi zaliv (Blue bay)	123 Lenina St., settlement Koktebel	36-331,35-289, 36-284
Krymskoye Primorye (Crimean Seaside)	settlement Kurortnoye	38-372, 38-430
Yakor (Anchor)	settlement Koktebel	36-285
SUDAK		
Voyenny sanatory (Military sanatorium)	1 Naberezhnaya St.	21-673, 22-590
Zvyozdny (Star)	81 Lenina St.	22-480,22-498
Sudak	1 Naberezhnaya St.	21-606
Voyenny sanatory (Military sanatorium)	Biryuzova St.	21-673, 92-589
Sokol (Falcon)	21 Primorskaya St.	21-009, 21-810
Sudak	89 Lenina St.	21-606, 21-965

KERCH		
Kerch		34-257
Mechta (Dream)	8 Ordzhenikidze lane	34-122,35-063
Parus (Sail)	16 Suvorova St.	45-206, 47-417
Skazka (Fairy-tale)		20-076, 79-116

In order to call to any settlement of the Crimea one should dial 8, then 10 - access to international communications, then 38 - international code of Ukraine, then the code of the settlement and the telephone number. If you are in Ukraine, after 8 you should dial at once the settlement code and the telephone number. At the territory of the Crimea the code is simplified, instead of 065 dial 2.

CODES OF AUTOMATIC INTERTOWN TELEPHONE COMMUNICATIONS

Settlements	Codes
Azovskoye	06564
Alupka	0654
Alushta	06560
Armyansk	06565
Bagerovo	06557
Bakhchisarai	06554
Belogorsk	06559
Belokamensk (Inkerman)	0692
Beregovoye of Bakhchisarai district	06554
Gaspra	0654
Gurzuf	0654
yevpatoriya	06569
Zaozyornoye	06569
Katsiveli	0654
Kacha	0692
Kerch	06561
Koktebel	06562
Koreiz	0654
Kurortnoye of Sudak district	06566

Населенные пункты	Коды
Kurpaty	0654
Livadiya	0654
Massandra	0654
Novy Svet	06566
Ordzhonikidze	06562
Oreanda	0654
Otradnoye	0654
Parkovoye	0654
Partenit	06560
Ponizovka	0654
Primorsky	06562
Sevastopol	0692
Simferopol	0652
Saki	06563
Sanatornoye (Melas)	0654
Simeiz	0654
Stary Krym	06555
Sudak	06566
Feodosiya	06562
Foros	0654
Chernomorskoye	06558
Shchebetovka	06566
Shchelkino	06557
Yalta	0654

In order to call to Yalta, for example, from Moscow, dial:

8 *(whistle)*-**10-38-0654**-**XX**-**XXXX**;

to Yalta from Kiev:

8 *(whistle)*-**0654**-**XX**-**XXXX**;

to Yalta from Simferopol:

8 *(whistle)*-**24**-**XX**-**XXXX**.

SCHEDULE OF FLIGHTS CARRIED OUT FROM THE AIRPORT SIMFEROPOL WITHIN THE BORDERS OF UKRAINE

No. of flight	type of AV (air vessel)	direction	take off	arrival	days of the week	price of ticket (UAH)
5Ж122	АН-24	Vinnitsa	17.30	19.10	ВТ	220
36-310	Як-40	Dnepropetrovsk	14.40	15.50	ПН, ПТ	160
УДЦ3568	АН-24	Donetsk	17.40	19.00	ПН, СР, ПТ	160
ЛФ8947	АН-24	Zaporozhye	17.00	17.50	СР, ВС	75
6У8102	МД-80	Kiev (Borispol)	21.05	22.30	ЧТ	250
VV106	Б-737	Kiev (Borispol)	11.15	12.35	ВС	250
VV106	Б-737	Kiev (Borispol)	15.25	16.45	ПН	250
VV106	Б-737	Kiev (Borispol)	12.00	13.20	СР	250
VV106	Б-737	Kiev (Borispol)	20.00	21.20	ПТ	250
VV106	Б-737	Kiev (Borispol)	15.20	16.40	ВТ	250
VV106	Б-737	Kiev (Borispol)	18.30	19.50	ЧТ	250
VV206	Б-737	Kiev (Borispol)	20.30	21.50	СБ	250
Х9-304	ДС-90	Kiev (Borispol)	14.15	15.30	ВТ, ЧТ	250
OP 3363	АН-24	Kiev (Zhulyany)	15ю45	17.55	every day	250
OP 3365	АН-24	Kiev (Zhulyany)	08.40	10.50	every day	250
OP 3369	АН-24	Kiev (Zhulyany)	13.40	15.50	ПН-ПТ	250
OP 3373	АН-24	Kiev (Zhulyany)	11.00	12.50	СБ, ВС	250
OP 3385	АН-24	Kiev (Zhulyany)	18.45	20.55	every day	250
ТЖМ8941	АН-24	Kiev (Zhulyany)	15.00	17.00	ПТ	250
УРП8242	АН-24	Kiev (Zhulyany)	19.30	21.30	every day	250
УРП8244	АН-24	Kiev (Zhulyany)	11.00	13.00	ПН-ПТ	250
УРП8246	АН-24	Kiev (Zhulyany)	08.00	10.00	every day	250
УРП8248	АН-24	Kiev (Zhulyany)	16.30	18.30	every day	250
УРП8250	АН-24	Kiev (Zhulyany)	18.00	20.00	every day	250
УРП8252	АН-24	Kiev (Zhulyany)	09.30	11.30	every day	250
УРГ 456	АН-24	Krivoi Rog	12.00	13.10	Пт	140
ЛУ3682	АН-24	Lugansk	13.30	15.10	Сб	200
5Ж 122	АН-24	Lvov	17.30	20.00	ЧТ, ПТ, ВС	270
5Ж 122	АН-24	Lvov	17.30	20.45	ВТ	270
ЛФ 8945	АН-24	Nikolayev	07.50	08.50	ПН, ЧТ	75
TVR2302	ЯК-42	Odessa	07.05	08.00	ПН, ПТ	150
УНР3975	Л-410	Odessa	12.00	13.40	ВС	150
УНР3975	Л-410	Rovno	12.00	16.40	ВС	220
ЛУ3684	АН-24	Severodonetsk	13.40	15.20	ВС	200
УНР3975	Л-410	Uzhgorod	12.00	18.50	ВС	250
ХФ4410	АН-24	Kharkov	14.30	16.30	ВТ, ЧТ, СБ	160

Privileges for children:

- the cost of a ticket for children under 5 amounts to 10% of the cost of a ticket for adults (without giving a place);
- the cost of a ticket for children from 5 up to 12 amounts to 50% of the cost of a ticket for adults (with giving a place).

SCHEDULE OF TRAINS TRAFFIC

SIMFEROPOL

All the trains following from Sevastopol pass through Simferopol

No.	Communication	DEP	ARR	Days of running
12	Simferopol - Kiev	16-35	7-52	Every day
56	Simferopol - Sumy	16-10	7-35	On odd days
68	Simferopol - Moscow	12-22	11-17	Every day
82	Simferopol - Kharkov	22-48	8-29	Every day
86	Simferopol - Lvov	8-58	12-07	Every day
88	Simferopol - Kovel	11-36	14-26	Every day
100	Simferopol - Minsk	14-36	17-48	Every day, from 16.09 on even days
158	Simferopol - Dnepropetrovsk	22-05	7-05	Every day
182	Simferopol - Minsk	21-42	5-10	from 2.06 on even days
188	Simferopol - Kislovodsk	0-22	6-30	from 3.06 on odd days
202	Simferopol - Khmelnitsky	15-00	14-51	From 3.06 on odd days
216	Simferopol - Sverdlovsk	15-22	13-51	Every day
242	Simferopol - Lugansk	18-44	11-42	Every day
294	Simferopol - Mogilyov	9-38	18-11	From 16.06 up to 4.09 every day
615	Kerch - Simferopol	20-30	5-31	Every day
616	Simferopol - Kerch	23-30	7-16	Every day
631	Simferopol - Yevpatoriya	8-14	9-53	Every day
645	Simferopol - Sevastopol	9-55	11-50	Every day
650	Simferopol - Odessa	17-15	6-59	Every day

SEVASTOPOL

No	Communication	DEP	ARR	Days of running
08	Simferopol - St. Petersburg	9-20	19-00	From 4.06 up to 20.09 every day
26	Sevastopol - Moscow	17-00	19-42	Every day
28	Simferopol - Kiev	18-00	11-46	Every day
40	Simferopol - Kiev	14-30	9-36	From 19 VI - Every day
454	Sevastopol - St. Petersburg	16-25	9-34	From 6.06 up to 2.09 on Th. and Fr.
646	Sevastopol - Simferopol	18-28	20-08	Ежедневно

YEVPATORIYA

No	Communication	DEP	ARR	Days of running
18	Yevpatoriya - Moscow	19-30	20-29	From 26.05 up to 2.10 Every day
126	Yevpatoriya - Dnepropetrovsk	21-11	6-15	From 11.06 up to 19.09 on odd days
144	Yevpatoriya - Moscow	19-06	21-52	From 26.06 up to 1.09 every day
352	Yevpatoriya - St. Petersburg	18-20	9-34	From 4.06 up to 31.08 on Tu., Sat.
366	Yevpatoriya - Minsk	20-46	5-10	From 3.06 up to 29.08 on odd days
394	Yevpatoriya - Kiev	20-20	15-04	From 1.07 up to 3.09 on odd
632	Yevpatoriya - Simferopol	10-08	11-44	Every day

FEODOSIYA

No	Communication	DEP	ARR	Days of running
104	Feodosiya – Moscow	14-58	15-50	From 28.05 up to 30.09 every day
106	Feodosiya – Kiev	11-06	5-01	From 11.06 up to 15.09 every day
124	Feodosiya – Moscow	19-48	22-42	Till 28.06 on Th., from 29.06 up to 1.09 every day
154	Feodosiya – Kharkov	22-10	10-04	From 11.06 up to 7.09 on odd days
340	Feodosiya – Dnepropetrovsk	20-35	6-15	From 2.06 up to 31.08 on odd days

KERCH

No	Communication	DEP	ARR	Days of running
102	Feodosiya – Moscow	23-10	5-53	On odd days
128	Kerch – Moscow	23-55	5-53	From 28.05 up to 30.09 every day
182	Kerch – Kiev	18-10	15-04	From 11.06 up to 2.09 on even days
616	Kerch – Simferopol	20-30	5-21	Every day
656	Kerch – Kherson	0-27	11-38	Every day

SCHEDULE OF ELECTRIC TRAINS TRAFFIC

TO YEVPATORIYA

No.	DEP	ARR	Days of running
6634	5-40	7-41	Every day
6636	6-40	8-50	summer
6638	7-28	9-35	Every day
6642	8-33	10-08	Every day
6644	10-08	12-08	Every day
6646	11-34	13-20	Every day
6648	13-02	15-21	Every day
6650	14-06	16-12	summer
6652	15-36	17-37	Every day
6654	17-03	19-11	Every day
6656	20-20	22-44	Every day

FROM YEVPATORIYA

No.	DEP	ARR	Days of running
6677	5-05	7-27	Every day
6679	8-01	10-25	Every day
6681	10-11	11-50	Every day
6683	10-58	13-19	Every day
6685	12-30	14-35	summer
6687	13-27	15-42	summer
6689	14-35	16-29	Every day
6691	15-58	18-00	Every day
6693	16-43	19-05	Every day
6697	18-58	20-49	Every day
6699	20-27	22-18	Every day

FROM SEVASTOPOL

No.	DEP	ARR	Days of running
6529	4-50	5-38	To Bakhchisarai, every day
6531	5-26	7-43	Every day
6533	6-50	9-02	Every day
6535	8-35	10-58	Every day
6537	11-12	13-27	Every day
6539	14-00	16-10	Every day
6541	17-15	19-45	Every day
6543	20-17	22-33	Every day

FROM SEVASTOPOL

No.	DEP	ARR	Days of running
6530	5-58	6-49	To Bakhchisarai, every day
6532	5-01	7-15	Every day
6534	8-15	10-44	Every day
6536	10-19	12-42	Every day
6538	12-48	15-22	Every day
6540	14-18	16-43	Every day
6542	17-10	19-34	Every day
6544	20-08	22-16	Every day

FROM DZHANKOI TO YEVPATORIYA

No.	DEP	ARR	Days of running
6695	6-31	9-55	summer

FROM YEVPATORIYA TO DZHANKOI

No.	DEP	ARR	Days of running
6696	17-38	20-57	summer

FROM SIMFEROPOL - NOVOALEKSEYEVKA

No.	DEP	ARR	Days of running
6618	6-15	9-55	Every day
6622	11-13	14-55	Every day
6624	12-52	17-00	Every day
6626	13-52	16-34	Every day to Solyonoye Ozero (Salt Lake)
6628	18-03	22-16	Every day
6616	5-00	8-50	every day

FROM MELITOPOL - NOVOALEKSEYEVKA

No.	DEP	ARR	Days of running
6619	5-36	8-58	Every day
6623	12-32	16-08	Every day
6625	15-20	18-55	Every day
6627	16-51	19-29	Every day to Solyonoye Ozero (Salt Lake)
6629	17-28	21-00	Every day
6631	18-47	22-06	Every day

TO NOVOALEKSEYEVKA

No.	DEP	ARR	Days of running
To Melitopol			
6616	5-00	8-50	Every day
To Dzhankoi			
6620	8-45	10-50	Every day
6630	20-52	22-49	Every day
To Urozhainaya			
6614	3-15	5-00	every day

FROM NOVOALEKSEYEVKA

No.	DEP	ARR	Days of running
To Simferopol			
6631	16-50	18-47	Every day
From Dzhankoi			
6617	5-30	7-37	Every day
6621	11-21	13-33	Every day
From Urozhainaya			
6615	5-24	6-48	Every day

FROM NOVOALEKSEYEVKA TO GENICHESK

No.	DEP	ARR	Days of running
6779	2-50	3-20	Every day
6781	6-20	6-50	Every day
6783	9-00	9-30	Every day
6785	10-40	11-10	Every day
6787	15-15	15-45	Every day
6789	17-10	17-40	Every day
6791	19-00	19-31	Every day
6793	22-05	22-35	Every day

FROM GENICHESK TO NOVOALEKSEYEVKA

No.	DEP	ARR	Days of running
6780	3-40	4-10	Every day
6782	7-10	7-40	Every day
6784	9-50	10-20	Every day
6786	11-30	12-00	Every day
6788	16-10	16-40	Every day
6790	18-00	18-30	Every day
6792	19-51	20-22	Every day
6794	22-55	23-25	Every day

TABLE OF DISTANCES BETWEEN TOWNS OF THE CRIMEA

Alushta													
83	Bakhchisarai												
90	85	Belogorsk											
138	131	140	Dzhankoi										
109	102	111	100	Yevpatoriya									
246	256	171	236	282	Kerch								
155	148	157	56	97	292	Krasnoperekopsk							
90	83	92	105	19	263	110	Saki						
128	45	130	176	93	301	193	74	Sevastopol					
45	38	47	93	64	218	110	45	83	Simferopol				
93	142	57	133	168	153	189	149	214	104	Sudak			
176	169	178	156	67	349	117	86	160	131	235	Chernomorskoye		
148	158	73	138	184	98	194	165	203	120	55	251	Feodosiya	
41	86	133	179	150	287	196	131	80	86	134	217	189	Yalta

A

Avinda - a mountain with a conic peak covered with pines; the highest point of Nikitskaya mountain pasture, at a distance of 5 km to the west of Gurzuf.

Avrorina skala (Aurora's rock) - an precipitous eastern projection of the cape Monastyr-Burun. The castle "Lastochkino gnezdo" ("Swallow's nest") is situated on it. The name was given in the XIX century: the rock protrudes to the side of the dawn, Aurora, rise.

Agarmysh (in Turkic "agarmysh" means "grey-haired") - a wooded mountain with a flat peak at a distance of 4 km to the west of the Old Crimea's centre.

Adalary - two small rocky islets at the sea to the south-east of Gurzuf.

Ayu-Dag and rocks of Adalary

Ai-Petri - a massive mountain with majestic rocky jags and crests near the peak. It is situated at the southern edge of the Ai-Petrinskaya yaila, at a distance of 2 km to the north of Alupka.

Aisavskaya dolina (valley) or Dolina Roz (Valley of Roses) - a valley, partially built-up, with clearings, groves, and roses plantations to the north-west of Sudak. In the valley they revealed the ruins of Saint Savva medieval cloister.

Ai-Todor - a high rocky cape dropping off into the sea by three juts, to the south-east of Gaspra. On the cape there was a medieval cloister dedicated to Saint Feodor.

The cape Aiya

Ai-Yuri, or Drakon (Dragon) - a toothed rocky mountain range with a tunnel-underpass of the new Sevastopol highway, forced in it, is situated to the north of Yalta.

Aiya - a high cape formed by rocks steeply dropping off, at a distance of 9 km to the south of Balaklava.

Ak-Kaya, or Belaya skala (White rock) - a spacious treeless plateau at a distance of 5 km to the north of Belogorsk.

Alchak (in Turkic "alchak" means "low, mean") - a naked cape with vertical rocky walls locking the Sudak bay from the east.

Angar-Burun (in Turkic "angar" means a wide valley, canyon) - a dome-shaped peak on the south-eastern jut of the mountain-mass Chatyrdag.

Angarsky pereval (pass) (in Turkic "angar" means a wide valley, canyon) is on the way from Simferopol to the South Coast of the Crimea, at a distance of 9 km from Alushta.

Ayu-Dag, or Medved gora (Bear-mountain) - a hump-backed wooded mountain between Partenit and the children's camp "Artek".

B

Babugan-yaila (in Crimean-Tatar - belladonna) - a hilly upland region, the highest section of the Main ridge.

Baidarskaya dolina (valley) - a spacious amphitheatre surrounded by wooded mountains, is situated above the Chernorechensky canyon.

Bakalskaya kosa (spit) - juts out into the Karkinitsky bay by the village of Steregushcheye.

Belbek - the most abounding in water river of the Crimea.

Bakla (in Turkic "bakla" means haricot beans, beans) - a spacious plateau-shaped height in which numerous grottoes of a settlement of the same name had been cut out, at a distance of 2.5 km to the east of the village of Skalistoye.

Belbek

Binbash-Koba, or Tysyachegolovaya peshchera (thousand-headed cave) - a karst cavity with a low entrance leading to the only hall, is situated at the mountain-mass of Chatyrdag. A medieval burial ground was here.

The big canyon

Bolshoi Atlesh (Big Atlesh) (in Turkic "atlesh" means fire) - a rocky cape with an arch made by waves at the southern shore line of the peninsula of Tarkhankut.

Bolshoi kanyon (Big canyon) - a narrow deep cleft on the bottom of which the river of Auzun-Uzen flows.

C

Chatyrdag, or Trapezus (in Turkic "chatyr" means a marquee) - a spacious mountain range with the rocky peaks Angar-Burun and Eklizi-Burun looks like a trapezium from many points of vision.

Chernorechensky kanyon (canyon) - a deep canyon of the river Chyornaya (Black) of length 8 km is below the Baidarskaya valley.

Choban-Kule (in Turkic "chobankule" means a shepherd's tower) - a naked precipitous cape at a distance of 4 km to the west of the village of Morskoye.

Chokrak - a salt lake in the north of the Kerchensky peninsula, is known for its curative mud.

Churuk-Su (in Turkic "chyuryuk" means "rotten") - the right tributary of the river Kacha, begins by the eastern outskirts of Bakhchisarai.

Chufut-Cheargan-Burun (in Turkic means the cape of calling for Israelites; in this part of Mangup the Karaites lived) - a mountainous cape in the north of the plateau Babadag.

D

Darsan - a hill with park plantations, the lower stage of the mountain range Lograf, is situated in the northern part of Yalta. One can ascend it by a rope-way.

Dvuyakornaya bukhta (Two-anchor bay) is situated between the capes of Saint Illya and Kiik-Atlama, to the west of Feodosiya.

Demerdzhi (in Turkic "demirdzhi" means a blacksmith) - a dome-shaped peak with grassy slopes, at a distance of 2 km to the north of village of Luchistoye.

Dzhangul - a five-kilometre section of the peninsula of Tarkhankut high north-western shore.

The Valley of ghosts

Dzhau-Tepe - a naked conic height in Kerchensky peninsula, a former mud volcano.

Dzhur-Dzhur - a powerful waterfall on the river Ulu-Uzen at a distance of 1.7 km to the north-west of the village of Generalskoye.

Diva - a pointed rock by the sea in Simeiz.

Dolina privideny (Valley of ghosts) - a steep wooded gully with stone "sculptures" on the south-western slope of the mountain Demerdzhi.

Donuzlav (in Turkic "domuz" means a pig) - a salt lake, the largest in the Tarkhankut group.

Kachi-Kalyon

E

Eklizi-Burun - a trapeziform naked peak, the highest point of the mountain range Chatyrdag.

Emine-Bair-Khosar - a cave with an entrance-well on the lower plateau of Chatyrdag.

F

Fiolent (in Italian "violente" means "violent"; perhaps, because of frequent heavy seas) - a high precipitous cape at a distance of 8 km to the west of Balaklava.

G

Genuezskaya skala (Genoese rock) or Dzhenevez-Kaya - a massive rocky pyramidal boulder in the south-eastern part of Gurzuf.

Golubaya bukhta (Blue bay) - the westernmost bay of Novy Svet, is situated between the cape Kapchik and the mountain Karaul-Oba.

Gurzufskoye sedlo (Gurzuf saddle) - a pass between the Gurzufskaya and Babugan-yaila.

Gyaur-Bakh (in Turkic "gyaur" means an adherent of a different faith, "bag" means a garden, a vineyard) - a rocky precipitous canyon in the mountain-mass Karadag.

The mountain range Karagach

I

Iograf - a steep wooded mountain range to the west of Yalta.

Iosafatova dolina (valley) - a vast ravine to the east of Chufut-Kale. A Karaite cemetery is situated here.

Ifinogeniya - a stepped rock wall in the west of Greater Yalta.

K

Kazantip (in Turkic "kazan" means a cauldron) - a peninsula in the Sea of Azov with rounded contours and a hollow in the centre.

Kanaka (in Turkic "khanaka" means a cloister of religious ascetics) - a sloping gully to the east of the village of Rybachye.

Kanly-Dere (in Turkic "kanly" means "bloody") - a narrow canyon at the southern outskirts of Bakhchisarai.

Kapchik, or Peshcherny mys (Cave cape) - a long cape with a narrow neck cut through by a grotto-tunnel; divides the Sinyaya (Dark blue) and Golubaya (Sky-blue) bays in Novy Svet.

Karabi yaila - the most spacious and desert upland region in the Crimea.

Karagach - a rocky mountain range with numerous figures of weathering in the western part of the mountain-mass Karadag.

Karagol (in Turkic "karagol" means a black lake) - a small forest lake on the slope of the mountain Mogabi near the highway Yalta - Bakhchisarai.

Karadag - a mountain range of a partly volcanic origin between the settlement of Koktebel and the village of Kurortnoye.

Karaul-Oba - a mountain at a distance of 2 km to the west of the settlement of Novy Svet.

Kastel - (in Greek "kasteli" means a small fortress) - a wooded mountain at a distance of 2 km from the southern outskirts of Alushta.

Khameleon (Chameleon) - a narrow lengthy cape steeply dropping off to the sea from all sides, locks the Koktebel bay from the east.

Mangup

Kiik-Atlama - (in Turkic "kiyik" means a wild goat, "atlama" - a jump) - a naked precipitous cape jutting out far into the sea, to the south-west of Feodosiya.

Koba-Kaya - a high rocky mountain above the settlement of Novy Svet.

Kuchuk-Yenishar - a wavy treeless mountain range to the north-east of Koktebel. Here the M. Voloshin's grave is.

Kyz-Kermen - (in Turkic "kyz" means a girl, "kermen" - a fortress) - a medieval settlement to the west of Bakhchisarai.

Kyz-Kule - the Sudak fortress tower most high situated.

Kyzyltash - a reddish cliff by the village of Krasnokamenka, near Gurzuf.

L

Laspi - (in Greek "laspi" means "clay, dirt") - a wooded amphitheatre restricted from the north and the east by rocky precipices of Baidarskaya yaila.

Lukull - a southern entrance cape of Kalamitsky bay.

M

Malakhov kurgan (barrow) - a steep-sided height with a flat peak on the Korabelnaya storona (side) in Sevastopol.

Maly (Small) Atlesh - a pointed flat-peaked cape on the southern coastline of the peninsula of Tarkhankut.

Mangup-Kale (in Turkic "maglyup" means "smashed up, defeated"; perhaps, the name appeared after the Turks had smashed up the town) - a medieval settlement on the plateau Babadag.

Martyan - a cape to the south-east of the village of Nikita.

Medvezhonok (bear-cub), or Kuchuk-Ayu - a small rocky cape in the eastern part of the Partenit bay.

Mitridat - a humpbacked height in the centre of Kerch.

The cape Tarkhankut

The cape Fiolent

Moinaki - a salt shallow lake at the western outskirts of Yevpatoriya.

N

Nikitskaya yaila - a plateau-shaped southern spur of the Main ridge.

P

Parsuk-Kaya - a rocky mountain at a distance of 1.5 km to the north of the village of Solnechnaya Dolina (Sunny Valley).

Perekopsky peresheyek (neck) connects the Crimean peninsula with the mainland.

Perchem-Kaya (in Turkic "perchem" means a forelock) - a massive mountain with a range of rounded peaks to the west of Sudak.

Petrovskiye skaly (rocks) - precipices of the plateau-shaped height in the south-east part of Simferopol.

Plaka - a flat-peaked cape on which the settlement Utyos (Cliff) is.

R

Roman-Kosh - a dome-shaped naked peak in the western part of Babugan-yaila, the highest point of the Crimea mountains.

S

Salgir - the longest river of the Crimea.

Sarych - a humpbacked cape with a more sloping southern side at a distance of 3.5 km to the west of Foros, the endmost southern extremity of the Crimean peninsula.

Sasyk-Sivash (in Turkic "sasyk" means "swampy", "syvash" means "to stick") - the largest salt lake in the Crimea is between Yevpatoriya and Saki.

Sudak, or Alepkhor (in Turkic "sudak" means a brook, a tributary) - a river formed by confluence of the rivers Suuk-Su and Adzhibei.

Shaitan-Merdven, or Chyortova lestnitsa (Devilish stairs) - a mountain pass to the Ai-Petri yaila.

Chufut-Kale

T

Taraktash (in Turkic "tarak tash" means a stone crest) - a powerful rocky crest above the settlement of Dachnoye.

Tarkhankut (in Turkic "tarkhan" means "freed from taxes, having privileges" - a peninsula in the north-western part of the Crimea.

Tepe-Oba, or Tete-Oba (in Turkic "tepe" means "hilly") - a long height near the southern part of Feodosiya.

Teshkli-Burun - a narrow mountainous cape, the north jut of the plateau Babadag, one of the capes of Mangup.

Tokluk-Syrt - a long wavy mountain range to the north of the village of Bogatovka.

U

Uzun-Syrt, or gora Klimentyeva (Klimentyev's mountain) - a height with a flat wide peak at a distance of 5 km from Koktebel. Is used for glider sports.

Uspenskaya skala (rock) - the rocky precipices along the canyon Maryam-Dere. By its foot churches and cells of a cloister are cut out in the stone.

Uchan-Su (in Turkic "uchan-su" means "falling water") - the biggest Crimean waterfall.

Y

Yuz-Oba (in Turkic "yuz oba" means a hundred peaks) - a treeless height at the southern outskirts of Kerch with a range of barrows along the peak.

Uchan-Su

A

Aivazovsky, Ivan Konstantinovich (1817-1900), Russian painter. In 1980 he founded in Feodosiya a picture-gallery which together with his works of art was left by him to the town by his will testament.

Ivan Konstantinovich Aivazovsky

Aleksandr II (1818-1881), Russian emperor, ruled in 1855-1881.

Asandr (?-21/22 B.C.), tsar of Bosporus(49/48-21/20 B.C.). Son of tsarina Dinamia. Had strengthened the Bospor state borders, was at war with Scythians and Tavrs.

B

Beibars Zakhir Seif-ad-din as-Salikhi, sultan of Egypt, ruled in 1260-1277.

Bertye-Delagard, Aleksandr Lvovich (1842-1920), historian, archaeologist. From 1874 up to 1887 worked in Sevastopol, was in charge of restoration of the town destroyed during the period of the First defence, built the first town water pipe-line. The seaside boulevard had been laid by his project.

Bogayevsky, Konstantin Fyodorovich (1872-1943), artist - landscape painter.

Botkin, Sergei Petrovich (1832-1889), physician, one of the founders of scientific clinical medicine, Aleksandr's III physician-in-ordinary.

Bronevsky, Semyon Mikhailovich (1763-1830), Feodosiya governor in 1810-1816, founder of the Feodosiya museum of antiquities.

Bulgaris, Yevgeny (1715-1806), priest, scientist.

D

Dasha Sevastopolskaya (from Sevastopol) (about 1836 - about 1910), daughter of a sailor, the first Russian medical nurse. During the period of defence of Sevastopol she voluntarily worked at dressing stations on the North side. In November, 1854 she was the first from Sevastopol women to be awarded a gold medal "For zeal".

Dinamiya, ruler of Bosporus, daughter of Farnak, granddaughter of Mitridate VI Yeupatore.

Aleksandr Lvovich Bertye-Delagard

Diofant, military commander and diplomat under Mitridate VI Yeupatore.

Dolgorukov-Krymsky, Vasily Mikhailovich (1722-1782), prince, general. From 13 - in the Russian army of Field-Marshal Minikh sent to the Crimea.

F

Farnak (97-47 B.C.), tsar of Bosporus state, ruled in 63-47 B.C. Son of Mitridate VI Yeupatore.

Firkovich, Avraam Samuilovich (1787-1874), well-known collector of antiquities.

G

Gasprinsky, Ismail Mirza (1851-1914), Crimean Tatar enlightener, publisher and editor of the first Russian-Crimean Tatar newspaper.

Gireis, khan dynasty which ruled in the Crimea in the XV-XVIII centuries and had been founded by Khadzhi Devlet Girei. From 1475 Gireis depended on Turkey as its vassals.

Golubev, Vitaly Nikolayevich, professor-botanist, doctor of biological sciences.

Grin, Aleksandr Stepanovich (his real surname is Grinevsky, 1880-1932), writer, author of romantic works.

Gubonin, Pyotr Ionovich (1825-1894), prominent Russian businessman and industrialist. In 1875 he received the title of a gentleman by birth, had become a large-scale landowner (the estate Gurzuf and others). Founder of the first in Russia sanatoria and health resorts complex (Gurzuf).

Homeros (between the XII and VII centuries B.C.), ancient Greek poet, author of the epic poems "Iliad" and "Odyssey".

I

Iosif (Joseph) II (1741-1790), Austrian emperor.

Istomin, Vladimir Ivanovich (1809-1855), rear-admiral (1853), hero of the Sevastopol defence of 1854-1855.

Ifigenia, in Greek mythology a daughter of Agamemnon and Klitimnestra.

K

Kazarsky, Aleksandr Ivanovich (1797-1833), commander of the legendary brig "Merkury".

Kazas, Mikhail Moiseyevich (1889-1918), Karaite painter, graphic artist. A native of Sevastopol.

Khanzhonkov, Aleksei Alekseyevich (1877-1945), Russian businessman and cinema figure, founder of the oldest in Russia joint-stock company on films production "Khanzhonkov and Co.". In 1916 founded a constant shooting base in Yalta on the basis of which the Yalta film studio has grown.

Keppen, Pyotr Ivanovich (1793-1864), ethnographer, bibliographer, author of the first generalizing work about the Crimea archaeological monuments "About the antiquities of the Crimea South Coast and Tavrichesky mountains" (1837).

Konstantin (Kirill) Filosof (about 827-869), Slavonic enlightener, creator of the ancient Slavonic alphabet (Cyrillic alphabet).

Vladimir Alekseyevich Kornilov

Kornilov, Vladimir Alekseyevich (1806-1854), vice-admiral (1852), hero of the Sevastopol defence of 1854-1855.

Krasnov Nikolai Petrovich (1865-1939), academician of architecture, by his projects in the Crimea more than 60 buildings have been built.

L

Lazarev, Mikhail Petrovich (1788-1851), Russian naval commander, geographer and hydrographer, admiral (1843). Chief commander of the Black Sea Fleet and ports, from 1834 up to 1851 - military governor of Nikolayev and Sevastopol.

Vladimir Ivanovich Istomin

M

Milgauzen, Fyodor Karlovich (1775-1853), physician, meteorologist, botanist.

Mitridate VI Yeupatore (132-63 B.C.), tsar of Pontus from 113-112 B.C.

N

Nakhimov, Pavel Stepanovich (1802-1855), admiral. One of the chief organizers and leaders of the Sevastopol defence of 1854-

Nikolai II

1855; commander of the Sevastopol port, temporary military governor of the town.

Nikolai (Nicholas) I (1796-1855), Russian emperor, ruled in 1825-1855.

Nikolai (Nicholas) II (1868-1918), Russian emperor, ruled in 1894-1917, was shot in 1918.

P

Pallas, Pyotr Simon (1741-1811), Russian naturalist, geographer, and traveller. In 1793-1794 investigated the south of Ukraine and the Crimea.

Pirogov, Nikolai Ivanovich (1810-1881), Russian surgeon, founder of military surgery.

Potyomkin, Grigory Aleksandrovich (1739-1791), grand duke Tavrichesky,

Pavel Stepanovich Nakhimov

Russian statesman and military figure, Field-Marshal-General, favourite and immediate assistant of Catherine II.

Pushkin, Aleksandr Sergeyevich (1799-1837), Russian writer and poet, forefather of new Russian literature.

R

Revelioti, Feodosy (about 1774-1850), major-general. Commanded the Balaklava Greek infantry battalion.

Rubo, Frants Alekseyevich (1856-1928), Russian painter of panoramas.

Grigory Aleksandrovich Potyomkin

S

Spendiarov, Aleksandr Afanasyevich (1871-1928), Armenian composer, conductor.

Steven, Khristian Khristianovich (1781-1863), Russian botanist and entomologist, founder and the first director (1812-1824) of the Nikitsky botanical gardens.

Suvorov, Aleksandr Vasilyevich (1729/30-1800), Russian military leader. In 1776 - commander of infantry of the Crimean corps, in 1778-1779 commanded the Crimean and Kuban corpses, took political and military measures on preparation of annexation of the Crimea by Russia and on defence of the Crimea.

In 1792-1794 - commander of the army of the south of Ukraine.

Avraam Samuilovich Firkovich

Sumarokov, Pavel Ivanovich (1760-1846), writer, lawyer. Author of the books "A journey along the whole Crimea and Bessarabiya in 1799" (1800) and "Spare time of a Crimean judge, or the Second journey to Tavrida" (1803-1805).

Shalyapin, Fyodor Ivanovich (1873-1938), Russian singer (bass), reformer of opera art. From 1922 lived abroad.

T

Tolstoi, Lev Nikolayevich (1828-1910), Russian writer, participant of the Crimean war.

V

Vardan Filippik, emperor of Byzantine, ruled in 711-713.

Vernadsky, Vladimir Ivanovich (1863-1945), Russian naturalist, the first president of Academy of Sciences of Ukraine (1919-1921). Professor and rector (1920-1921) of the Tavrichesky university.

Vladimir Svyatoslavovich (?-1015), Kiev grand duke from 980. During the Vladimir's rule the unification of eastern-Slavonic lands as parts of Kievan Rus was completed, Christianity had been introduced as the state religion.

Voinnovich, Marko Ivanovich (?-1807), count, rear-admiral. Commander of the first Black Sea Fleet battleship "Slava Yekateriny" ("Yekaterina's glory") (1783), commander of the Sevastopol squadron from 1786, chief commander of the Black Sea Fleet in 1789-1790.

Voloshin, Maksimilian Aleksandrovich (his real surname was Kiriyenko-Voloshin; 1877-1932), poet and painter.

Aleksei Alekseyevich Khanzhonkov

Vorontsov, Mikhail Semyonovich (1782-1856), Russian statesman, Field-Marshal-General (1856), prince. Novorossiysk (from 1823) governor-general and deputy (from 1828 - governor-general) of Bessarabia.

Y

Yekaterina (Catherine) II the Great (1729-1796), Russian empress, ruled in 1762-1796.

Greetings from the Crimea!

You can cut out this symbolic picture postcard, to write some warm words, and to send your greetings from the Crimea to your friends or relatives

Three mobile communications operators are represented at the territory of the Autonomous Republic of Crimea: JV "Ukrainian Mobile Communications" (UMC), the Company "Kievstar G.S.M.", and the Company "Digital Cellular Communications of Ukraine" (DCC).

The South Coast of the Crimea, large towns and territories adjoining the most important transport arteries of the Autonomy, and also the water space along the peninsula sea-coast are covered practically in full by mobile communications operators. Lately all the companies carry out intensive work both on increase of the coverage zones and on improvement of the quality of service.

The tourists who are not clients of the mobile communications Ukrainian operators and do not wish to support the international roaming may apply to local operators.

RENT OF A MOBILE TELEPHONE

From 2001 the Company "Digital Cellular Communications" (DCC) renders services on the D-AMPS standard mobile telephone lease in the Crimea

ADDRESSES OF THE UMC COMPANY'S OFFICES IN THE CRIMEA:

SIMFEROPOL,
2 ROZY LYUKSEMBURG ST.

SEVASTOPOL,
21 BOLSHAYA MORSKAYA ST.

YALTA, HOTEL "YALTA",
50 DRAZHINSKOGO ST.

ADDRESSES OF THE "KIEVSTAR G.S.M." COMPANY'S OFFICES IN THE CRIMEA:

SIMFEROPOL,
4 SAMOKISHA ST.

SEVASTOPOL,
2 GENERALA PETROVA ST.

YALTA,
1/6 MOSKOVSKAYA ST.

ADDRESSES OF THE "DIGITAL CELLULAR COMMUNICATIONS OF UKRAINE" (DCC) COMPANY'S OFFICES IN THE CRIMEA:

SIMFEROPOL:
115 KIEVSKAYA ST.
28 KIROVA ST.
64 POBEDY AVE.

YALTA:
4 IGNATENKO ST.
HOTEL "YALTA", 50, DRAZHINSKOGO ST.

YEVPATORIYA: 81 FRUNZE ST.

FEODOSIYA: 5 LENINA AVE.

ALUSHTA: 10 GORKOGO ST.

SUDAK: 57 LENINA ST.

GARDENS AND PARKS ABOVE THE DNIEPER

The cosiest place of the city. Along the green Dnieper slope there stretch the Vladimirskaya gorka (Vladimir's hill), Kreshchaty park, City garden, Mariinsky park, park "Askoldova mogila" ("Askold's grave"), park of Eternal Glory, Botanical gardens.

THE VLADIMISKY CATHEDRAL

The most outstanding complex of the late XIX century sacred painting. The paintings of the cathedral - the works of wonderful artists V. Vasnetsov, M. Nesterov, M. Vrubel, and others had a considerable impact on the home and European art.

THE ENSEMBLE OF KRESHCHATIK

The most grandiose architectural ensemble of the Soviet era. The central street which has been ground into ashes by the war - and has revived as a solemn chord of beauty and optimism

THE KIEV-PECHERSK LAVRA

The most holy place among the European Orthodox objects of worship. The architectural-artistic complex and the museum settlement are connected here with the burial of imperishable relics of God's saints' bodies at Near and Far Caves worshipped for hundreds of years by pilgrims

We recommend to begin the acquaintance with the Ukrainian capital having in hand the guide-book "A promenade along Kiev" recognized as the best tourist-regional publication in the rating **"The book of the year 2002".**

The guide-book has been awarded to the decoration "Crystal stork" from the Tourist Association of Ukraine as the best tourist book of the year.

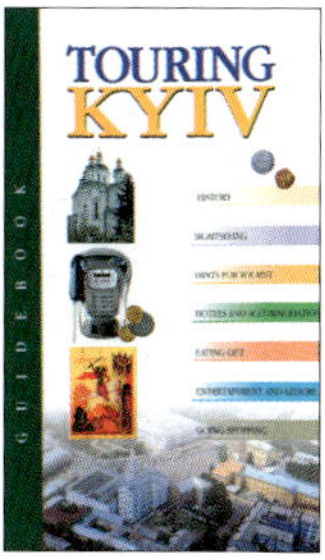

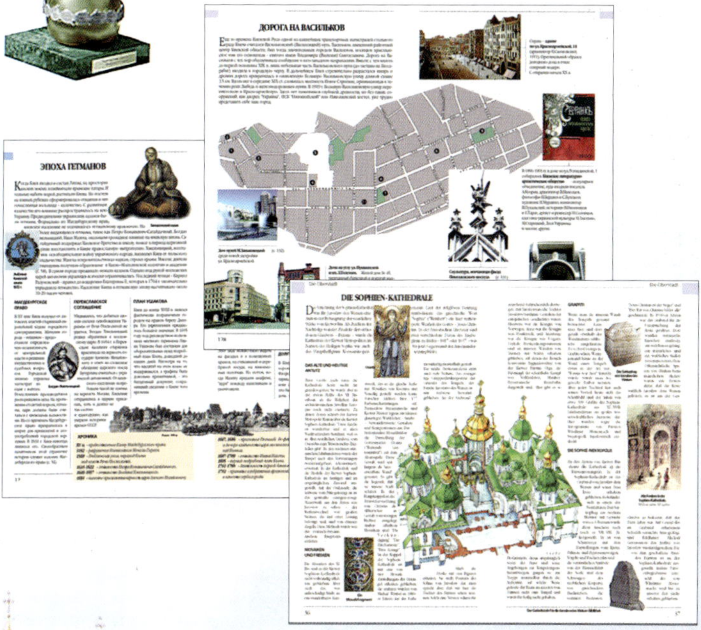

LIST OF ABBREVIATIONS

AMLLHE - Alushta museum of local lore, history, and economy
YeMLLHE - Yevpatoriya museum of local lore, history, and economy
CRMLLHE - Crimean Republican museum of local lore, history, and economy
CEM - Crimean ethnographic museum
SAM- Simferopol arts museum
FMLLHE- Feodosiya museum of local lore, history, and economy
BSMLLHE- Black-Sea museum of local lore, history, and economy

Days of the week:
MON. - Monday
TU. - Tuesday
WED - Wednesday
TH. - Thursday
FRI. - Friday
SAT - Saturday
SUN - Sunday

In the reference part:
DEP (departure)
ARR (arrival)

KHERSON
Tsiuriupinsk
Radensk
Novaia Maiachka
Golaia Pristan'
Malyie Kopani
Bol'shyie Kopani
Brilevka
Askaniia-Nova
Petrovk
Sivashskoie
KHERSONSKAIA OBL.
Gladkovka
Vinogradovo
Chaplinka
Novotroitskoie
Gromovka
Novonikolaievka
Mirnoie
Novomykhailovka
Krasnoznamenskii kanal
Kalanchak
Kakhovskii kanal
Krasnoie
Skadovsk
Zaliv Sivash
o. Kuiukfuk
Azovo-Sivaskskii natsional'nyi park
o. Churiuk
Lazurnoie
Dzharylgachskii zaliv
Armiansk
p-ov Chongar
o. Dzharylgach
Krasnoperekopsk
Karkinitskii zaliv
Zapovednik Lebiazh'i Ostrova
Ishun'
oz. Aigul'skoie
m. Peschanyi
Voinka
Bakal'skaia kosa
Razdol'noie
SEVEROKRYMSKAIA
oz. Bakal'skoie
Pervomaiskoie
Dzhankoi
75
RAVNINA
Vol'noie
44
Azovskoie
Berezovka
Chernomorskoie
Tarkhankutskii p-ov
136
Krasnogvardeiskoie
TARKHANKUTSKAIA
Krymskii p
179
Novoselovskoie
Chernomorskii kanal
Krasnogvardeiskii kanal
Olenevka
Novoozernoie
oz. Donuzlav
VOZVYSHENNOST'
Vinogradovo
Piatikhatka
m. Uret
Mirnyi
Oktiabrskoie
Amurskoie
Sadov
oz. Oiburskoie
Leninskoie
Salgir
Yevpatoriia
oz. Sasyk
Zaozernoie
Saki
Gvardeiskoie
Zuia
Burul'cha
oz. Sakskoie
Novofedorovka
Urozhainoie
Tsvetochnoie
oz. Kyzyliar
Aeroflotskii
Gresovskii
Komsomol'skoie
Agrarnoie
Zuia
Kalamitskii zaliv
SIMFEROPOL'
Molodezhnoie
Nikolaievka
441
108
Kol'chugino
Bulganak
Pochtovoie
Chisten'koie
Al'ma
Vilino
Pereval'noie
per. Angarskii
752
Kacha
111
Bakhchisarai
Kacha
Krymskii zapovednik
1527
KRYMSKIIE
Alushta
Kuibyshevo
Chuchel'skii per.
Sevastopol'
Inkerman
m. Khersones
1545
g. Roman-Kosh
Partenit
Krasnokamenka
Yalta
Gurzuf
m. Fiolent
zapovednik «Mys-Mart'ian»
Nikita
Massandra
g. Ai-Petri
per.
527
1234
Koreiz
Yaltinskii gorno-lesnoi zapovednik
Baidarskiie Vorota
Gaspra
Alupka
Foros
Parkovoie
Sanatornoie
Simeiz
CHERNO
46°
45°
33°
34°
37
54